C000241087

THE APPLEMAN AND THE POET

THE APPLEMAN
AND THE POET

Hubert Butler

Edited by Antony Farrell

THE LILLIPUT PRESS
DUBLIN

First published 2014 by
THE LILLIPUT PRESS
62–63 Sitric Road, Arbour Hill,
Dublin 7, Ireland
www.lilliputpress.ie

A CIP record for this title is available
from The British Library.

1 3 5 7 9 10 8 6 4 2

ISBN 978 1 84351 267 7

Set in 10 on 12 pt Palatino by Marsha Swan
Printed and bound in Spain by GraphyCems

Contents

'TO THE HOUSE OF MY HOSTS IN OCTOBER'

The windfalls from your apple-trees
Fall thick on windy nights like these,
And like a sea-swept strand resound
The taller trees that stand around.

May every chance and lot that falls
Be fortunate, within your walls;
And may you breathe a peaceful air
Ring'd round by trees that speak you fair.

Maurice James Craig, *Some Way for Reason* (London 1948)

PREFACE AND ACKNOWLEDGMENTS

If ever Lilliput had a mission statement it resides in bringing to light the works of Ireland's most elegant and far-reaching prose writer of the past century. With the essays in *The Appleman and the Poet* that task is fulfilled. Only the Selected Letters remain.

As an aspiring young publisher, grounded in London during the 1970s, leaving Trinity College Dublin in 1972, and now re-engaging with Irish life and culture on my return in 1980, I uncovered this treasure-trove of material with the excitement of a Schliemann at Troy. I had just set up The Lilliput Press with Tim Robinson's *Stones of Aran*. We were hungry for material and I hastened to meet this man as old as the century, who awaited his first publication.

An instant groundswell of support, reviews and readership came with the publication of Hubert Butler's *Escape from the Anthill* in May 1985. That essay volume was constructed over a previous year of week-end exchanges of mss and typescripts, trafficked down the Midlands corridor linking Westmeath to Kilkenny. Three further volumes of essays, with themed selections chronologically framed, followed down the years – *The Children of Drancy* (1988), *Grandmother and Wolfe Tone* (1990) and *In the Land of Nod* (1996) – as the drawers, desks and bookshelves of Maidenhall yielded up their bounty.

Much of the material had been previously unpublished (see Note on sources below) but the bulk had been preserved in small specialist periodicals – weeklys, monthlies, quarterlies – that lined Butler's shelves: *The Bell, Enyoy, Peace News, The Church of Ireland Gazette, The Twentieth Century, The Listener, The Dublin Magazine, The Kilkenny Magazine, The Irish Review, Hibernia,* the *Journal of the Butler Society,* and others; transcripts from the

BBC and Radio Éireann, *The Irish Times* and *The Irish Press* also surfaced. These organs kept the intellectual juices flowing and the spirit of debate and reflection alive in often diverse communities that had little else in common, tactile projectiles that allowed great freedom of thought in a more leisured and unhurried age than our own, creating a world-wide web of connectivity reaching into the future.

As the writer and politician Conor Cruise O'Brien declared, ending his memorial address for Seán O'Faoláin at Glasthule Church in Dublin on 4 May 1991, saluting the three great Irishmen of his day: 'You won, Owen Sheehy Skeffington, Hubert Butler and Seán O'Faoláin ... you won.'

Butler's earliest champions in the public domain included the journalist Eoghan Harris in his page in *Image* magazine, who also launched *Escape from the Anthill* on that memorable May day at Butler House in Kilkenny; the historian Roy Foster, who persuaded the *TLS* editor to open up his august columns to Butler in a substantive review; Dervla Murphy in *The Irish Times*; Monk Gibbon in the *Irish Independent*; Ulick O'Connor in the *Sunday Independent*; Chris Agee in *The Linen Hall Review*, Hugh Breedin at *Fortnight*. My fellow publisher-editors overseas took up the torch: Paul Keegan of Penguin in London, Elisabeth Sifton at Farrar Straus and Giroux in New York and Samuel Bruxelles at Anatolia in France, fortified by his Nobel-Prize-winning friend the poet Joseph Brodsky.

Behind the scenes, Hubert's wonderful wife Susan ('Peggy') Butler, a woman of formidable wit and concomitant warmth, held to a constant belief in her husband's genius as she presided over the serene household that was Maidenhall. His US-based daughter Julia Crampton and imperturbable son-in-law Richard Crampton were also powerful enablers, as were their children Cordelia, Suzannah and Tom; and, by extension, Joseph Hone and Eleanor Burgess: a formidable familial phalanx. From Oxford, Rob Tobin, author of *The Minority Voice: Hubert Butler and Southern Protestantism, 1900–1991* (2012), archived the family papers and lent invaluable support to us all.

There was an inexpressible ease, gentleness and quiet determination about the Butler I knew for eight years. It is a huge cause for joy in now knowing that his spirit and work endures, and will continue to inhabit and to nurture our minds. The small standing that The Lilliput Press has in Irish cultural life owes everything to his legacy.

A.F.
Arbour Hill, Dubin 7
12 February 2014

NOTE ON SOURCES

'A Stroll Around Leningrad': Unpublished typescript, 1932.

'Leningrad in 1932': Unpublished typescript, 1932.

'On a Russian Farm': Unpublished typescript, 1933.

'Those Russians': Unpublished typescript, 1933.

'Specialists in a Soviet school': the *Dublin Review* number 9, winter 2002–3

'Soviet Literature – A Survey': *The Irish Times*, 25 May 1946.

'Letter from Ireland': *Peace News*, 4 March 1949.

'Pacifism in Ireland': *Peace News*, 13 May 1949.

'Wanted: Unofficial Travellers': *Peace News*, 1 July 1949.

'*Friendship*: Personal or Official': *Peace News*, 22 July 1948.

'Autoantiamericanism': *The Bell, May 1951*.

'Trieste': *Peace News*, 20 November 1953.

'Yugoslavia Today': *Peace News*, 5 August 1955.

'Tito's Marxist': *Peace News*, 21 November 1958.

'Ireland and Neutrality': *Peace News, 7* March 1953.

'Home and Bigshotte Royles': Unpublished typescript, 1970.

'Charterhouse': Unpublished typescript, 1970.

'On Sex': Unpublished typescript, November 1962.

'About Deafness': Unpublished typescript, 30 August 1989.

'The Appleman and the Poet': Unpublished typescript, 1977.

'Stock-taking in the Irish Provinces': *The Twentieth Century*, October 1953.

'No Petty People': *The Irish Times*, 13 May–8 June 1955.

'Reflections of an Unjustified Stay-at-Home': *The Twentieth Century,*
October 1955.

'Protestantism and Unionism: Are They the Same Thing?': *The Plough*,
September 1957.

'Protestant Timidity': *Hibernia*, 25 July 1975.
'A Protestant Predicament': *Hibernia*, 25 July 1975.
'By-Products': *The Kilkenny Magazine,* summer 1960.
'An Encounter with Lord Ormonde': Unpublished typescript, 1945.
'Walter Butler: A Talk at the First Butler Rally': *Journal of the Butler Society*, 1970/71.
'Butlers' Island – Georgia': *Journal of the Butler Society*, 1973/74.
'The Butlers of Priestown': *Journal of the Butler Society*, 1973/74.
'Forewords': *Journal of the Butler Society*, 1978/79; 1988/89.
'Jonathan Swift': *The Kilkenny Magazine*, autumn – winter 1963.
'Enid Starkie': *The Bell*, February 1942.
'W.B. Yeats': for *The Kilkenny Magazine*, unpublished, 1944.
'Vienna – 1838' : Unidentified source, 1976.
'Denmark's Finest Hour': *The Irish Times*, 22 November 1963.
'The Ant at the Top of the Hill': *The Irish Press,* 10 July 1978.
"Some Irish Saints': *Church of Ireland Gazette*, 7 September 1950.
'Horace Plunkett and the Irish Co-operative Movement': *The Bell,* December 1951; *Irish University Review*, autumn 1977.
'Good Men and True': *The Irish Times* Book of the Day, 27 October 1964.
'The One and the Many': *The Irish Press*, 3 February 1977.
'Teilhard de Chardin': Unidentified source, 1977.
'Rebecca West in Yugoslavia': *The Irish Times*, 17 September 1977; the uncut version.
'Ronald Reagan and the American Wall of Separation: A View from Ireland in 1985': *Journal of the Butler Society*, 2010; *Princeton University, Library Chronicle*, 2010.

FOREWORD

THE PRIVATE INVESTIGATOR

Fintan O'Toole

'I was glad I belonged to an insignificant nation.'

In an essay written in 1975 and collected here, Hubert Butler recounts the eighteenth-century fable of the hen and the horses: 'A hen, finding herself alone in a stable with nowhere to roost, addressed herself to the horses: "Let us agree, kind sirs, not to tread upon each other!"' One might see some parallels with Butler's own situation, but also a crucial difference. He was a little hen in the stable of grand twentieth-century ideologies, a man of no great consequence, an 'English-Protestant Irishman' from a marginal part of an insignificant nation. He had no party, no Church, no institution, no power – often, even, no publisher. The only time he was much noticed, even in his own country, was when he was ostentatiously ostracized. And yet, unlike the deluded hen, he sought no agreement with the big beasts. With intellectual poise and literary elegance, he trod on them all the time. And as this late windfall of writings so amply demonstrates, he left an enduring footprint on their backs.

The Butler we find here is a man in a gap – or perhaps several gaps. In the gap between cynicism and scepticism, there are these wise and richly pleasurable essays. Butler is one of the twentieth-century's great sceptics. He is suspicious, quizzical, unshakeably unimpressed by the claims of systems, nations, alliances, crusades, totalities. He weighs those claims against the concrete realities he observes so sharply and finds them hollow. What he retains from his Protestant heritage is the idea that personal judgment is not just a right but an absolute duty. Butler is that rarest of things – a private investigator without a client. He looks into corners, pulls at threads, pursues contradictions. But he is searching for nothing more than the best approximation of the truth he can manage. He has the freedom of his own 'insignificance'. He is unburdened by the delusion that he will be heeded.

This scepticism is written into his prose. Butler does not raise his voice. In part, this is because there is no point in shouting when the only people who will hear you are likely to be close at hand anyway. 'What is the use', he asks, 'of a few grains of red pepper in an ocean of soup? Would it not be better to keep them to flavour a small cup?' It is striking, indeed, that the most peppery essay in this collection is an attack, not on a distant enemy, but on a friend and fellow-inhabitant of the small cup of Irish liberal dissent, Seán O'Faoláin. For the real enemies – the great tyrannies of the twentieth century – Butler reserves a cool, quiet, playfully humorous and unnervingly civil tone. That civility is itself a political statement, the only rebuke the writer can give to murderous hysteria and toxic cliché.

Time and again, Butler draws blood, not with the bludgeon but with the surgical incision. One of the great joys of these essays is the discovery of sentences as sharp and lithe as a Toledo rapier. No one can skewer an entire system with such economy and precision as Butler. Stalinism in nine words? 'To prove a theory a nation is being vivisected.' A century of Anglo-Irish relations in a sentence? 'The Union failed because the English, like the Irish, were unwilling to accept the equation that it implied.' The complex attitudes of most Irish people to the grand project of reviving Gaelic as their vernacular language? 'The average man treats the revival of Gaelic culture as one of those conventional aspirations, which it is bad form either to take seriously or to criticize.' The ways in which Tito shifted, for the West, from gallant anti-Nazi ally to Communist fiend, and back to gallant anti-Stalin ally? 'Tito quarrelled with Moscow and became no longer an ex-friend enemy, but an ex-enemy friend.' There's a steely glint to this tautly concentrated scepticism that would be cruel were it not so clearly truthful.

The attempt to be truthful, to see through the haze of contemporary enthusiasms and lies, is what makes Butler's essays so eerily prescient. The reader often has to look at the dates to confirm that they are not, indeed, written with hindsight. The collapse of the Soviet system through incompetence and self-delusion is prefigured in his calmly brilliant reports from Russia, written at a time when even his greatest critics credited Stalin with awe-inspiring power. The rise of religious fundamentalism in the politics of the United States is spotted early. The dilemma of Muslim women in relation to the wearing of the veil leaps out at us from the 1950s. The fear that American anti-Communism might

shade into a willingness to make use of fascists, expressed so power-
fully here, is entirely justified by subsequent events, especially in Latin
America. Even Ireland's acquiescence, in our own time, to rule by the
international debt-collecting Troika, is foreshadowed in a sentence that
shivers with anticipation: 'We have a respect for the registered and certified *fait accompli* that makes us at our best the most tolerant of people, at
our worst the most slavish.'

There is nothing mystical about this prescience, of course. It is the
fruit of a courageous scepticism that consists in seeing, and saying, the
obvious. At this level, Butler's genius is quite simple – it is the art of
recognition. He sees what is there to be seen. At another level, though,
Butler is complex. For against his own scepticism, he retains a stubborn,
equally unyielding idealism. He is as far from cynicism as he is from
gullibility. In one half of his mind there resides that most eighteenth
century of dreams, the search for universal love. Butler seems, not so
much to believe in this ideal, as to believe in nothing else. It is what he
is left with, after seeing Stalinism and Nazism, internecine hatreds in
Yugoslavia and Ireland, petty and appalling cruelties. Butler's idealism
is entirely of a piece with his lack of illusion: he believes in love because
he knows the alternatives only too well. The rubric for his essays might
be Auden's 'We must love one another or die.'

Love, though, is not so much a consolation as an agonizing question. The search for apparent impossibilities – a neutrality that is not dis-
engaged, a localism that is not parochial, an individualism that is not
merely individualistic – accounts for the restlessness behind the compo-
sure of his prose. He is tormented by the question: where can love live?
Not in the State: 'Isn't it obvious that in our highly organized world the
kindness and humanity and intelligence of the individual are commodities like any other to be hawked about by governments?' But not in the
family either: 'The family is too small a unit for tenderness and talent to
prosper side by side in its shade, the State is too large.' Nor is Butler, as
he is sometimes portrayed, a simple localist, for he knows that his own
patch of ground, however devoted he is to it, can never be enough for
him: 'Our affections are not really tethered to our neighbourhood. We
have not found it possible to coordinate our loyalties, which stray away
in contrary directions.'

All great writers have a large uncertainty at the heart of their work,
and this is Butler's: he is never quite sure what kind of collective can
express the 'kindness and humanity and intelligence of the individual'.
But he occupies this uncertainty as an open space. Just as he works in
the gap between scepticism and cynicism, he also places himself in the

small but radiant fissure between Either and Or. Butler's experiences of both Stalinism and Nazism in the 1930s give him the moral strength to be equally sceptical of both sides in the Cold War. He is an anti-Communist and an anti-anti-Communist.

With typical prescience, Butler, in Leningrad in the 1930s, imagines a future in which Communism has stampeded the world 'into two great parties': the competing blocs of the post-war world. Neither party is his. The real-world knowledge of Stalin's Russia so eloquently articulated here inoculated him against Communism. But 'the furious campaign against godlessness and Communism that is surging round us in Ireland' (a campaign of which he became an accidental victim) repelled him too. If he was "insignificant" in the Cold War years it was because he refused to amplify his own humane and sceptical voice with the booming rhetoric of either set of crusaders. That kind of insignificance was, in the long run, highly significant.

Hubert Butler lived through terrible decades when to refuse to be Either/Or was to be nothing. He made that refusal, in his own way, into not just something but everything. Early on in this luminous collection, Butler, in Russia, poses for himself a fundamental question about how to react to human suffering: 'Should we look away in disgust and horror or should we follow every tremor of the victim with sympathy and intense scientific curiosity?' At first glance, that final 'and' looks like it should be an 'or'. Most writers would pose 'sympathy' and 'scientific curiosity' as opposites – the one emotional and warm, the other intellectual and cold. Butler's glory is that he does not recognize such polarities. He writes with the cool detachment and fearless curiosity of a scientist. But every sentence is guided to its target by an unabashed and irreducible human sympathy.

PART ONE

Russian Dispatches
1932–1946

1

A STROLL AROUND LENINGRAD

Breakfast is over at the October Hotel and some tourists wish to blow away the memory of stale buns and bad eggs with a breeze from the Neva; guidebook in hand, they have negotiated the islands of October Square and find themselves gazing helplessly up the majestic length of the Nevsky, which they never can remember to call October Street. Trams groan up it like monstrous hydras, bulging arms and legs and faces. The wreathed mass of struggling bodies is borne slowly along while at every halt there is a frantic battle. IT IS ONLY ALLOWED TO ALIGHT FROM THE FRONT OF THE CAR. Dozens pour out and at the other end scores shove in, bells clang, wheels clank, and the rusty monster creeps into the middle distance.

The tourists are daunted.

If one is wealthy one can take a droshky but it is unlikely that one is as wealthy as all that. There are a few bearded isvoschiks in long blue coats driving spanking, well-fed horses in traditional harness. But now, instead of entrancing demi-mondaines or elegant loungers, they contain pince-nézed officials or Red Army officers. The droshky is becoming self-conscious, an anachronism, and that is uncomfortable in Russia. One may pay a few extra kopeks and take a bus but as they are less frequent than the trams they are just as crowded, and sometimes lie on their sides when too ruthlessly overloaded. Bicycles are seen occasionally. They would not be recognized by their working brothers in Oxford or Cambridge – as soon trot to your lectures on a race-horse as hack one of these shining sports models to the factory every morning.

But you can walk! The broad pavements of the Nevsky Prospekt are flagged with pantiles, grey and beautiful, and never since when they were laid down by Peter the Great have they seen such hard service as today.

Two hundred years before the Five Year Plan was conceived, in the bad old days of exploitation and hugger-mugger, St Petersburg was planned. Planned and built to a plan, indomitably dignified, the city imposes a certain order on its inhabitants. The trailing mobs of cotton-clad foot passengers move in regular streams up the expanse of Nevsky, and the fine buildings in the intersecting streets dwarf the heterogeneous crowds to a stylized uniformity. If you want to reach the Republiky Most in good order you must keep to your own side of the pavement.

It is impossible for the bourgeois visitor to avoid sentimentalizing as he elbows his way along, however proletarian his sympathies. He wonders whether Nevsky does not cry for rattling carriages, shining horses and lovely ladies. As he passes under the arcade of the Gostiny Dvor, richly dressed phantoms linger among the arches and flutter past him into discreet shops. Closer inspection will reveal the shops to be displaying a few white cabbages on doubtful linoleum swarming with flies ... but sentimentalists can ignore such trifles of fact. Do the painted walls of historic buildings gladly foil bright peasant handkerchiefs and hard brown peasant faces? The bourgeois wonders.

Maundering in this way, he will probably trip over a pile of masonry and rubble; streets are up, workers' dwellings going up, and churches coming down, debris is everywhere. On the Fontanka not only is the road under repair but a barge of firewood is being unloaded and piled along the pavement. Through the fine old wrought-iron railings of the canal one sees the reflection of deserted mansions, Italianate palaces and fin-de-siécle flats; this was once a fashionable street. On the Moika, on either side of the canal, the road is up and lorries bound recklessly off mounds of cobbles into pits of sand, the racing engines and smoking radiators intriguing the audience every motor can command in Leningrad.

Here you may even see a brand new Buick or Lincoln tipped at an angle of 45 degrees waiting for its tourist cargo to emerge from the Yusuppov Palace, now a club for scientific workers. These shining newcomers to Leningrad transport the First Class tourists rapidly from sight to sight. They are driven with reckless brutality and skill; they speed down the empty thoroughfares

4

at 60 mph, cutting their way through tram queues and peasant carts with small regard for either traffic regulations or human life. Light signals, operated by small boyish militiamen in neat grey, obviate the most bloody calamities; all the same there is a large road fatality for so pedestrian a city. Trams sometimes spill their contents wholesale, sometimes a struggling body is squeezed off and cut in two, sometimes two trams collide, at midday, travelling at 5 mph. The streets are never dull; you may see an ancient automobile expiring gloriously in smoke and flames, the passersby solemnly attentive. Or, on a frosty morning when the streets are slippery, you may see a distinguished citizen in a fur coat lying on his nose in the gutter, blind-drunk, and completely ignored by everyone.

But Uritzky Square is a haven for nervous pedestrians, an oasis of peace in a restless city. In the summer it was more like a ploughed field than a palace yard, but the small island of asphalt in the centre under the Alexander Column has gradually spread over the whole great expanse. The shifts were working day and night to complete the task, under the burning midday sun, dazzled by the sand and dust, and at night, when the Neva rolls darkly past and the silhouette of Peter and Paul was faintly visible across the water.

Wandering through the galleries of the Hermitage one passes imperceptibly into the main building of the Palace, used now as a public gallery, where one is torn between looking at the pictures on the walls and at the great square laid out like a handkerchief at one's feet. A glance through the vast windows of the Winter Palace of the Romanovs does something to illuminate the mentality of Imperial Russia; even the puny tourist from the home-counties catches his breath and savours the faint aftertaste of intoxicating power. The whole area of impudently splendid buildings enclosing the square, is so confident, so solid with authority and tradition, so apparently impregnable. Steam-engines rolling the square below are dwarfed to the dimension of beetles and the painters at work on the Palace itself are insignificant as flies. It is only when one glances through another window into the little vulnerable face of a painter suspended between heaven and earth that one abruptly realizes the tremendous importance of these human flies and the monumental stupidity of the arrogant shell they are whitewashing. No British workman would trust himself in the cradle used by this painter, a roughly knocked-up affair of fragile splinters; but lack of security does not seem to worry him and in November the freshly painted Winter Palace is a monument to his methods. The authorities decided to do up all the principal stucco buildings of the city in their original colours and the resulting ochres and lilacs and blues and greens are very delightful.

Unless one has lots of time, shopping in Leningrad is a hopeless business; time means nothing to most Russians, who prefer to wait half an hour for a tram rather than reach their destination in ten minutes on foot. Queues are ubiquitous and are not confined to bakeries and co-operatives and other purveyors of necessities. Should you wish to have your photograph taken you must queue up and listen to endless discussion between the photographer and his clients, chiefly sailors; whether to be taken in uniform, or with the shirt open at the neck or perhaps the whole torso without any shirt, this is the kind of question that has to be decided. Married and engaged couples do arty snuggles and cuddles under the lens and are tweaked into position by the operator. All this takes time. Even bookshops have the animated appearance English people associate with Great White Sales; young people stand three deep at the counter choosing picture postcards that are cheap and excellent; you will find coloured reproductions of modern painters among which Cezanne and Van Gogh are well-represented, admirable coloured drawings of animals, and studies of old Russian customs and village life, almost pre-Raphaelite in their careful realism. The cards are chosen for their cultural and propagandist qualities and are immensely popular with all-comers. What Englishman could resist sending his aunt the card on which an American dentist in solar topee and eyeglass (British officer), is threatening an innocent black man with a dog whip? A Bible is sticking out of the British officer's pocket. There are not many bound books in stock as owing to the paper shortage books are rationed and only a limited number of intellectual books are produced. Elementary educational, propagandist, and technical pamphlets, cheap and easy for beginners, take precedence over poetry, novels and philosophical works.

At the street corners are stalls attached to the big bookshops where stationery, pamphlets and postcards may be bought as well as the daily papers. A few street vendors peddle cigarettes singly out of grubby boxes and display toothpicks in enticing bunches; in the summer evenings hoydens with flowers tease the drab passers-by and tempt them with the fresh gaiety of their bouquets. Each blossom may cost 30 to 50 kopeks but there is so little else to buy that people often take some home. The banana plant, which readers of nineteenth-century novels associate with Russian interiors, has survived the Revolution and many windows in the dreary cliffs of apartment houses are thick with its unappetizing greenery.

In Leningrad even the shoeblacks have their queues; they are an elderly grizzled fraternity with uninterested eyes who crouch on their little stands day-long, and are always busy. People in top-boots should be avoided at all costs in a queue because it takes several minutes to polish the leg of a top-boot, and as the legs in the boots often belong to soldiers or officials the shoeblack lingers over them till he can see his reflection in the glossy cylinder. Pushing young women wear smart, high-heeled, coloured leather shoes but the great mass of the people walk around in wretched bark pampooties, heel-less slippers, or the kind of speckled sandshoes one connects with suburban gymnasiums. The leather brogues of a foreigner are a treat to the shoeblack and he turns back the foreign trousers reverently from the beautiful foreign shoes.

Perhaps the climax of the shopping experience is reached in the General Post Office, in the stamp queue. After ten minutes of waiting it is your turn to approach the guichet and you request a group of ladies in blouses behind the counter for half-a-dozen stamps. 'Stamps?' says the spokeswoman briskly, 'Stamps? I haven't any at present but if you'd like to wait I can send out for some!'

But it would be a pity to wait because there is still so much to see in Leningrad.

[1932]

2

LENINGRAD IN 1932

'Nine million tons of pig iron is the estimate for 1932,' said a Soviet official, adding wearily, 'Yes we have made great progress in education and the theatre and the films are all excellent, but we haven't enough to eat.'

There was nothing very surprising about this admission (indeed it was self evident) except that an official should have made it. Never till this winter have the Communists been so frank about the hardships that the Five Year Plan is imposing on the Russian people. It is now nearing its end and the strain is at its greatest. Never since 1920 have the people been called upon to face a more cheerless winter, if they endure it without collapse there seems to be no limit to what can be borne. Whatever we may think of the goal they are striving towards, the chances are that they will stay the course.

There are plenty of inducements dangled in front of them it is true. The next Five Year Plan is to develop the light industries and to raise the standard of living. Many of the great industrial undertakings will already be working at full capacity and there will be less need for foreign capital and foreign brains. They will not have to export food, but the finished products of their new factories and the collective farms will be well under way. Because of this there will be butter and eggs and sugar and tea and bacon in plenty for the housewives.

This is an old, old story, and the Russian citizen does not question its truth – but the prospect of good dinners a few years hence is cold comfort for an empty stomach.

Torgsin, the foreigners' shop, is the most splendid of all the food stores. Cotton curtains hide the display from the street, and the doorway is barred by an old man, who says, 'Only foreign currency or gold.' It is a great privilege to be able to shop there, even a walk round provides the simple with a thrill. When our maid Masha went to buy eggs and butter, she tied a clean red handkerchief round her head and took a friend. Once through the door, except for the long queues and the seething crowds, one might be in Liptons or the Home and Colonial. There are mountains of butter and eggs and white loaves, cheeses and tins of fish and fruit, cream cakes, pear drops and strawberry jam. I can hear English spoken with an American accent; the cashier has to fumble distractedly in German marks, Greek and Italian money, and seldom produces the right change. It is a foreigners' shop yet the mass of customers are Russian. The Russians are of two types. There are stocky peasant women who have probably exchanged a gold cross or their wedding ring for Torgsin bonds. A prosperous peasant in the old days seldom invested his money in anything but gold ornaments for his wife. Banks break, currency becomes worthless but gold never loses its value. The Soviet government has always been aware of the wealth of gold in private hands and has tried to extract it in various ways. It has used laws and threats, violence, even torture, but endurance is one of the lessons that Russia has learnt from her past.

Torgsin is a more humane mode of extracting it. You may not get a great deal for your gold but you get something and even the thriftiest find it hard to resist the temptation of the well-filled shelves. The other class of Russian who shops in Torgsin has seen better days. Though they are bourgeois a few have married into Communist families or used their brains to get positions of trust. Others are too old or too deeply committed to the old order of things to adapt themselves to the new. They belong to a liquidated class yet they have a certain value to the Soviets for their relations who emigrated and send them foreign money, which they exchange for Torgsin bonds. But bad times in Paris and Prague, Berlin and Belgrade, and all the haunts of refugees, have checked the flow of gold to Russia; the geese have stopped laying golden eggs, it is time to sell them. A few weeks ago it became possible to ransom one's relations from Russia.

Only a very small proportion of the inhabitants of Leningrad can hope to shop in Torgsin, for the others there remains the co-operatives and their various categories. Third-Category workers can be sure of little but bread and vegetables, the Second can count on rice, buckwheat and millet, macaroni and sugar and butter, while the First Category can often get such delicacies as sausage or dried fruit. The prices are very low but the quantities allowed on each ticket are small. The majority of people supplement their ticket by purchasing it in the open market. Prices may be ten times as high as in the co-operatives but purchases are usually to be found.

There is a big market building filled with stalls not far off the Nevsky where the produce of the collective farms is sold, the surplus that the government has not commandeered. It is moderately filled but to reach it one must pass through a narrow lane seething with excited traders. It is in this small lane and not in the spacious official hall that the bulk of the business is transacted. Rows of countrywomen stand around holding slabs of butter or meat, while some are re-selling at a profit sugar and meal and delicacies purchased at Torgsin or the co-operatives. Not far away stand others, haggling about galoshes or old leather coats. To get regular meals in Leningrad, if you are not in a factory with a factory dining-room, you often need ingenuity and patience. It is sometimes too much of a bother, and to save trouble one misses a dinner or supper. Yet for a special occasion, for a marriage or a name day or a big party, no effort will be spared. For weeks beforehand the whole family will be collecting and contriving for delicacies. A cousin who is on the stage will get them a cake through the theatrical co-operative. Relations in the First and Second categories will bring gingerbread and sausages and smoked herring and pickled cucumber. A German engineer will be asked to bring sprouts and Caucasian wine and Marie biscuits from Torgsin. The maid will be sent home on holiday to bring back a couple of chickens or some home-cured bacon, and her work of waiting in the bread queue will have to be undertaken by the members of the family.

The party is the blossoming of weeks of effort. The tables groan with food and drink. There are toasts and jokes and songs and laughter. At two or three o'clock some of the guests go home, while the rest go to bed on the floor and tip-toe out in the early morning – then the family sleep on in no hurry to awake. Food achieved, they sleep the sleep of the replete. Pinching, planning and privation are over – till tomorrow.

3

ON A RUSSIAN FARM

I

Most visitors to Russia expect to be shown a collective farm, but many return frustrated and disappointed. The farms that were on the programme of their tour turn out on investigation to be not collective but state farms, and between the 'Kolkhoz' and the 'Sovkhoz' there is all the difference in the world. The 'Sovkhoz' is a state-run experimental farm: it has laboratories and model crèches, English-speaking foremen and nice tourist lunches, and like all experimental farms all over the world it has no pretentions to being economically self-supporting. There are lots of them at home and the tourists, having patted the babies in the crèches and digested the lunches, become querulous and suspicious. Was it for this that they jollied for two hours on hard seats across the monotonous swampy plains? They feel that they have been cheated and made fools of and they distrust everything they see. Why are the test-tubes and the samples of soil in the laboratory always so tidy and the professors always at their lunch? Then why can't they be seen at this lunch? And what, anyway, do they have for lunch? A harassed, overworked guide prevaricates and tells them that unless they run they'll miss the train. As they wait for those quarters of an hour on a draughty, derelict platform their feeling of disappointment and frustration deepens. They forget the lunch and the babies and that not even in England are foreigners shown professors dining, and remember only that they have seen nothing that they came to see, not even a cow or a haystack. Call that a farm!

The fault, of course, is partly with the tourists and with the whole system of tours. Tourists are often considered frivolous, useless people, and no one would want to interrupt the work on a real farm, to have them trooping across the young corn, distracting the manager, leaving the gates open. On no farm in the British isles would a 'surprise visit' of thirty foreign tourists be welcomed, why should they be welcomed on a collective farm in Russia? So it is that, part cynically, part from a genuine desire to please, the 'show farms' are 'shown' – everything is prepared, the babies are there to be patted, the ledgers to be examined, the tall tenement houses clean and irreproachable around the office and the laboratory. Far away on the horizon, inconceivably remote, is a little dot; it may be a silo or a cow or a farm-hand, but between it and the tourists lie acres of mud and slush and marsh – and they have no change of boots. When at last they have been jostled back into the train they realize with a pang of remorse that it was the little dot and not the offices and the crèches that they came all the way to Russia to see.

Russia is full of collective farms, but they are inaccessible and it was not till that I had been there several months that I succeeded in seeing one. The officials declared that there were none to be seen within a wide range of Leningrad and that it was the wrong time of the year. When at last through a friend I heard of a 'Kolkhoz' within easy reach of Leningrad, I could be sure at any rate that it was not an 'official' farm. There would be haystacks and cows, even if there wasn't a crèche.

We left in the frosty early morning, the canals were already frozen over and we had to keep rubbing the windows with our train-tickets to see out of them. One caught a glimpse of the Finland railway station and the great black figure of Lenin with hand outstretched on the very spot where fifteen years before he had delivered his first speech on his return to Russia. The train took us on to a sandy district where there were small dilapidated villas scattered among pine trees and at last came to a stop almost on the borders of Finland. To our left were still pine trees and sand, slopes and a glimpse of a cold blue lake and more pine trees beyond it stretching to the Finnish Gulf. To the right the prospect was more typically Russian, such pine trees as there were, were swallowed up in the distance, tillage and fields were small patches in an indefinite wilderness. On the edge of it lay the K – collective farm.

The houses of the Kolkhozniki, or collectivized farmers, lie along a sideroad: they are large, two-storied wooden dwellings, more like villas than farm-houses. In the old days it was easy to get summer visitors here to rest in the pine woods, and the country people must always have had a good deal of town sophistication and shared a little in the prosperity of St Petersburg. Nevertheless they held their land on the primitive strip system, universal in the Russian contryside. The strips started from the back of each house and ran parallel away from it. The absurdity of this previous system must constantly be borne in mind when the collective agriculture is criticized. There was little opposition when in 1928 the collective farm was organized. Those who refused to join in were allowed to retain patches of land in one particular section, but for various reasons they soon abandoned it and preferred to work in Leningrad.

There are 720 hectares in K-farm and it is comprised of the union of 70 different holdings, and 17 families, who were admitted without holdings. Altogether there are 285 members of the Kolkhoz, about 100 of whom are able-bodied workers on the farm. There are four people in the manager's office, a book-keeper, two clerks, and a technical expert; as the crops were all gathered, there was little work on the farm and they were ready and eager to answer questions and show us around. My friend had himself been working on a collective five years before and was interested to see what progress had been made. There were 135 head of cattle on the farm, including 83 dairy cows, 54 horses, 56 pigs and 10 piglets. There were 65 hectares under oats, 25 under sunflowers, there was a silo almost complete, which would hold 350 tons of feeding stuff, composed mainly of sunflowers, cabbage leaves, potato peel and weeds. Owing to the proximity of Leningrad they were able to devote about 60 hectares to market gardening, cabbage, turnip, potatoes and tomatoes. They had also a few acres under roots for the cattle.

In the winter the horses work in the town carting wood, and all the year round, in exchange for milk, the farm gets slops and scraps from the restaurants and the hotels, which it feeds to the pigs and dairy cows. In these and other ways K- is affected by the vicinity of a great city and neither its members nor its methods are entirely typical. In its constitution and rules, however, it can be taken as representative of all the collective farms of Russia.

One of the most interesting and most involved of its aspects is the system of payment. The unit for which payment is made is called 'a day's work', but this is judged not by a time-valuation but by a certain standard of achievement varying with the class of work. Each dairy-maid, for instance, at K- has about 10 cows under her charge and 'a day's work' is judged at about 40 litres of milk, more or less according to the season. She may, in this way, achieve more than 'a day's work' in the day. Ploughmen and cattleherds are similarly paid according to a standard of achievement. In addition to these considerations there are five or six grades of labour for which the 'day's work' is calculated differently: someone whose job is light and unskilled, such as minding poultry, may find his day's effort only calculated at half a 'day's work'; the skilled clerks, though, find their daily office-hours are reckoned at two day's work, and jobs demanding inter-mediate degrees of skill are calculated accordingly. The office of book-keeper on a collective farm is obviously no sinecure.

In 1931 the pay per 'day's work' was 3 roubles 10 kopecks. This year the final assessment will probably be 4r. 75k. It is not known till the end of the year when the proceeds of the farm have been calculated at what rate the 'day's work' can be paid, but till the final reckoning is made, every month the wages are paid according to an estimate made at the beginning of the year. The difference is paid up at the end of the year, when the books are finally made up. In the year 1932, for instance, though it was anticipated that the 'day's work' would be 4r. 50k. actually it has proved to be 4r. 75k., so only 3r. a day were paid in advance every month. What was owing was made up at the end of the year, partly in roubles, partly in actual produce.

II

On K-farm the sale of the produce is also conditioned by various regulations. A large proportion is bought by the government at a fixed price and is used for the supply of rest-homes, government shops, etc. What is left over may be sold in the private market at competitive prices and the proceeds divided among the Kolk-hozniki. In the last few months, in order to stimulate production, the amount appropriated by the government has been greatly reduced – hence far more is available for the private market.

The Kolkhoz is often confused with the Sovkhoz, a different, far more drastic system of collectivization, whose forcible extension was checked by Stalin himself in the spring of last year. Under the Sovkhoz, all property is held in common, and the individual peasant may not even keep poultry. Each member must sacrifice all his private property to the Sovkhoz, and in return is fed and clothed and schooled by it. The Sovkhoz system has now been abandoned and under the collective farm a large measure of private property is allowed. We visited the private farmyard of one of the Kolkhozniki and found a cow and several pigs and a great many hens, all thriving and well looked after.

The collective dairy cattle are kept in a long wooden shed with wooden flooring, scrupulously clean and lit by electricity, for electricity is now in use even in remote farmsteads in Russia. Milking is done by hand but as far as conditions allow modern dairy methods are in use. This year it has been difficult to keep up the proper rations for the dairy cattle and the pigs; each cow has a fixed diet according to its milk yield, hung over its stall, varying proportions of hay, straw, ensilage and restaurant scraps but the dairymaid admitted that in the last few months these had had to be modified. Some of the pigs especially bore traces of their reduced rations.

K-farm has not been long established and its workers have fewer social amenities than those of neighbouring farms. A big building, mainly of wood, was in the process of erection alongside of the road. It was to house the club and reading-room; on the ground floor there was to be a common dining-room. There is a farm orchestra on K-farm, but 'culturally' K-farm considers itself backward and is not pleased with its progress.

On the office wall hangs the current copy of the wall gazette, a universal feature of all Soviet institutions. It is the joint production of all the members of the farm, its columns are open to mutual criticism, grievances are discussed and settled, slackers are reproached, workers are commended and to give it spice personalities and even caricatures are allowed of rather a savage kind. Occasionally there are even some jokes. This issue is the jubilee number for the fifteenth anniversary of the October Revolution and it is richly illuminated with red stars and flourishes. I had time to read something very sarcastic about a muddle-headed clerk and a drunken ploughman and the following appeal called 'The Plea of the Children': 'We, the children of brigade three, ask our parents and elder friends not to take us out with them all day riding on the hay wagons etc because it interferes with our homework and we hear them using bad language and learn to use it ourselves.'

After reading this wall gazette it was almost a relief when I returned to Leningrad to see naughty boys throwing stones at tourist's motors and making slides on the pavement like their capitalist contemporaries. Juvenile literary contributions in an earnest and reproachful vein are universal in Russia. I remembered the Soviet slogan pinned-up in the playroom of a crèche at one of the state farms. 'Play is not just fun but a preparation for toil.' There are Sovkhoz workers even in the nursery, but the toddlers, who were romping in the playroom, did not seem to be worrying their heads much about the texts on the wall.

Nothing but Russian is spoken at K-farm. England and Ireland are unknown there. I was shown a big white sow, whose family came from Yorkshire, and I believe that she was the only living things in the whole existence of K-farm connected with these islands. Yet it was impossible not to wonder whether all that one saw there would be purely national in its effects or would one day affect one's own country too. To this there is no satisfactory answer.

It would be possible to come away from K-farm, as from many other such farms through the length and breadth of the USSR, with very comforting conclusions for western European agriculture. I have not tried to translate the rouble wages of farm labourers into their equivalent in our currency, because the rouble has only internal value and attempts to equate it with our money would be misleading, but it would not be hard to prove that in the necessities of life the Russian farm labourer is at present much poorer than the labourers of Sovkhoz. All the same, whether collective agriculture survives in Russia will not depend on the economic prosperity of any particular farm, perhaps not even on the economic success of all the collective farms in Russia. Collectivization linked up closely with the essential doctrine of Bolshevism, and I think the Soviets would be prepared for any economic sacrifice rather than abandon it.

To prove a theory a nation is being vivisected. It is a clumsy piece of surgery, whatever we may think of its motives. Should we look away in disgust and horror or should we follow every tremor of the victim with sympathy and intense scientific curiosity?

[1933]

16

4

THOSE RUSSIANS

Most people who have been to Russia, even if it's only for a week, feel that they are imposters if they do not return with notebooks crammed with horrors and statistics. How many churches have been desecrated? How many farms collectivized? What about pig-iron and the GPU [State Political Directorate, under the Council of Peoples Commissars of the USSR; successor to the Cheka]? Those who live any length of time in Russia must find their appetite for this sort of thing steadily declining. They either quickly become immune to figures or else go mad, for it is easier to extract prophesies from the proportions of the Great Pyramid than to get political generalizations from the labyrinth of Soviet society.

Firstly about the figures – they are meaningless or else misleading. Anyone who has had the experience of changing money in a Russian state-bank, and seen three people with pencil and paper, a bead abacus and an American adding-machine working out a simple proportion sum for twenty minutes and then working it out wrong, will not believe that figures about cotton production in Turkestan carried to three decimal points are going to be very informative. He will conceive a distrust for Russian figures that will never leave him. Neither under the Tsar nor under the Bolsheviks have the abstract sciences flourished. Not only statistical research but also elementary book-keeping were always the handmaids of political dogma. That this is so in present-day Russia does not take long to discover.

Last year the Soviet government appointed an eminent authority on intelligence classification to find out in the American method in what section of the community the highest degree of intelligence was to be found. After very careful experiment and statistics he found a slight superiority among children of non-proletarian origin. He was told promptly that he must have made a mistake in his calculations and a second scientist was sent to collect the information.

This extreme reverence for the results of statistics and the very lighthearted way of arriving at them are characteristic, all the same, not of Bolshevism but of Russia. A civil servant, who knew Russian officialdom both before and after the Revolution, told us that on the whole Bolshevik book-keeping and general clerical efficiency is a degree higher than those it replaced, and bribery, once universal as a means of securing the right results, is now practically unkown. In this connection it is interesting to remember how minute has been Russia's contribution to scientific thought, to mathematics or physics, to any experimental work that demands not brilliant generalizations but precise laborious calculation. Perhaps the exact sciences require a leisured, settled world, a sense of freedom from exploitation and oppression that the Russian people have never had.

Another reason for being indifferent to statistics is of course the vast size and diversity of Russia; a sixth of the whole world, it is of considerable importance in which particular pocket the statistician alights with his notebook. I met in north Russia a woman who till a few years ago had been managing her own estate. Our maid in Leningrad was the daughter of quite a prosperous farmer, who had somehow escaped dekulakization; they lived in the heart of collective Russia yet kept their pigs and their cows and hens and wove their own clothes; she came back every time from her holidays laden with country produce as she might have done twenty years ago. There must be many such still in Russia. Naturally they are very popular with their employers.

Those who travel will see merely by looking out at the small station platforms the infinite diversity of Russian conditions. The train passes through a zone of watermelons; the melons disappear and give place to chickens; then comes a zone of overripe cucumbers, a zone of small green apples or corn cobs, or nothing at all. The collapse of transport accounts largely for the fact that the food is so badly distributed; there are pockets of plenty in a wilderness of starvation. In the same way there are factories and collective farms that flourish, others that decay, and in both cases there are a thousand other causes more important than the Communistic theory working for their success or failure. There is the same absolute diversity among the people themselves; romantically minded tourists may find princessess selling matches in the gutter, old generals hawking little plaster busts of Lenin; it is not so easy to identify the princess who is a manager of a big workers' club or the general who is working in the GPU. If it is power, and not a comfortable life, that they enjoy, in many cases they find more scope for it in the new life even than in the old, but they are not going to boast of their origin to the statistician. It is significant that those much maligned guides, who 'show you only what they want you to see', are drawn almost exclusively from the former landowning and professional classes, for only there was a knowledge of foreign languages to be found. The tables were turned, but it is probable that now, after fifteen years, a pushing bourgeois stands as good a chance as a pushing proletarian – discriminations are made against him, but on the other hand he has the traditions of leadership and the relics of a good education to help him. Probably there is much the same scum and sediment in the new world as in the old.

In Russia it is easy to form conclusions, but it is hard to see their relevance to the outer world. Yet it is obvious that Russia and Communism are now established as levers in the political life of other countries and topics of conversation in every home. Exotic, eastern bogies, they haunt the most peaceful suburbs and it is too late now for mere argument to exorcize them. Russians themselves do not discuss Communism in the home and are surprised at the interest and enthusiasm or the horror of the foreign visitors. They are as bored as an Englishman would be should a party of foreigners come over to find the exact workings of the national government. Why do all these people, I was repeatedly asked, want to see our bakeries, our crèches? Have they none at home? They are equally baffled by the indignant suspicious members of parliament, who aren't allowed to see the inside of political prisons, to attend secret meetings of the GPU, to see factories that aren't working and farms that don't pay. Are those the sort of things that we show our visitors? But outside Russia the talk is all of Communism. Those who know Russia may find it hard to say what Communism, as they saw it, is, but they won't find it hard to say what it is not.

In most people's minds at the present day it seems to stand

for any revolutionary creed whatever. Land confiscation, that is Communism; attacks on the churches, attacks on the banks, that is Communism; Communists burnt the Reichstag and shot at President Roosevelt, and so on down to bank robberies, free love, obscene literature, and Mr Gandhi. But the Communism of Lenin is, after all, only one of six or seven revolutionary policies, which by a mere accident captured the Russian government in 1917 by the very un-communistic device of giving the land to the peasantry.

What has happened to all the other revolutionary parties, who Lenin regarded as his bitterest enemies, more hateful, because more insidious, than the landlords and the priests themselves? Do they never shoot and burn? No, it is always the Communists! Is this just a new method of classification on the part of journalists and politicians, or has the world genuinely grouped itself into two violently opposing parties? Has the success of Leninism in Russia (I use success in the sense that there is no sign yet of its collapse) acted like a magnet to which all the discontented people of the world have been drawn, from which all the comfortable contented classes have recoiled? Has it stampeded them all into two great parties? Whether it has or not, probably the most indefatigable advertisers of Communism have been its opponents, who treat it not as political theory but as a virulent disease. Its diagnosis must often embarrass them.

Who are the worst enemies of the Bolsheviks? Probably the Letts, the Estonians, the Poles, people who have had racial as well as political and economic grievances against the Russians. They fought against the Communists and defeated them but when the Baltic peoples set about establishing their new states, the bulwark for the rest of Europe against Communism, one of their first moves was to confiscate the major portion of the property of the landlords and also of the Church. Neither has regained its lost territory since. There are German noblemen as pitifully dispossessed as any in Russia living in small rooms in Riga or Reval, who are the victims not of Communism but of its bitterest enemies. The Letts, who claim that this adoption of revolutionary method saved Latvia from Communism, may or may not be right but at any rate it should narrow down a little our definition of Communism.

The history of the last few weeks in Germany should also dispose finally of the notion that violent methods, the suppression of freedom of speech and thought, the attack on private liberty, are in any way a Communist monopoly. They are the natural accompaniment of any violent change of government. The Bolsheviks have not been able to suppress nationalism in their own people and the Nazis too will find that Marxism can no more be refuted by suppressing newspapers than relativity can be refuted by suppressing Einstein.

Is it too late now for us to think of Communism out of its Russian setting? It is a theory of economics evolved not in bloody massacre in Russia but largely in the Reading Room of the British Museum by Marx and Lenin, and only other economic facts can combat it. The original conception is no doubt erroneous and out of date. Marx, for instance, wrote *Das Kapital* with a highly industrialized country like England in view, and he prophesied that Russia, owing to its large individualistic agricultural population, would be both the last and the least fitted to receive the gospel. At the meetings of the Communist International the Russian delegates were regarded with contempt by all the others; they were thought factious and unconstructive and animated too often by bitter personal hostilities. Above all, they brought an Eastern fanaticism, born perhaps of their religion and the oppression of the Tsars, to bear on the discussions. Marx, like Lenin after him, became not an economist but a Messiah, and a dozen prophets sprang up among the Russian exiles, each with a different interpretation of their gospel. There is no doubt that if Marx had lived to see the development of the social sciences, of psychology generally, he would have made many modifications in the creed, but of such modifications the Russian exiles could not admit a trace, and it is characteristic that it was Lenin, the least compromising of them all, who finally won. It is natural though that we should still think of Communism with a rather Oriental tinge, just as if Liberia were the only republic or Babylon the only empire our views on democracy and imperialism would be very differently cast.

It is probably because Russians are such fervent individualists that they have always had to be ruled by dogma and dynamite. Stalin learnt his brand of it in a theological college in the Caucasus, where he founded a small revolutionary society among the other students. He demanded from them the same unquestioning faith that his teachers demanded from him. He was impatient of anything unorthodox. When he left Russia he visited Capri where Maxim Gorki had founded a Communist university on a humanistic basis. There were lectures and debates and everything was freely discussed and disputed, but Stalin was revolted by it and halfway through his course bolted to Lenin in Paris. Lenin, who had quarrelled with Gorki, met him grimly with the words, 'You won't find intellectual liberty and right of public judgment here. The Central Committee rules here!' Stalin was delighted and became his most devoted disciple from that time on.

Now the whole Russian empire is ruled according to his beloved dogma.

What about the Communist attack on religion? The brutality and venom with which it has been persecuted has disgusted the whole world, but the position of Russian Christians has been made greatly worse by ecclesiastical denunciations of Communism, whatever salutary effects these may have had at home. If no Christian can be a Communist, then in a Communist state a Christian must, *ipso facto*, be an enemy of the state and the government seem to be given a better justification than Nero ever had for acting against them. This year more churches were pulled down than ever before; the largest cathedral in Moscow, the Spasetel, has been destroyed and the Kazan Cathedral in Leningrad has joined the Isaki Cathedral as a museum of waxwork figures illustrating the evolution of superstition from Egyptian and Babylonian down to Christian times. Nobody, who wishes to know about Russian religion, need stay long in either of these cathedrals; the exhibits are crude and unfair, the pictures of the deification of the Imperial Family are probably fakes, so are many of the documents. In any case the shafts of ridicule are directed, nowadays, mainly against the rival spiritual leaders outside Russia, such as Gandhi or the Holy See. The home front, in their eyes, is well in hand.

The leaders of the Soviets and of the Churches agree that Christianity is incompatible with Communism, but they probably both have the Russian brand in view. They may be right in general as well, but there are particular reasons why the Russian revolutionaries and the Russian Church should always be at loggerheads. As evidence for that we don't need the anti-religious museums. Wallace, a Victorian writer who described Russia at the end of the last century, spoke of the sluggish corruption of the clergy and the close ties that bound them to the Emperor, whose ministers had in fact the appointment of the synod and all the bishops entirely in their hands. The village priest was often expected to be a political agent, as well, reporting any suspect in the neighbourhood. He tells how Moscow noblemen, who wanted matins celebrated, used to send out their footmen to haggle with the priests who stood outside the Kremlin: the priests had breakfast rolls in their hands and threatened to break their fast with a bite if the fee was not large enough. It was clear that the Russian Church would not for long survive the Tsardom.

The Bolsheviks have attacked the Orthodox Church in several ways – by actual persecution and confiscation, by taxation, by imposing disabilities on churchmen or more subtly by promoting schism in the Church itself. These are the methods they use with adults, whom it is easier to intimidate than to persuade – but for the young there is the whole battery of anti-religious propaganda. I think that is mainly the reason for the extreme crudity and simplicity of Bolshevik propaganda. It does not aim at converting the old or sophisticated; those who have resisted fifteen years intensive persecution must be pretty tough and would in any case be unreliable converts, so they are allowed to go their own way. That there are many such, and that they are not interfered with at present anyone who was in Leningrad on Alexander Nevski day last September would have seen without a doubt. It was a day when all the Alexanders and Alexandras in Russia used to celebrate their nameday with parties and flowers before the Revolution in the big monastery called after their patron saint at the end of the Nevski Prospekt. Even in 1932 one could see many people rushing about with bunches of dahlias and bags of cakes, and a great crowd of many thousands was pressing in through the gates of the monastery. I saw a Red Army officer whom I knew, called Alexander, among the crowd, but when I congratulated him on his birthday he went very red and said the day of the month had never entered his head. He had just happened to be passing by. All the same, he came with me into the church, and we saw three priests gorgeously dressed, blessing, head by head, a long procession of worshippers. The congregation was mainly elderly, such young ones as there […] and anonymous bits of metal and woodwork all painted glaring colours.

Everybody who visits Russia feels bound to investigate the condition of the churches – but in Russia itself it is hard to get evidence either of great persecution or great devotion. I should say that nobody there except the elderly is religious from habit, but I met a few young people who were religious from conviction. Most of the young who were mystically minded have been ridiculed by their teachers and schoolfellows, by wireless talks,

and school lessons, out of their parents' faith and inoculated successfully with Lenin worship and the Five Year Plan. Christians
are represented as sneaky and underhand and unathletic, lacking
those virile and true womanly qualities that make a good Komsomol. Among schoolboys and schoolgirls, of course, this form of
propaganda is far more effective even than torture.

If religious enthusiasm revived in Russia I think it would not
be among the unhappy survivors of the Orthodox Church but
among the fully-fledged Communists themselves. They are bored
with the boy-scout virtues of the Komsomol, but to a Russian
soul mystical enthusiasm is indispensable. Five Year Plans cannot
go on forever and Lenin himself is an arid figure on which to
focus so much supernatural fervour. Pious hands have collected
and edited every scrap he ever wrote. Russian literary criticism
is moulded on his perky schoolboy style – even his scribbled
annotations on a volume of Hegel have recently been edited.
These consist of marks in the margin like, 'Fool!' 'Stupid German
sausage!' 'Sheer idealistic childishness!' How long can this last?
There is one thing to be said about Lenin. He would have been
profoundly surprised at the Lenin cult, a new opiate for the
people, for under the cloak of Leninism a mass of measures have
been taken of which he would have profoundly disapproved.
Perhaps there are already some indications that the Bolsheviks
will be content with the overthrow of the Church and will not
demand that Christianity itself be uprooted. One of the leading
Russian novelists, who is also a Communist, has ventured to
make his most sympathetic character a Christian and his friend a
nobleman. His political orthodoxy is well known but all the same
his book is thought very daring.

There is no country in which unoffending people are persecuted so outrageously and cynically as in Russia, but the foreign
press, which represents this as systematic or calculated, is usually
wide of the mark. Misfortune, when it falls, falls like a thunder-
bolt – there is a wild attack of hysteria and nerves at headquarters, a hunt round is made for a victim – as likely as not they have
forgotten the address of the most suitable scapegoat (I think the
all-seeing eye of the GPU is a romantic fiction) and somebody
completely innocent finds himself hauled off to justice. When I
was in Russia, though the Torgsin shops had started, there was
a great deal of talk still of the hot and cold rooms into which citizens, who were suspected of hoarding gold, were being made to

stew or freeze alternately until they gave it up. Many people died before they told. I only met one woman to whom this had happened; she was taken away in a GPU lorry in the middle of the night and kept without food or drink for fifteen hours standing in a crowded steaming room. Then, when she was almost dead with exhaustion, she was taken out and put through a gruelling examination by a GPU inquisitor. It was only when it was halfway through that she found she was being addressed by the name of the woman who had tenanted her flat several months before. The officer made a suave apology and let her go: she said he had beautiful manners and was quite obviously a former aristocrat.

Another man was sent to Solovki Island in the White Sea because he defended Platonism at a party. It shocked a Marxist present; but a little later I met someone who was bringing out a translation of Plato's *Laws* through a government publishing house – and nobody thought anything of it.

Very often when people are denounced it is by their own friends in a moment of spite or jealousy. There was a party of four or five friends last summer in Leningrad, at which two men who had drunk too much toasted Pilsudski as a joke. They were reported to the GPU and banished for a year to a remote town in central Russia. I knew two of the other guests, and both of them told me privately that it was the other one that had denounced the two to the GPU and gave good reasons for supposing so. Eventually they challenged each other face to face; they were neither of them angry and walked down the stairs debating it gravely. As it never turned out who had denounced whom, they remained good friends with each other and the two scholars. The latter found they had landed on their feet, because while work was short in Leningrad they found there was a whole new library to be organized in Orel, and they will probably stay on after the sentence has expired. These five people were all of bourgeois origin and they were acting more probably as Russians than as Marxists.

One might go on multiplying instances of the haphazard inconsistencies and the cruelty of Soviet Russia and yet not feel that one touched on the merits or demerits of Communism. In the first week everybody fits into boxes and compartments but after a month or two all the labels get shifted. The fierce Jew Communist who follows one round with savage black eyes is not as one thought at first a spy. He is anxious to make friends so as to get an English fishing-rod without paying duty, or a Swan fountain-pen.

He would like too to get his overcoat lined at Torgsin. On the other hand the small refined woman who looks like an English headmistress was one of the most bloodthirsty agents of the Cheka; with her own hands she carried out sentences of execution, which she herself had passed on countless young officers. Now she is bored with the squalour and monotony of Soviet existence; she is pining for a trip to the South of France but she will never get it for the Soviet will almost certainly refuse her her visa. One day I caught a glimpse of what she must have been like in the good old days of the Cheka. Stonyfaced and unrelenting, she sat at her desk, while two girls sobbed and pleaded; they were bourgeois, and, what was worse, they were pretty, and they had been expelled from college, because they had registered their names a day late. Through this institution lay their only chance of a foothold in a hostile society; scores of other students had been just as unpunctual and been forgiven, but in this case Anna Petrovna was inexorable. They must go.

I have successfully avoided so far all reference to the Five Year Plan or to collectivization. People who live in Russia are so stupified with constant repetition of these words that after a bit even if one wanted to, it is impossible to listen. Often on a dark night one will come to a deserted square. There is nobody there, but all the same there is a loudspeaker attached to the corner of a house, blaring out the latest figures of grain returns in the south. Aeroplanes write them in the sky, and every village concert starts and ends with a long recitation.

Neither collectivization nor the Five Year Plan seem to me to be particularly typical of Communism, for large tracts of the Russian land were always held collectively years before the Revolution. What is novel and barbarous about it is the forcible introduction of our modern agricultural methods from the West. These have been thrust wholesale upon a reluctant, dull-witted peasantry with unheard-of enthusiasm and bottomless inexperience; there has probably been more widespread frightfulness in making people use tractors who didn't want to than in the widely advertised expropriations and shootings.

We are shocked to hear of whole villages being shifted bodily from central Russia to the shores of the Arctic Ocean, but anyone, who travels down the Volga, will see every day whole townships doing it for themselves, and they have always done so for hundreds of years. The landing stages are crammed with seething masses of peasants, struggling and screaming; they have brought bedding and food and tables and chairs, and in many cases have had to sleep a couple of nights on the platform before they can get accomodation on a down-going ship. Perhaps they are still a migratory people. The Bolsheviks who treat them like cattle are merely following the precedent of generations of their rulers.

Similarly, the Five Year Plan is not particularly typical of Communism. It is simply the adaptation of Western industrialism including many of its capitalist methods, with a mystical fanaticism that the West has never dreamt of. We hear a great deal of the bacillus of Communism, but I should say that the damage it has done is trivial compared to the misery that has been caused in Russia by our particular industrial bacillus. She has been forced to enter the arena of capitalist competition. In 1926, before the Plan started, there was plenty in Leningrad, fat chickens and bottles of wine and fancy bread were on every table, but year by year the stock of food has grown less and less. Everything that might conceivably tempt the prosperous West has been exported or sent to the tourist hotels. For six weeks this winter there was no sugar, few people ever see meat or would care to try it if they did but this is borne uncomplainingly by the bulk of the population, for they are told that capitalism must be defeated by our own methods. We must be smothered in food and produce. The hunger in Leningrad is largely due to trouble on the collective farms, but I think that the greater part of it is deliberate: the export figures must be kept up so that machinery may be bought and foreign industrialism defeated.

I met many English, Irish and also German and American Communists in Russia. They were mostly homesick and I think unhappy. They were like people with religious mania who cannot rid themselves of obsession, and two or three of them seemed on the verge of a nervous breakdown. They were not able passively to endure like their Russian colleagues, for they were constantly judging things by standards of which the Russians were not even aware. It was not that they had lost faith in Communism, but they did not understand people who when they came to a tight screw threw their spanners into the works in a fury. Many of them come home disgusted with Russia and with more open minds about political theory than when they went there.

After a month or two, though, in a capitalist country, they usually forget all the discomfort and disillusionment of Russia;

they forget that as unemployed in England they are often better provided for than as paid workers in Russia, and they are sensitive to the strain of humbug that underlies so much anti-Communist propaganda. They remember that when they were ill, as most of them were, they were well cared for by their factories and that they convalesced in beautiful country villas. It seems preferable now to them to starve where everybody else is starving than to be undernourished in the midst of comparative plenty. In a very short time, as a general rule, they find their old sympathies returning.

For fifteen years now foreign newspapers have been prophesying a speedy end for the Bolshevik rule. They will probably go on prophesying for another fifteen years. Those who live in Russia and who have suffered most under Bolshevism do not look at the future with such cheery optimism. However wretched they are, they know that it will not be overthrown in Russia without bloodshed, in which many of their own friends will suffer. Their children have grown up under Bolshevik rule, many of them have married Communists or by their intelligence or ceaseless effort have got for themselves a foothold in the new regime; they are officers in the Red Army or in the GPU.

If Russia was delivered from the Bolsheviks, what sort of treatment could these people expect from the savage exiles who would pour back from Paris and London and Constantinople? They would be exchanging whips for scorpions. I knew a Russian aristocrat who had served under the Bolsheviks for three years and at last escaped to London. He expected to be welcomed by the White Russians there, to get some relief from the White Cross, but he found all doors closed against him. He had served under the enemy. English people helped him to get work, but last autumn he lost it. A foreigner cannot expect to be employed when Englishmen are out of work. He is not eligible for the dole and if he must starve he would prefer to starve among his own people. If he could be sure that the Bolsheviks would forgive him his treason he would return to Russia.

Some Russians see no hope of a change of government except through foreign intervention. They are rather shamefaced in expressing this view, for it is an admission that the fervent nationalism of the Tsardom was correctly diagnosed by the Bolsheviks. The bourgeois, they claimed, exploited it as long as they were on top, in order to keep the poor distracted, but now that they have been disposed of they are all too ready to call in the foreigner.

Can one conceive of any peaceful and happy issue of the Bolshevik experiment? The success of the Five Year Plan will of course improve materially the condition of the workers, and relax the stringency of the laws. Will they then turn their attention to the rest of the world, crippling our trade with their colossal output and deluging our workers with propaganda? Most foreign experts are not scared by the bogey of this trade competition. Though Russia may rival other countries in the quantity of her output, she will not for many generations be our equal in quality. For a long time too she will have her hands full consolidating Communism in her own country. She has not got a superfluity of money to send abroad, and the agitators she has sent have too often forgotten to agitate and succumbed to the fleshpots of the bourgeoisie.

What would happen, I often asked, if Communism were to start in another country – Germany for instance, the home of its origin? Would Moscow remain the capital of the Soviet States of Europe, and Moscow Communism be the only orthodox faith? 'Oh, of course,' they said, as if it wasn't worth discussing, but I believe there would be a very fruitful cause for argument here and that national pride might revive in the most unlikely quarters. Is it not possible that a new and vigorous convert to Communism might prove more dangerous to Stalin's crazy structure than all the capitalist opposition of the West? In such a topsy turvy world almost anything is possible.

[1933]

5

SPECIALISTS IN A
SOVIET SCHOOL

The specialist is the most characteristic human product of our time: not unnaturally for the modern state requires that its intellectuals should be amenable. Arrogant in his own sphere, the specialist is extremely docile and adaptable in everybody else's. 'Get on with your own job and don't put your nose in what doesn't concern you!' is his favourite maxim, and hence he has shown himself the fittest to survive the storms that have swept over the cultures of Russia and Central Europe. It is not surprising, therefore, that in Fascist countries human life used to be reorganized on professional lines, while in the USSR a subservient aristocracy of specialists has come into existence. The 'Navochny Rabotnik', the scientific worker, is there a privileged being. Next to the army and navy and GPU, he has the first claim on food and fuel and clothes, he has special shops and eating places, and on house committees and in clubs takes precedence of ordinary workers. 'Scientist' is a title of honour and it is conferred even on teachers or actors or artists, for in the USSR science is a word of generous application.

Under the more sophisticated dictatorship of the West, the specialist is tamed by kindness rather than by force, but in the USSR the whole business is on a cruder and more candid footing. We see it as a violent and at the same time as an inevitable process. In Inyazmass, the college where I was for sometime teaching, it needed brutality to weld a number of intelligent and experienced individuals into a successful institution, but the result once achieved was harmonious and consistent. There was so little friction that it was often difficult to realize that the bourgeois 'specialists' on whom it depended had undergone a cultural revolution. The parts of a machine that had broken down had been drastically reassembled and that was all.

There were three separate principals in Inyazmass but I never discovered the precise distinction of their functions. Comrade Chashkaya was apparently the most important and certainly the most formidable. She was very small and thin and the skin on her face was so tight that the small apologetic smile she habitually wore seemed to have been pulled into position. Her hair, too, was sparse and tightly screwed back and her whole appearance was academic rather than alarming. She twittered in a low voice, twisting her meagre withered torso from one listener to another. This twittering and twisting never ceased, nor did the little rat's smile. She was like a marionette. All the same I dare say she would have passed muster in any representative gathering of headmistresses even in England.

It was her experience not her face that was unique, though one of her charges traced everything back to her face. The Revolution, he said, had given to women like her the supreme opportunity for compensation. Comrade Chashkaya had been famous for her severity as a commissar. She used to execute her prisoners herself, and to shoot the young and the handsome and the well-born with especial relish. Now that she was a principal her victims were of her own sex, and her motives ordinary female jealousy rather than '*spretae injuria formae*'. There was a rule that every student must register his name ten days before term began; Comrade Chashkaya never attempted to enforce it regularly but every term used it as a device for expelling the unwary beautiful ones. This happened to two while I was there: they cried and sobbed and pleaded that all the rest of the college had defaulted too, but it was no good — they must go. And once expelled from that college they would never get a chance anywhere else.

The political director was superficially far more alarming. He was a terror to look at, a big burly man; a Jew from Armenia, he wore the high-necked black shirt of the Party member and had a great black lock of hair straggling over his heavy sullen face. He sat at the entrance to the classrooms, lowered over a pile of papers, and casting sombre glances at everyone who passed through the room. His business was to see that the ideology of the teachers and the lessons were orthodox – every time I felt his eyes travel over me I was uneasily conscious of my bourgeois appearance, I trembled for my ideology and crept past him as if he was a wild animal. Later on I was relieved to hear from a friend that he thought me a 'zolotoy chelavyek', a 'golden man'. I asked him out to tea, and had so far overcome my awe that I forgot I had asked him. It was an hour and a half there and back to my lodgings, but the next day he gave me the same firm scrutiny: he bore no resentment, and seemed, if anything, embarrassed by my apologies. He was gentle and stupid and simple and he scowled, I found, not because he was savage but because he was puzzled. He had a simple man's reverence for learning: he was typical of the proletarian political supervisors and I believe I should have found him easier to work with than the middle-class mass-man, who in Russia, as in fascist lands, is superceding him as the dicta-tor of culture.

Those who destroy without knowledge can never be so thor-ough as those who have a little, and the stranglehold of political theory on literature and culture in Russia only became serious when in the last few years the middle-classes started everywhere to oust the proletariat from power. Comrade Nalbandian and his like were too unconcentrated, too natural and spontaneous to be good at the ruthless application of a system. A revolution to them was a matter of blood and violence: the patient and scientific extermination of intellectual liberty that is being carried out in Central Europe by the 'bloodless revolution' would have struck him as undignified and pettifogging. When I knew him better he even seemed to me a vaguely beneficent influence, as he crouched over his desk. The little slips of paper that he was writing on were not the names of suspects but laundry lists, cuttings from pro-vincial papers, sums that wouldn't tot up; he pawed them over vaguely like a squirrel rummaging in his larder. He was studying Aramaic and sometimes he would show me with pride some new characters he had learnt to scribble on the blotting paper. He was so surprised and delighted with his own learning that he could afford to be tolerant of the intellectual vagaries of others.

The functions of the third principal, Alexander Spiridonich Dashkov, were purely intellectual. He arranged the timetable and, subject to Nalbandian and Chashkova's approval, the curriculum and classes. He was efficient, intelligent and charming, but his ideology was all wrong, indeed at a glance one could see that it was all so wrong as to be hopeless. Because of that nobody interfered with him or persecuted him. There was no need. He was handsome and smiling and serene and always beautifully dressed. His face was not ravaged with suffering like the faces of other aristocrats, who had spent themselves resisting. All the same it was clear that he was elegantly fading away like a tropical plant in a derelict conservatory. He had been the director of a great St Petersburg academy, a famous man. The conditions in which he had flourished had been elaborate and artificial, but he was not a simple product of them: he was an artist and had realized that his environment was plastic up to a point and hence all its shapes must be transient. This scepticism must have helped him. His attitude to the bleak Soviet world seemed ironical and indulgent, and full of faint surprise and gratification that he should still be adaptable enough to come to any terms with it at all, that it should bring even a small fraction of his talents into play. I met him only rarely and he seemed to me to be contented enough, but I saw in him the tragic figure of the modern intellectual, who has sold his integrity to the masses in exchange for bourgeois comforts and respectabilities. Now, when the masses repudiate the bargain and give him neither the liberty to think nor the opportunity to be comfortable, he can only grumble or shrug shoulders. He has no longer the moral right to the savage indignation that alone can create a united front of the spirit and save European civilization.

These three were the spiritual leaders of Inyazmass, and such 'ideology' as existed in the college was the fruit of their co-operation. I should say that their association was no accident and that everywhere where Communism is preached in Russia it filters through some such amalgam of warring elements, blended together in the white heat of the Revolution. There are many Chashkayas. The emotional impetus, the driving power, comes from those who have been spiritually frustrated, cheated, disillusioned. Bolshevism gave them a knife to cut the knot they were unable to untie. Their materialism is the more formidable because it is inspired by a spiritual grievance. Political theories are colourless till they are interpreted and collectivism has its peculiar character in Russia, because it was interpreted by injured individualists.

Nalbandian's part seemed an inactive one, but he was a symbol of something formidable. It was his class, the economically depressed, which had provided the brute strength behind the movement. Their grievances were purely material but they must not be allowed to accept a purely material satisfaction. They must be roused to new wants before they have forgotten the old. If inducements are no good, they must be kept stimulated with privations. They must learn by experience that suffering may be individual but relief can only be collective. At all costs they must not be allowed to sink back into lethargy.

As for plausibility, coherence, all the intellectual trimmings of an 'ideology', the Dashkovs are there to supply them. They are those, who for some reason or other, passively lend their intelligence to interpret a theory, which means their own extinction.

What has happened in Germany and Russia is a proof that the independence of learning and intelligence is fiction. It can exist only so long as it is not openly challenged by circumstances or so long as it is allied with a vigorous personal emotion. Enthusiasm can only be resisted by enthusiasm and the Dashkovs had nothing but a specialized and subsidized intelligence to oppose to the vehement and primitive emotions of the Revolution. Intelligence can be so refined by institutionalism, so purged of all human irrelevance, that it becomes mere skill or speed in establishing connections. Modern scientists are more than self-effacing, they are self-destroying. They have forged a weapon, so sharp and bright and easily manipulated that the simplest and least skilled can handle it. Today not only science but the scientific intelligence itself is being turned against the dispassionate individualism from which they developed. It is better to have no arms at all than that your arms should fall into the hands of the enemy.

There were a dozen or so other teachers in the school and since the principal teaching was on foreign language and literature, and knowledge of these was formerly a monopoly of the upper classes, it was not surprising to find that the majority of the staff were bourgeois. If anyone still preserves any faith in the solidarity of bourgeois culture, it would have been rudely shattered by the composition of that teaching staff. To all appearances they were autonomous, it should have been a stronghold of 'bourgeois ideology'. Chashkaya and Nalbandian knew no European language but Russian and though they had a pupil in every class told to observe the ideology of the teaching, they were neither of them sufficiently subtle to be expert at unmasking heretics by eavesdropping or informing, and in general I believe that the proficiency of spying in Russia is exaggerated. Heretics were mainly detected mechanically and passionlessly by looking up back-files and card-indexes or else by sudden impulsive swoops of jealousy or distrust.

In spite of this the dozen bourgeois teachers never revealed any inclination to preach heresies. They performed their duties conscientiously and well. They even seemed to take a pride in their work and in their ingenuity in fitting everything into a framework of Marxism. Leonov has a story of a Russian landlord who found he could make his mouzhiks work hard in his absence if he left his spectacles on a tree trunk beside them. It was a splendid success till one of the mouzhiks thought of covering the spectacles with his cap. In the same way there was no need for a strict supervision of the teachers in Inyazmass. The sight of Nalbandian's galoshes or of Chashkaya's portfolio were still enough by themselves to recall these former landowners and civil servants to their duties and their Marxian principles. Nor did they teach with conscious cynicism, witholding their own personal beliefs from what they said. It is hard to do that for long. They had committed themselves spiritually and uncompromisingly to the new doctrines and would have been shocked and pained as well as alarmed if they had heard them criticized. I met many former bourgeois in Russia, and though I heard constant criticism of particular acts and persons I never heard the fundamental tenets of Marx questioned, except perhaps by the 'lishentai', those unfortunates who have been deprived of all rights and have nothing more to lose.

The most completely bourgeois were the most acquiescent, the most critical were those who, before the Revolution, had been revolutionaries and rebels to their class. This is as one might expect, for the Russian Bolsheviks recruit their middle-class enthusiasts from the same types that produce Fascists elsewhere. They are those whose lives are filled with trivialities or are incapable of subjective criticism, who have no inner intellectual independence and fall easy victims to mass suggestion.

Most of the teachers were able and efficient men and women. Some of the older ones had high academic distinctions, for the college was not under direct control of the Communist Party and bourgeois antecedents were more readily condoned than in severely Marxist colleges. Professor Budkov and Professor Bachtin were survivals from the professorial staff of St Petersburg University, Professor Williams was agitated and pop-eyed and eager to please. He and his wife, Mrs Williams, had evolved a system of phonetics – incorporated in a brochure and gramophone records. It had a great vogue in the USSR and by means of it in a very short time his students learnt to speak with assurance a measured and toneless Lancashire. Professor Bachtin had been an eminent philologist and because of his knowledge of Anglo-Saxon had been put in charge of the English section, a tribute to his reputation rather than to his qualifications, for he could not speak a word of English.

Of the younger men, Sasha Gulsky was learned and slim and elegant. His father had been a wealthy professional man and by inviting all their friends and relations to stay they had managed to keep the whole of their old town flat. Young Gulsky's room was furnished in the Persian style. He had admiring pupils in Central Asia who brought him presents from Tashkent and the Caspian Sea. Like many other Russians, Soviet and emigré, it was his ambition to be mistaken for an Englishman and he believed that he looked rather like the Prince of Wales. He was as familiar with the literature of modern England as with that of Germany and Soviet Russia, and it was he who had first introduced the writings of Mr T.S. Eliot and Mrs Woolf to Leningrad. He dressed as he fancied an Oxford undergraduate dressed and liked his friends to call him 'Sandy'. He was completely happy under the Soviet regime, and he was popular with his pupils, for he was one of those freaks, more common in the upper than in the middle-classes, who enjoy discomfort and crudity, provided they are interested. His personal life was so full and exciting that problems of 'ideology' did not bother him.

Andrey Segalyevich had gold teeth, a military carriage and beautiful manners. He used to apologize for his 'Victorian outlook', which expressed itself in kissing ladies' hands, making other people go first through the door, preferring Tennyson to Joyce and buns to bobbed hair. He was genuinely kind and affectionate but he balanced his counter-revolutionary manners by giving information about his colleagues to the GPU.

There were other teachers, but these were the ones I remember best. They were alike in nothing except that they had all a more than average share of intelligence and knowledge, and most of them seemed to be conscientiously spending it in furnishing a new generation with the practical ability to suppress everything that gave meaning to their own education.

I do not think that the threat of hunger alone could have accounted for this wholesale subservience. It is easy to say that the educated bourgeois have prostituted their learning for position and security, but prostitution usually implies a breach of faith, a betrayal of some intimate belonging, whereas modern culture or 'science' belongs to nobody. Though it was begotten by individuals, it has been reared by the state, which bought the right to exploit it with the promise to defend it. If the cultured but acquiescent victims of Fascism or Bolshevism feel any remorse, it must be not for their 'betrayal of culture' but for the disastrous bargain that robbed the individual of the right and of the desire to defend his own.

[1935]

6

SOVIET LITERATURE — A SURVEY

What has happened to Russian literature? For some years before the war it appeared that its cultural influence in the West had ceased. A multitude of novels were translated, but they were so confidently, so deliberately boring and esoteric that there was no satisfaction even in reviewing them candidly. Clearly nobody cares whether they entertain us or not. They are like company reports that go on appearing year after year, though even shareholders, all but a few initiates, do not read them.

This is very strange. The Russians are among the most gifted and sympathetic of Europeans. They are not, by nature, parochial. Great Russian writers have become *pari passu* of great European writers. There was constant reciprocity with the West, the Russians giving more than they received and adorning everything they touched. They were oddly eclectic in their contacts. Tolstoi, for example, was influenced by Dickens but he also acknowledged the greatness of Miss Braddon and Canon Sheehan. Like alchemists, the Russians could turn the least-valued products of the West into gold. They had become indispensible to us and now they are no longer there.

One thing we can say, Russian literary talent has not perished from neglect. The Revolution was the product of the small educated minority and had been hatched in literary salons and coteries, so that in Russia the intellectual has never, as in other countries, ours for example, been ignored or belittled. From 1918 to 1946 Russian literature has been subjected to one regimen after another. It has been given every kind of dose and stimulant. It has had purges and prizes. NEP [New Economic Policy] relaxed the discipline; RAPP and VAPP [Russian and All-Russian Association of Proletarian Writers] tightened it up. The problem, which they have not yet solved, is how to transfer the craftsmanship and the experience of the bourgeois to his supplanters without infecting them with his reactionary spirit.

Over the early years of Soviet literature Maxim Gorki presided, keeping contact with the past and checking the absurdities of the fanatics. As he grew old his practical influence weakened, his personal prestige became enormous. H.G. Wells recalls a visit to his old friend in Moscow when he appealed earnestly for assistance in forming 'a thin web of Societies about the world, associated to assert the freedom and dignity of art and letters'. In the milder atmosphere of Leningrad, Alexey Tolstoi and others listened to him and his ideas took root, but Gorki was a Soviet divinity, who had long ago forgotten his old humanism. He suspected a capitalist intrigue. Though he failed, H.G. Wells certainly did more than any other man to pierce the barrier that stretches between Russia and us.

The apotheosis of Gorki was a strange and vital part of the Soviet literary programme. In his old age he became the symbol of all kinds of irrelevant ideas, and tributes were paid to his genius such as no writer had ever received before or since. The historic city of Nizhninovgorod was rechristened Gorki, which is as though Dublin should be called 'Yeats' or 'Shaw'. Even his death was charged with a lunatic significance. At the Moscow trials his doctor confessed that he had deliberately hastened Gorki's end by urging him to come to Moscow in the early spring and make bonfires in his garden. He knew, explained the doctor, that this would be fatal to Gorki's lungs. A martyred mythological Gorki [resulted], the friend of Chehov and Tolstoi, the chronicler and patron of the penniless and unwanted.

In the early days of the Revolution, when Blok and Essenin and Mayakovsky flourished, literature was freer than it has ever been since. Those were the 'Messianic' years. The Futurists conceived of themselves as allies of the proletariat. They were intoxicated with the wonder and horror and tremendous promise of the cataclysm. They imagined, like Marinetti and D'Annunzio in Italy, that when order developed out of chaos, there would still be a place for their inspired war cries. They proclaimed a new art that was to sing of 'mines and machines, mass-rebellion and the bustle of cities'. Blok's 'The Twelve' is a magnificent memorial of this strange period, which ended for most of them in misery and suicide and party discipline.

Only for a brief period, ending about 1921, was it supposed that a pure proletarian culture could be created. Countless Prolet-kult Studios were formed in which factory workers were coached into creativity by literary specialists from the bourgeoisie but not even a mouse of talent emerged from this mountainous organi-zation. The most that can be said is that a great many workers and peasants became aware of art and letters and the appetite for reading developed. From that time onward the leading Soviet writers have been, like Leonov and Romanov, Zoshehenko, Kataev and Alexey Tolstoi, of bourgeois origins and associations.

The bourgeois problem is still acute; one of the main jokes of satirists like Zoshenenko is that if you scratch a Communist, even a shock worker or a commissar, you may find an outraged petit-bourgeois. The Russian bourgeoisie has never been liquidated for it is not a class but a frame of mind and highly infectious. There is good reason for the sensitive *noli me tangere* attitude of the true Communist and his deep distrust of the West.

In the liberal NEP phase (1921-26) that followed, Futurism and Proletkult both ended and there was recoil to realism. There was freedom for private publishing companies and booksellers. There was great literary activity. The 'poputchiki' or fellow travellers, that is to say writers who were sympathetic to Communism but not party men, wrote with a candour that has not been possible since. The party issued a manifesto against 'hot-house proletar-ian literature'. One of the leading writers, Leonid Leonov, in his novel *The Thief* [1927, transl. Hubert Butler 1931], described with pathos and imagination the fusion of classes and the sufferings of those, like the drunken and dispossessed nobleman, for whom no place could be found. The pivot, the moralist, of this intelligent but chaotic story is a Russo-German Christian, whose advice to his friends was 'Steel yourself with suffering!' Leonov occupied, and still occupies, a high official position in Soviet literature and I do not think that the sincere objectivity of this book has ever been held against him. His other books written during the Five Year Plan, and a play, during the war, have been more conventional in treatment.

NEP was terminated abruptly by the Five Year Plan 1926-31. This era was memorable towards its close for the stringent RAPP campaign, a new attempt to hammer out a Soviet literature. A 'literary Magnetogorsk' was the target for the shock troops of letters. There were writers called 'Populists' and others called 'Onguardists', and special conducted tours for writers to collective farms and factories. Gladkov's *Cement* and Panserov's *Brusski* were the appalling results. These books, the most celebrated of the tractor school, sold over half a million copies each and were translated into many languages. They are almost unreadable, but till Gorki came down from his throne and denounced *Brusski* they continued to be read.

In 1932 RAPP was dissolved and from that time the writer has been able to choose his own subject within the limits of Socialist realism. Some interesting books have resulted, in particular those of Alexey Tolstoi and Ehrenburg. Émigré writers, who returned to the Soviets, they brought with them a welcome freshness and breadth of outlook. They are both of them highly original writers and their conformity to any known ideology is bound to be perfunctory. Tolstoi is happiest in fantasy about the future and imaginative reconstructions of the past. His novels *Peter the Great* and *The Road to Calvary* are the most important achievements of the past years in Russia. Ehrenburg's *Fall of Paris* is a disappointing book. It is a vivid journalistic account of the corruption of French life before the invasion yet it is marred by journalistic cynicism. It is a panegyric of the French working classes and a subtle analysis of their changing moods. He makes no mention, however, of the Soviet-German pact, and the dismay it caused in the ranks of French Socialists. It cannot, therefore, be said that his subject has been seriously treated.

Since the outbreak of war Russian literature has been stimulated with patriotism in large but careful doses. Not only Suvorov and Peter but Dostoievsky have returned to honour. Dostoievsky was a Slavophile, a champion of Russian Christianity, an antagonist of German influence. The word 'Russia' is frequently heard once more. It is unsafe, for the writer, to refer disrespectfully to patriotic saints like St Alexander Nevsky or St Dmitri Donskoi; he must watch his step if he talks against religion. The Soviets have many new Christian subjects, whose assimilation is a delicate business.

Yet it is too early to say that this nationalist phase will outlast the war for long or that it will be more favourable to the writer than those which preceded it. Literary taste can be controlled in

Russia as nowhere else and at any moment a change of strategy is possible. The great success of the 'liquidate illiteracy' campaign has brought a vast new region of the earth within reach of the printing press. There are almost no picture-papers, novelettes or sporting-sheets in this virgin soil and the new literates will read what they are told with excitement. As a result there is probably more serious reading – *Cement* is nothing if not serious – in Russia than anywhere else. How otherwise can we explain the deluge of Swift literature in fourteen Soviet tongues with which the Dean's centenary has been celebrated in Russia. This distinguished clergyman has received far less honour in the countries where he ministered and wrote.

Yet this is only literary strategy. It cannot convince us that the Russian genius, so daring and free, is not still asleep. Our vision is limited and easily distorted. Undoubtedly there are movements which we have not perceived. For long we were told that religion was extinct in Russia but we know now that this was never so. When the Orthodox Church disintegrated, many regional and peculiar Christian sects spawned in its place, whose existence neither the Communists nor the great dogmatic Churches of the West are anxious to acknowledge. Something of the sort has surely happened with Russian literature; we do not know what new ideas are fermenting in obscure and perhaps provincial coteries. For Russia is the land of 'cells' and 'brigades' and schisms. Truth and beauty will emerge again but in a form and in a place, where VOKS [All-Union Society for Cultural Ties Abroad] and Gollancz and Lawrence & Wishart are not likely to recognize them. Everything else about Russian literature is speculative, this is certain.

[1946]

PART TWO

Peace News Papers
1949–1958

7

LETTER FROM IRELAND

It would be easy to despair of a strong peace movement in Ireland. We are by temperament bellicose neutrals. That is to say we shall, as a nation, I think, keep out of future wars not on principle but because the war in question won't ever please us. We are, perhaps, like the Jehovah's Witnesses, waiting for the perfect war, the war of angels and devils, and indifferent to second-rate substitutes.

How, you will ask, can this be reconciled with the furious campaign against godlessness and Communism that is surging round us in Ireland? If you opened our newspapers, you would think that every Irishman was ready to leap to the arms to fight Russia, the enemy of all mankind. The front page is always now half-filled with reports of Cardinal Mindszenthy's trial and its sequels, with the protests that are being telegraphed, the Masses celebrated, the monster indignation meetings summoned in all our country towns. The excitement is so great that even Protestants are getting swept into this orgy of resentment, forgetful that we too once imprisoned and insulted bishops and that it is scarcely a century since in Ireland the Church of Rome was far more impressed than it is today in Hungary.

Turn then to the other half of the front page and you will note that the border question is being debated there with almost equal fury. But this time it emerges that we are not going into any war, good or bad, till our own domestic problems are settled first. We know well that War III will be against Russia and that we shall take no action against this great power unless Britain leads the way. But not even against Russia shall we stir till the Six Counties are returned to us. To that end we shall denounce our brothers in the north as if they were pickpockets and so inflame them that even the most amiable Ulsterman will resist us to the death.

What is the meaning of all this? We, who do not believe in wars, crusades, Atlantic pacts, find it ignoble but not alarming. Have you ever seen terriers after a cat? It is the silent ones that mean business. The fussy excited ones are quite satisfied to run round and round barking madly. They don't really want the cat. Cats don't taste nice and are apt to scratch.

I am not sure if you could call the hedge of argument with which we have surrounded ourselves a vicious circle. It seems protective rather than vicious. Once inside it we feel as if nothing in the world can happen to us. It runs like this:

Every Irishman is ready to fight Russia to the death.

But Ireland cannot fight at all while she is a mutilated nation, without Ulster.

But England could not possibly give up Ulster as a base for planes and troops and for the protection of convoys.

Ergo Ireland though ready to fight Russia to her last man will never be in a position to do so.

Ergo we shall remain neutral as in the last war and England is to blame for this not us.

Am I implying that we are a nation of cowards and hypocrites? No, we are a brave people but not brave enough to face what we know in our hearts, that war is in itself wicked and wrong and leads to worse wickedness and wrong. We concoct futile and disgraceful reasons for an abstention, which would be honourable if it were candidly interpreted.

The doctrine of pacifism is so revolutionary in Ireland as to be frightening, but one day it will be accepted. Arthur Griffiths, our first president, believed that Ireland could get her freedom by passive resistance on the model of the Hungarian resistance to the Habsburgs, but, of course, he was overruled. Pacifist theory had played an important though inconspicuous part in our independence movement and it is still influential. Tentatively our Minister of External Affairs has advocated a pacifist policy for Ireland. Some time we shall harmonize our words and acts with our thoughts and feelings. To be capable of this might be the definition of the educated man, but in Ireland we are not yet very educated.

We have the prospect of becoming a neutral nation, sitting on the fence like Switzerland, in full armour and sweating with tactfulness and apprehension. Would it not be better to be an openly pacific nation, going about our business in peace time, and, in time of war, helping the sufferers indiscriminately and refusing to believe that nature arranged men behind frontiers according to their merits, bad Russians and Bulgarians, good Dutch, etc.? I am afraid though we shall be what is known as a 'friendly neutral', which is about as exciting as the nursery game of Granny Steps. You take what steps you can against the enemy, so long as he or his consular representative doesn't see you. Most Irishmen in the last war were pro-British except for a handful of anti-British (the Germans hardly impinged). Neutrality is a state of mind wholly alien to us and I don't think even our officials ever quite reconciled themselves to it.

Once on the east coast an English plane made a forced landing. The local sergeant of the Garda, instead of interning the crew, took them to a friend's house and entertained them. His official superior came down from Dublin and reprimanded him for this breach of neutrality. 'But you see, sir,' said the sergeant, 'I couldn't remember who we were being neutral against!' Neutrality, though distasteful to us, may well be our destiny. There seems to be only one honourable way of avoiding it and that is by the fearless advocacy of peace, that peace which has nothing to do with neutrality or appeasement. It derives from the knowledge that all men are brothers and the unceasing effort to restore life and vigour to that tired platitude.

[1949]

8

PACIFISM IN IRELAND

In Ireland, if you told a fellow countryman that you believed in passive resistance he would look at you with surprise and dismay, but, if you added, 'You see I am a Friend,' a look of ready understanding would cross his features, 'Ah, I see!' he would exclaim with relief, 'Of course!'

Once an oddity has been classified, we will accept it more readily than any other people. We have a respect for the registered and certified *fait accompli* that makes us at our best the most tolerant of people, at our worst the most slavish.

On the other hand, the uncatalogued individualist will be more miserable in Ireland than anywhere else. Ireland, of course, has a reputation for wilfulness and eccentricity, but if you go into the matter you will find that most of the notable characters derive from the eighteenth-century tradition; they belonged to, or received countenance from, the Ascendency class. The Irish gentry had a privileged position denied to their English equivalents. Often they carried self-expression to extraordinary lengths. They believed and said exactly what they liked. They minded the disapproval of their compatriots so little that few found it worth while disapproving.

Now that is all changed. Those to whom privilege was a birthright have gone, and the new privileged are uneasy and self-conscious. They mind intensely what people say of them; they console themselves by thinking that there is almost no one that they cannot disconcert with their own sniffs of disapproval. Because of this, when anything unorthodox is said or done there

48

is a hurricane of sniffing and mocking. The inhibitions of centuries are let off like squibs, and an obvious target is the unusual person. That is why the passive resister will not come out into the open till our country is more established and self-confident.

At the moment, as a fellow-traveller of the Society of Friends, the war-resister can find reassurance and sympathy, but I don't think I am showing disrespect for that noble body if I say that their problems are different from those of the unclassified fighter for peace. Their insubordinate days are now over and it is hard to recall that they were once gaoled as disturbers of the peace, dangerous innovators and heretics. Their claims to be different have been admitted and they are pillars of society. And you cannot be a pillar of an essentially militarist society and also its whole-hearted critic. Their criticisms of society often seem part of an ancient rite and are listened to with bowed heads and wandering thoughts.

Inevitably, as the pioneers of pacifism, the Friends are its leaders. The man who does not belong to the Society of Friends would hesitate to teach his grandmother to suck eggs or distract her from what is now her primary occupation, the relief of suffering, the care of the bereaved, the dispatch of food and clothes. These are all honourable occupations and no one does them better than the Friends.

No, the problems of the born pacifist are very different from those of the convert. The convert is an impatient fellow and having turned his back on his friends and often his opportunities and his career, he is seldom content with relief work. He wants to change society, not just to rub healing ointment into its wounds.

What can he do here in Ireland? How can you in England help us to escape from the ignominy of neutrality and to play a positive, not a negative role in the building of peace? Direct pacifist propaganda has few prospects. In Ireland to go far off the beaten track is suicide.

Moreover I do not think that it is so necessary in small states to preach peace, a negative virtue, as brotherhood, a positive one. Those who have once tasted neutrality in a world war will be neutral till their neutrality is violated.

In a small state like Ireland, a peaceful foreign policy may be taken for granted. If war broke out, at most we might send an army of volunteers, such as went from Ireland to fight for Franco in Spain. But the suppression of volunteer armies that, for disinterested or mercenary motives, go to fight in foreign lands does not seem to me of primary importance. The great evil is when apathetic or unwilling people are forced to hate, to fear and finally to kill those towards whom they feel no spontaneous dislike. If we could strike at that crime the other evils would die of their own accord.

[1949]

9

WANTED: UNOFFICIAL TRAVELLERS

Ireland, like other small countries, is committed irretrievably to intercourse with other nations. It is too late to advocate, as some Gaels do, the peaceful, self-sufficient life of Fiji Islanders before the Europeans arrived. The peace that can be had by shutting the door cannot be had even by us, though we live as far away as we well could from the boiling point of war.

A generation ago, in times of peace, the talk was all of commercial relations with other countries, now it is of cultural relations. Our problem should be how to pass on the third phase, which is 'friendly relations'.

The present campaign for cultural relations is not as straightforward and benevolent as it sounds. It is full of hidden pitfalls. This year we have started in Ireland an association for making Irish culture known to the world. If it grows at all, it will follow in the steps of one or other of its big brothers, 'The British Council', the 'Institut Français', the 'Deutsches Haus'.

Surely the last word on the abuse of culture for political ends was said in that admirable book, *La Trahison des Clercs*, by Julien Benda [1927; trsl. R. Aldington as *The Betrayal of the Intellectuals*, 1928]? When he wrote, the treachery of the artist and the writer to the great international ideals of the past was not yet organized in a big way. Today, however, it all goes much more smoothly, so smoothly that the most scrupulous can travel down this primrose path without apprehensions as to where it is leading. Distinguished critics and authors can voyage to sunny lands at government expense in order to advertise Shakespeare or Georgian architecture or Mr Gladstone, as choice samples of the British Way of Life. They travel for British poets and musicians as one might travel for nylon stockings or combine harvesters. They open up new tracts of the earth for British culture, as their fathers did for British trade and their grandfathers for the British flag.

But ultimately the results are disastrous. Great writers, if they have a meaning for any but their countrymen, are great because they can transcend the narrow values of their native land and people. Tolstoy, at his best, was really a repudiation of the self-centred nationalism of Russia. Yeats, Shaw, Joyce, Æ represent a shocked recoil from the Ireland of their day. For such reasons it was painful to see a bust of Dostoievsky under a huge picture of Stalin in the Soviet pavilion at an exhibition in Zagreb. It is good that Dostoievsky should be honoured in Soviet Russia, which he would have hated so much, but not honoured in that way.

H.G. Wells was the last great English writer to put the matter clearly:

The reality of the case is that any writer or artist or teacher of repute, who allows himself to be put on a wire and dangled in this fashion according to the narrow ideas of some director of propaganda, Herr Goebbels or Lord Perth or Lord Lloyd or what not, fails to grasp his real significance in the world and is getting into low company. He is falling short of the essential aristocracy of his profession.

No, I do not think that understanding comes by government-supported councils for culture.

If officially directed 'travel' and 'social intercourse' is harmful and if direct peace propaganda is usually impracticable, what have we left? Travel, like sport, is often advertised as broadening the mind and bringing the nations closer together, but does it? I was amused when Osbert Lancaster said the other day, 'If there is one thing that creates more international ill-feeling than sport it is travel.'

Perhaps we have to go back a couple of centuries to get any inspiration. Arthur Young's *Tour of Ireland* [1780] is an admirable and conciliatory book. He went round Ireland as a private investigator, staying with private people. He rarely stayed at hotels or took counsel of government officials. He was not concerned with inflating national prestige.

9. WANTED: UNOFFICIAL TRAVELLERS

How can we reproduce in a democratic age the free social intercourse, the liberal interchange of views, ideas, experiences that were often possible in an aristocratic one? Relatively few people can afford independent travel, and the old tradition of private hospitality to strangers of enquiring minds, which existed in Arthur Young's days, has almost disappeared. The unofficial traveller is dying but he must be revived at all costs. It is the sponsored visitor who must die, for he carries with him the taint of propaganda wherever he goes. If he is paid by the country that sends him, he is thought to be a spy, if he is paid by the country that entertains him, he is thought to be a dupe. He does not bring friendship with him, he does not bring peace. Nobody trusts him, nobody believes him.

Is it possible to find a way around the barriers that divide the nations from each other? The question is worth a closer inquiry.

[1949]

10

FRIENDSHIP: PERSONAL OR OFFICIAL

When I was in Yugoslavia over a dozen years ago I held a travelling scholarship, which enabled me to go round the country. In the days before the Iron Curtain, to be foreign was, at the start, an asset, and when I arrived in some town of Bosnia or Macedonia I was made to feel welcome.

There was usually a little club, presided over by someone who had travelled abroad, and I was entertained. When I said I was Irish, sometimes my new friends were perplexed by this unnecessary flaunting of provincialism when I could have passed myself off as an Englishman.

They themselves were often at pains to explain that they were only Yugoslav by some accident of geography; spiritually they belonged to some great centre of culture and civilization – Chicago, Vienna or London. Those who were contentedly Yugoslav accepted me readily as an Irishman.

I was glad I belonged to an insignificant nation. It has never surprised me that in Abyssinia, before the Italian invasion, the most popular foreigners in that rightly suspicious land were those who hadn't any country — stateless people travelling on Nansen passports, French, English, German, Italian — to a thin-skinned native they seem to plant flags when they enter a café. It is hard for them not to use a national prestige to inflate their own small personalities.

While in Zagreb together with a Yugoslav friend, Mirko, an English teacher in Dalmatia, I worked out a scheme that still seems to me superior in many respects to the various official contrivances for 'cultural intercourse'.

I got in touch with a few small clubs and two or three Irish friends with enquiring minds and talents of some kind that would provide an excuse or a visit to the clubs, which mostly agreed gladly to entertaining a visiting stranger. But how was his ticket to be paid for? In Yugoslavia the Press Bureau used to issue free tickets. The first Irish visitor (I will call her E) was to bring a correspondent's card from her local paper (she would write an article for it when she returned). In this way I got her a free ticket for the Yugoslav railways.

While in Ireland I tried to make a corresponding plan for a Yugoslav visitor to Ireland. There were no clubs, no Press Bureaux, but from one railway company I got a free ticket for Mirko, from another, one at half price. I got an engagement for him on the Irish radio and a promise to accept two articles of his by the *Irish Independent* and an invitation to talk at the Mansion House in Dublin. Then he got an invitation to stay near a Technical School where a talk for him could be arranged.

On his part he discovered a cultural organization in Yugoslavia to finance his journey as far as Ireland. Financially all went well enough. Mirko paid his way with talks and articles and enjoyed himself. But the little unpretentious gatherings we had looked for did not materialize. We were only half appeased by being given sherry at the Mansion House. The Yugoslav consul was at the lecture and warned the audience against asking indiscreet questions about politics.

An important official atmosphere was generated, which is fatal to friendliness and understanding. All the same we felt we had laid down a rough track that could become easier and smoother as more people followed.

Back in Yugoslavia I started to prepare for E's visit. And here my story ends in a very unsatisfactory apotheosis. Just before E was to come, the British Council started.

I suggested to her that perhaps they would help her with fares to the frontier. They received her sympathetically, recognized her talents and engaged her as the first British Council Visitor to Yugoslavia.

The British Council was launched, my scheme died. With the coming of the Council a wave of excitement passed over the little clubs. British MPs were promised them, libraries, paid secretaries, scholarships. And with success came suspicion. A bomb was placed under the chair of the librarian of the British Council in Zagreb and both her legs were blown off.

As for Mirko — he would scarcely have been human had he resisted the temptation to cash in on his knowledge of English ways, and he has become an interpreter to Yugoslav delegations to foreign capitals. In Belgrade in 1948 I heard an English resident describe him as a 'government stooge'.

The Iron Curtain seems unexpectedly porous in parts, impenetrable in others. In Belgrade I found an American establishment exhibiting the American Way of Life. One window was full of New York fashions, another showed a model recommending the secret ballot. A big well-manicured hand was being inserted stealthily into the ballot box. In another was a huge plan of 'The Temple of Science', in which all the branches of science can be studied in pseudo-ecclesiastical surroundings.

Evidently, under government patronage, pseudo-science, pseudo-religion, sales talk and political preaching can filter through from the USA. The Iron Curtain cannot be as impenetrable as we are told.

I found a British Reading Room in Zagreb, with many good books and papers and, despite the Iron Curtain, many Yugoslavs reading them. But to the Yugoslav most Anglo-Saxon literature is escapist rather than stimulating, so little relation does it bear to his problems. Six friendly voices from England would be worth six tons of print from Fleet Street.

[1949]

11

AUTOANTIAMERICANISM

Seán O'Faoláin is normally the least traitorous of clerks, so it is disquieting to find him perverting Benda's famous phrase, '*la trahison des clercs*' to endorse a war-policy that would have horrified the French philosopher. 'The clerk', wrote Benda, 'by adopting political passions, brings to them the tremendous influence of his sensibility, if he is an artist, of his persuasive power, if he is a thinker, and in either case his moral prestige.' Elsewhere he condemns those writers, who 'think it is essential for them to belong to a powerful nation, which can make itself feared'. (Note here O'Faoláin's reference to our 'joke-army' and 'joke-navy'.) And also: 'When I see philosophers concerning themselves with the safety of the State and Ministers striving to bring about love among mankind, I think of what Dante said: "You turn to religion him, who was born to preach. Thus all your steps are out of the true way."' Here are three caps that might fit Seán O'Faoláin in his present mood, and if he doesn't want to wear them, he ought to withdraw his custom from Benda's.

You see not only does O'Faoláin concern himself with the safety of the state, bringing to that prosy problem an artist's sensibility and a thinker's persuasiveness and a great deal of political partisanship, but also he commends the American government for its effort 'to bring about love among mankind' by means of its Economic Cooperation Administration (Marshall Plan) etc. Now Benda's thesis, which seems to me wholly sound, is that it is the duty of the clerk, i.e. the O'Faoláins, 'to preach universal love and the abolition of frontiers and other spiritual things', while it is

57

the duty of the state to punish him and confine itself to the realist task of defence. He instances the life and death of Socrates, the destructive critic of the state; both Socrates and the government, which condemned him, acted in character and did their duty. So too did Zola and the Dreyfusards do their duty, when they stood up for justice, even though they thereby undermined the prestige of the French army – and so did the French government do its duty in resisting them.

Applying Benda's philosophy to Ireland, it is surely the duty of our 'clerks' to preach peace and brotherly love till they get shut up ('The modern clerks,' says Benda, 'have ceased to understand that the sign of an attitude truly in harmony with their function is that it should be unpopular with the layman'), whereas it is the duty of our government to concentrate on the safety of the state in the most realist way imaginable, choosing 'cowardly neutrality', as in the last war, or active participation, whichever is most likely to insure the welfare of Ireland.

And, in fact, the best clerks and the strongest governments always have behaved like this. While the democratic governments were still staving off the Nazis with pacts and promises, a handful of English clerks were using their sensibility, their persuasiveness, and their prestige, in the only legitimate way these can be used, not for war against Germany, but to give what help and encouragement they could to their counterparts, the clerks of Germany. For they knew that totalitarianism could not be killed by foreign armies, which would only rally the whole German people to the side of the Nazis; it must be destroyed by the Germans themselves. Therefore we find the usual group of honest clerks, a tiny one, Huxleys, Russells, Stephens and so on, and their colleagues in other democratic lands, securing the Nobel Prize for Ossietzky [awarded for Peace in 1935}, who was in Sonnenburg prison camp for his resistance to the Nazis.

We find H.G. Wells lecturing against the Nazis in Australia and threatened with expulsion by Mr Lyons, the premier, because of his 'insults to the head of a great and friendly power' (Adolph Hitler). If you want to see how official England was feeling about the Germans at this time, read *Ourselves and Germany* by Lord Londonderry or Neville Henderson on his mission. And forgive them if you can. As Ministers it was not their duty to be concerned about international morality. If the honest clerks had been more numerous, the Nazis would never have been able to persuade themselves that political accommodations were all that was necessary. Goering would never have come to England in 1937 for the coronation, confident that he would be well received. The hatred for Nazi cruelty that had to be soft-pedalled in embassies and consulates would have reached to those millions average Germans who acquiesced in Hitler from apathy rather than approval. Can you say that honest clerk was of no account? If so, why was he invariably the first to be blacklisted in invaded countries? Generals were forgiven, but honest clerks were pursued with every kind of rigour. They, not the soldiers, were the formidable ones.

The average intelligent American will frankly admit the wholly self-regarding nature of America's foreign commitments. Joseph Harsch, the American radio commentator, in his book *The Curtain Isn't Iron* [1950], writes in reference to them: 'We (Americans) do agree – most of us – that the function of government should be to govern for our material welfare, not for some purpose beyond our material welfare.'

Harsch too explains that from now on the struggle for survival in the West can no longer be expressed in that simple-minded Either-Or formula adopted by Seán O'Faoláin, 'either Communism or Capitalism'. Harsch shows, from innumerable examples, that the old capitalist elements are now completely submerged in most of the Eastern satellite countries. Apart from their helplessness, many of them compromised themselves with the invader; others have been dispossessed by earlier non-Communist governments. To attempt to resurrect these people as allies would be to focus upon them the undivided hatred of their countrymen and would be the surest way of exterminating them. No, Harsch maintains, the only suitable allies that the democracies must look for within the Communist countries are the Titoists, the disaffected Communists, who exist in every country, deriving from the revolutionary nationalism, that was in every country the real driving force behind the resistance movement. That is to say American policy, which is already seen operating in Yugoslavia, will be to support one set of Communists against the other.

It will be rather like Richelieu's policy in the Thirty Years War, when he persecuted the Protestants at home and abroad supported the Paladin of Protestantism, Gustavus Adolphus of Sweden, or like the Vatican support of William of Orange at a later date. That simple-minded crusade of right against wrong, white against red, into which O'Faoláin invites us, looks quite different when you examine it more closely. As for those compassionate souls who want a war to rescue the oppressed of the east, let them ponder Harsch's words: 'If there is going to be a war we had better say a requiem now over eastern Europe.'

And what would the realist policy be in regard to the European countries, over which America and England exercise influence? Would not the Americans be *obliged*, by force of circumstances, to resurrect the Nazis and Fascists who have had over ten years' experience in fighting Communism? Would they not be obliged to delude themselves and Mr O'Faoláin into thinking they were doing something different? He becomes almost incoherent about a moving experience he had in Calabria, which proved to him that Ireland too *must* join in the Atlantic Pact.

I too had a moving experience, which filled me with such helpless rage that only now can I write about it at all soberly. When I was working with the Quakers in Vienna, 1938, I walked down the street leading to the Prater a fortnight after it had been wrecked by the Nazis. You could still see the foul inscriptions on the broken Jewish shop fronts, which the officials had deliberately left there. '*Verholung nach Dachau*', 'On a Rest-cure at Dachau!' was the mildest of them. I have never before, in any Communist country, and I have visited several, felt myself enveloped by such an emanation of evil, of tolerated evil. And then I saw pasted on a wall in a small street near the Stefansplatz, the manifesto of the Austrian Catholic bishops applauding Hitler, and I heard how the leaders of the Austrian Evangelical Church had sent him an even more fulsome address, signing it, as did Cardinal Innitzer, with 'Heil Hitler.' If you don't believe me read them all, in toto, in the Dean of Chichester's *Struggle for Religious Freedom in Germany*.

Now, if at that time, when the world was not seriously menaced by Communism, such connivance was necessary, such *trahison des clercs* from those who should have been the foremost guardians of 'universal love and spiritual things', what sort of connivances can we not expect in a third world war, when the menace from Communism *is* serious? Will it not be necessary once more to give power to those who instigated the horrors of the Praterstrasse? Of course it will. It's happening already. We are being reminded once more of that much-advertised Austrian '*gemutlichkeit*' and how the Austrians were not really Nazis at all, whereas in fact any Austrian refugee will tell you that the Austrian

Nazis, of whom Hitler himself was one, were the most brutal and remorseless of them all. I do not doubt that many American strategists have in mind a solution of the Eastern problem by the resurrection of a federalized Austro-Hungary but Tito must first be vigorously supported and then as vigorously attacked. First the whitewash, then the tar.

What is left of O'Faoláin's Either-Or crusade? It is as inconsequent as a nursery game but there is wickedness in its frivolity. 'Oranges and Lemons, darling?' ... But it doesn't matter which you choose really for 'Here comes a chopper to chop off your head!' and the kind old uncle has a real chopper under his Father Xmas robes, and sometimes he'll use it against the Communist lemons and sometimes against the Capitalist oranges. It all depends. 'The function of government should be to govern for our material welfare.'

But I think the source of O'Faoláin's confusion is that he equates private benevolence and public. He compares cynical ingratitude for the bounty of America with scepticism of the motives that prompted the great reformers Howards and Wilberforce. What a fatuous comparison! The bounty of America is on par with the bounty of the Irish taxpayer to the old-age pensioner and the county home. There is kindness and enlightenment of course in it but so diluted with compulsion and the desire to make the state take over the moral obligations of the individual that Miss Bennett is perfectly justified in looking the gift-horse hard in the mouth. Did anyone give us a halo because of the gifts that we sent to starving Europe after the war, disproportionately large, I believe, in relation to our income? Public and private benevolence must be judged by wholly different canons. The honest clerks, the Howards and the Wilberforces, were hounded by their governments before prisons were reformed or the slave trade abolished. Behind every generous act of government there is always the desperate pressure and often thankless effort of a few honest clerks.

Because of that, let Mr O'Faoláin give all his admiration to those efficient, idealistic Americans, who are transforming the Calabrian countryside – to some, I feel sure, it is much more than a job for which they are well paid, it is a mission. But let him be wary of giving the credit, which belongs to individual Americans, to 'America', for 'America', means the American government, which hasn't even a right to be disinterested.

Isn't it obvious that in our highly organized world the kindness and humanity and intelligence of the individual are commodities like any other to be hawked about by governments? I remember hearing from a Pole after the terrible bombardment of Warsaw of the wonderful efficiency of the German relief service, which arrived with hot dinners in thermos plates and kind frauleins to pat the heads of sobbing and mutilated orphans (Aryan). The kind fraulein, whose kindness is not simulated, with her nourishing soup-cubes and her piccy-books (German), is as much a part of a well-made modern bomb as its detonator. The illusion of stern justice tempered with mercy has to be conveyed by every modern dictator, and if O'Faoláin thinks that the USA are in some way unique in their dramatic charities, he has had very little experience of modern Europe.

Has he forgotten about Mussolini, who abolished slavery in Abyssinia, and brought cinemas and libraries to benighted Arabs in Libya and Tunisia, while all the time at his front door this suppurating misery of Calabria, which O'Faoláin so graphically described, was tolerated, till foreigners from another continent arrived on the scene? It was tolerated because Mussolini counted on the landlords to support his regime, and because it is always easier to take the more out of your brother's eye than the beam out of your own.

O'Faoláin would undoubtedly see what I mean if he went to Macedonia, or if he even read the account of H.N. Brailsford, who has known that land for fifty years, from the time when Uskub, now Skoplje, was a derelict Turkish town. Brailsford was in Macedonia when O'Faoláin was in Calabria. Their experiences were much the same. The transformation that Brailsford, a hard-bitten and experienced old journalist, discovered, he describes as 'a barely credible miracle ... After centuries of stagnation and oppression ... for the first time in history her own young men are in charge of her affairs.' The Marxists are anxious to claim the credit for the transformation of Macedonia, the Western democrats for the transformation of Calabria, but in point of fact nothing is proved by either except that miracles can be achieved by science allied with a team of respectable well-paid technicians. An honest clerk would look in these manifestations not for justifications for the American or the Communist way of life but for the presence of that 'universal love', which Communism and Capitalism can exploit and harness and misinterpret but never-effectively stifle. And I think in both cases he could find some evidence.

Without the acknowledgment of a common spirit at work, which Benda would call 'universal love' and that has nothing to do with Communism or Capitalism, all this regeneration is in vain. Look at the map! Calabria and Macedonia, lying over against each other, are on the frontiers of the opposing powers. If the opposition is as sharp and irreconcilable, as O'Faoláin claims, Calabrians and Macedonians are for it and it doesn't matter much whether there are sewers in Lucania or Skoplje or not. If the Russians don't destroy them, the Americans will.

Yet if we recognize this universal love, the picture of the conflict is transformed. It no longer looks like a wolf seeking to devour a little lamb or even like one wolf intent on destroying another. It is more like an alligator with a defective nervous system biting its own tail (if I am not overburdening this simile, I would say that 'the nerves' are 'the honest clerks'). Once the alligator got it into its poor bemused brain that the fierce protuberance, which it saw through the corner of a bleary eye, was its own, the lashing and the gnawing might come to an end. It seems to me that the brains and the teeth and the eyesight are at the Western end of the alligator and therefore that the chief blame for the misunderstanding, as well as the chief hope for dispersing it, is with us.

But Seán O'Faoláin's worst offence is his defeatism. For I submit that either he believes in the inevitability of that war that nobody (we all know) can win, or else his logic is at fault. For example he says, 'Nobody is free to dither indefinitely.' Everybody must take sides because of 'a global war.' Now what does he mean by that? Doesn't he see that the Atlantic Pact means either a permanent dither on the edge of war for a generation or two or else war itself? In the zone of Russian power there are already two tolerated ditherers, Communist Yugoslavia and anti-Communist Finland. As time goes on there may be more. China might have dithered, had it not been for MacArthur, and she still may. Blessed be the ditherers! Harsch shows how for each loss of face on one front the Soviets must compensate themselves by a victory on another. If there are no neutrals in the Western bloc, there will be no neutrals in the Soviet bloc either.

So what? Mr O'Faoláin dared to misrepresent Benda grotesquely so he shall have a bath of Benda. Let the Irish government be as squalidly realist as it possibly can. On the other hand let the clerks (a comprehensive term surely for those who are not swayed chiefly by national self-interest or material values) be as idealistic as they want. Let them go and fight for civilization in Korea, if they really believe that is where the issue will be decided. Or let them try to do in Connemara what the Americans are doing in Calabria. But if they want to intervene abroad in some other way than fighting, let them forget about the barriers as Nansen did, when he organized relief for the Volga famine at the height of the Bolshevik Revolution. Think wherever possible of the people and not of the governments that represent or misrepresent them.

Does this sound vague? I could give many instances of how we could act in this spirit. We are a small people and whatever we do may be small, though if you come to think of it Nansen and the Red Cross both originated in small countries. Seán O'Faoláin has always, in practice, acted as an honest clerk, so let me illustrate my point by a recent action of his.

When Ivo Andritch, an honest Yugoslav clerk, if ever there was one, came to Dublin to the Inter-Parliamentary Conference, crowds formed in the streets to boo and hiss at him, because he came from a Communist country and it was assumed that he believed in persecution, the imprisonment of priests, the closing of churches and so on. He is one of Yugoslavia's foremost writers and neither before nor after the revolution has he written a line approving of one of these things, or suggesting any values of conduct or character other than those accepted by all civilized people. He returned home hurt and bewildered. O'Faoláin was one of the few in Ireland who resented this treatment and wrote to the papers denouncing it. It was a small thing but important. For half a second the alligator was forced to recognize its own tail. But the alligator's head does not become its tail by acknowledging a shared identity. The danger that we might become Communists by reciprocal relations with them in their country or ours is not great. We are as likely to infect them with our heresies as to be infected by theirs. Let us not close any doors (and pacts and 'line-ups' are all doors) on this possibility of friendly, critical reciprocity.

O'Faoláin rightly resents the hypocrisy of selling our assistance in 'the defence of Christendom' for the Six Counties. But does he really think we should become less, rather than more, pleased with our 'lily-white hands', our 'pure souls', if we joined the Atlantic Pact? Would not our ignorant smugness increase a hundred-fold?

Is it impertinent to suggest that what is behind O'Faoláin's stirring call-to-arms is not apprehension of invasion or gratitude to America or concern for the Calabrian peasant but simply exasperation with our small-mindedness? Does he mean possibly that a bit of war-fever would be *good* for us? Tennyson and Ruskin dared without blushing to prescribe war as a tonic for the anaemic Philistinism of the British. Nowadays, perhaps, the flutter of preparing for a war that will never take place – Americans in Mullingar, money flowing, tongues wagging, planes roaring – might be a substitute for the exhilaration of a Victorian war. And how broadening it would be for us to 'line up' with India and Pandit Nehru on the 'the problem of Asia,' instead of with Miss Cook on the problem of Baltinglass! Yes, indeed, it might be good for us and even if it wasn't so good for Asia, Asia could take it.

But all this is very different from the O'Faoláin of ten years ago! We were far more gravely threatened then than now. There were many more pro-Germans in Ireland than there are pro-Russians today. But in O'Faoláin's brilliant and pugnacious articles in *The Bell* the philosophy of Either-Or and the shamefulness of dithering was scarcely adumbrated. It is true that in the series, which he called 'One World' (not 'Half a World'), he argued that isolationism was becoming impossible, but he did not argue that it was immoral, while it lasted. Without being in the least parochial, he made us feel that we had battlefields at home in which we could expend all the strength we had.

And now why has he started haranguing us as if he were Lord Roberts or one of the bulldog breed himself? It sounds phony to me. For Seán is no gun dog or watchdog; he is an Irish terrier and at his happiest chasing the next-door cat. Did you notice, for example, how Kingsley Martin, that typically English intellectual, has only to poke his head once over the garden wall and talk about 'the problem of Ireland' and, as always, there is a wild scuffle and hurroosh, and Asia, Russia, Communism, Calabria are all completely forgotten. And then just suppose for a moment it was Pandit Nehru, who poked his head over the garden wall to settle 'the problem of Ireland' – and he'd have a perfect right to reciprocate this attention ...! Golly!!

O'Faoláin is trying to use the contemporary war-scare as a means of rousing us out of our spiritual stagnation. But I submit that it is a poor way and that there are many better ways of performing this necessary task.

[1951]

12

TRIESTE

Has opportunist diplomacy ever had such a devastating exposure as over the question of Trieste?

A Free State was established after the war in an attempt to reconcile the Yugoslav ally and the Italian enemy. The task was difficult and in a few years the occupiers wearied of waiting for the dove of peace to walk into the neat hutch they had prepared for it.

The Italians were well-bred and sociable, the Slovenes surly and suspicious, and, as it became clear that Italy was more friendly than Yugoslavia to the Western democracies, there was some relief felt, I think, among the Anglo-Saxon intruders when Italy was suddenly promised Trieste. At last they could go home.

But before the promise could be carried out, the situation changed.

Tito quarrelled with Moscow and became no longer an ex-friend enemy, but an ex-enemy friend. He had to be encouraged so Trieste was not handed over.

And then recently another change. Extremists threatened to get control in Italy and the Italian government declared that their collapsing prestige must at all costs be bolstered up by the recovery of Trieste.

The Western Allies decided to take the risk and Mrs Clare Luce, the American ambassador in Rome, is said to have prophesied that Tito would make a fuss but come to heel in the end.

Was there ever so false a prophecy! There is a wild chauvinistic screeching from Rome and Belgrade, there are threats and riots. Will the curtain go up on an Italian Trieste as promised, or has it stuck a second time? Behind the scenes one can hear the frantic shifting of furniture and the stage is, I hope, being set for an altered programme, but what a way to do it!

In the meantime not quite so many stones are flying through the windows of Anglo-American cultural institutes in Belgrade but a lively fire has opened on their associated offices in Rome (one sad aspect of the government patronage and publicity for the arts is that the arts have lost their old international prestige. Shakespeare and Dante have to climb down from Mount Olympus in order to become commercial travellers and whipping boys for rival Foreign Offices).

What is to happen?

Obviously in her present vengeful and chauvinistic mood, Italy cannot be given Trieste. Under the pretext of anti-Communist measures the large Slovene minority would be crushed or forcibly Italianized. Reprisals would be taken in the Yugoslav-controlled Zone B and that would lead to further Italian territorial demands. Signor Pella's prestige would have to be fed with pound after pound of Slovene flesh.

Obviously the only possible policy is to give the Free State a longer and fairer trial.

It is objected that there is something artificial about its autonomy and it is true of course that it has not had a long history of freedom like the Hanseatic States, but its Italianita, despite all the braying, and rioting and flag-wagging, is equally artificial.

Trieste owes it size and importance to a Rhineland baron, who conceived the idea of expanding a small Slovene fishing village into a great port for Austro-Hungarian commerce. Italians poured in from outside to fill an empty shell reared by Teutons and Magyars in a Slav countryside.

The Triestini are, and in their less excitable moments will admit to being, a Mischvolk.

Of course there was a Roman Tergeste, but that has as much bearing on the situation today as Roman Verulam or Roman London.

There was never a Venetian Trieste. Indeed to escape the suffocating embrace of Venice the little medieval port flung herself into the arms of the Habsburgs.

When I was last in Trieste I found there was a small but sturdy and serious group of Triestini who believed in the Free State and its power to develop organically if it could be nursed through this terrible epoch of reprisal and counter-reprisal.

In the 1952 elections this party polled 22 per cent of the votes.

Not very many, you will say, till you remember that the two annexation parties have powerful states at their back while the occupying powers are scrupulously neutral.

Of the twenty-odd newspapers of Trieste, *Trieste Sera*, the organ of the Independentists, was perhaps the poorest of the lot, crippled for office space and only able to appear twice a week.

What can one hope for?

I do not feel justified in recommending the pure milk of pacifism but only a rather adulterated kind.

The occupying troops obviously cannot at present be withdrawn. Yet something could be done to support the only party of reason and reconciliation.

Can we not urge publicity, propaganda, research on behalf of this struggling group, which would like to be the mediators between Slav and Latin, between the culture of revolution and the culture of tradition?

If reason were restored to her throne in Italy, from which she has so often ruled the world, she might welcome such a state, where Slav and Italian enjoy equal rights. Yugoslavia might be ready to enlarge the frontiers of the little state with the adjoining regions whose inhabitants now under Yugoslav rule have the same mixed inheritance as the Triestini.

Is this all a fantasy? When we consider the terrible alternative we can reject no peaceful plan because it is difficult and likely to be slow in fulfilment.

[1953]

Zone A, including the city, was held by the Italians, with popular support, under UN protection as the 'Free Territory of Trieste' between 1947 and 1954. Zone B, to the south, came under the control of Yugoslavia. Border issues were finally settled with the Treaty of Orisino in 1975. (Ed.)

13

YUGOSLAVIA TODAY

There have been three good books on Yugoslavia in the past few weeks; an autobiography by King Peter II, a travel record by a Swedish writer, M. Sommelius, and lastly this work of Mr Tennyson.*

Alone of the three writers, the King was personally involved in the great catastrophe that swept away a still medieval kingdom and left a question mark in its place, while M. Sommelius brought a poetic vision and a certain Nordic honesty to the study of this enigma upon the Adriatic. Mr Tennyson brings a Quaker seriousness and cheerful matter-of-fact optimism (but I am not certain whether, as organizer of various international Quaker undertakings, he was acting as a Friend or as a Friend of the Friends).

To me Mr Tennyson's book is the most congenial of the three. Without being a professional middle-of-the-road man, he is beautifully objective, or let us say, rather, that he observes other roads in Yugoslavia besides that which runs between Communism and democracy. The Marxists and their opponents are only indirectly involved in many of the sad crises and conflicts that are inevitable when an ancient people is pushed by circumstances from medievalism to modernity.

Consider the sad dilemma of many Moslem women today. The Communist law prohibiting the veil has been supported by the religious leaders, the Hodjas and Immams, who declare that its origin is not in religion but in custom. Yet the tradition is strongly

---

* Hallam Tennyson, *Tito Lifts the Curtain, The Story of Yugoslavia Today.*

cherished and many a Moslem wife sits indoors all day, terrified to walk out of doors unveiled lest she infuriate her husband, or to walk out veiled lest she be prosecuted by the police.

There are many bad old customs, which, like the veiling of women, have been handed down reverently from generation to generation. Only the dynamite of some crude revolutionary philosophy will abolish them, yet one is not obliged to commend the liberating violence, but rather to deplore the strange impotence of the humane and educated, who acknowledge the necessity of reform, but leave its execution to bandits or bureaucrats. If the Hodjas acknowledged that the veil should be abolished why did they leave it to the infidel to enforce the abolition?

Mr Tennyson has certainly no illusion about the tact of the new Communist evangelists, but he is touched by their simple zeal. His enthusiasm for the old Macedonian dances worried his Communist friend in Macedonia who expressed himself like this:

We must be modern. We have to put the nix on dervishes, witches, beggars, ballad singers and these here long festivals up in the hills. Maybe they was useful in the olden days ... But today they waste the precious time when the farmers ought to be improving their livestock and their agriculture ... You won't write only 'bout them dances, will you, comrade? You won't forget the pottery and the tobacco refinery and the fruit packing plant and the hydro-electric station?

Despite his admiration for the dances Mr Tennyson recognizes the sincerity of this lament, for in many villages where Orthodox Catholics and Moslems were present together there were as many as 200 holidays in the year excluding Sundays.

Mr Tennyson declares that in Yugoslavia he would 'as a believer in God and party politics' have been no more than 'a second-class citizen with limited rights' but he considers that in a country, where new things are happening every day, the individual and his decisions may have an importance that they lack in a land like Britain, where the individual's rights have long been assured and democracy rolls along effortlessly on traditional rails.

Justifiably he plays down the influence of doctrinaire Marxism in contemporary Yugoslavia. 'Materialism,' he says, 'for the average Marxist boils down to no more than a vague feeling that this is the only world we are likely to know and therefore we had better make the most of it.' It is probable that, even without the breach with Moscow, Yugoslav Marxism would have had to adapt itself to many strong regional and cultural idiosyncrasies. Mr Tennyson is doing a good work for peace, when he shows that the way of dogma, which the Yugoslav Communists have built against the Christian world, has many gaps in it and is not at all formidable to the sincere explorer.

[1955]

14

TITO'S MARXIST HERITIC

Most of the heroes of history have had enthusiastic communities behind them, giving them moral support when they fail, looking after their posthumous glory when they succeed. Milovan Djilas is one of the exceptions.*

As a former Vice-President of Yugoslavia, he is too deeply implicated in Communism and probably too proud to qualify for the laurels that the West bestows on those who defy the Marxists in their citadels.

He cannot be represented as crusading for anything much except free speech and yet that is too vague a cause to be glamorous. Yet he thought it worth going to prison for, and this book with its unemotional account of his boyhood in Montenegro does much to explain his decision.

It is a sober account of a small society intoxicated alternately by religious, racial and political passions, and rarely have these violent disorders been chronicled with so little bias by one so intimately involved. Montenegro, to which the poet prince Nejegosh gave the name Land Without Justice, was famous for its crusading heroes, their epic deeds and independent personalities.

There can have been few countries where the distinction between peasant and aristocrat was so slight. It was a democracy achieved by levelling up rather than by levelling down, and the humblest was able to behave with the eccentric freedom of an eighteenth-century English nobleman. It was a moderately united

---

* Milovan Djilas, *Land Without Justice.*

land while the Turks were still there to focus upon themselves the concentrated ferocity of the Christians, but in Djilas' boyhood the Cross finally triumphed over the Crescent.

Alas, it was a political and not a moral victory. Barbarous cruelties were practised on the defeated Moslems. Those who restrained themselves from murder looted. Djilas saw one of his uncles forcing a Moslem child to squeeze through the narrow window of a mosque and bring him the carpet, another uncle specialized in Moslem chickens, Djilas' mother acquired a load of wheat. By the time he grew up there were few savage disillusionments for which this young Montenegrin was unprepared.

Very soon the Montenegrins were at war with themselves, for some wished for incorporation in Yugoslavia, others wanted their independence and their king. Young Djilas observed with loving but candid eyes how his family and friends were swayed first by one loyalty, then by another, and finally came to be guided by self-interest alone.

His father was a slightly modernized descendant of a long line of peasant warriors who had won deathless glory in fighting against Turks and Austrians. He had scruples and hesitations unknown to his ancestors, and sometimes felt embarrassment when engaged on a crusade. Once vengeance was being taken on the villagers of Rovchi, who were reluctant to be incorporated in Yugoslavia: 'There were many routine things to be done, the women had to have cats sewn up in their skirts and the cats had to be whipped, old men had to carry young soldiers pick-a-back across the river and much else.' The elder Djilas, as he stood beside the cannon that was demolishing the village, began to falter.

What had these villagers done to deserve this? Had he not once like them been a supporter of the king; was he not really in his heart a supporter still? Suddenly reassurance came to him. He remembered that some men who had stolen his bull, Spot, had probably come from Rovchi. Now he felt comforted.

After every volley of the cannon he cried out: 'Ha! My bull, Spot! Ha!' Montenegrin justice was vindicated.

It is difficult to praise as it deserves this book, which is a picture of a primitive society in violent collision with the sophistication of the West. The new ideas that fly like sparks from an anvil under the furious impact of the modern world do not always seem to us very new at all. Sometimes chapters end with weighty reflections that are in themselves as trite as cracker-mottoes.

Yet recently quarried from experience, they seem to have a vigour and dynamism lacking in our most venerated truisms. The book has been translated by an anonymous American professor. I like his version, though the narrative remains rather rugged and uncouth and patently translated. He does not waste time searching for smooth English equivalents. The English *mot juste* is often a dreary veteran, while those Montenegrin kinsmen of our platitudes are still fresh and lively.

The injustices and squalors of which Djilas writes often do not seem to belong to any time or nation. *Homo Homini lupus* is his theme. He narrates how in the First World War a young Czech doctor joyously came over to their side, confident of a welcome from his brother Slavs, and how one of these brother Slavs, a neighbour of Djilas, blew his brains out to get his watch.

He remembers the small shabby incidents that chroniclers of epic deeds usually forget. 'The Montenegrins,' he recalls, 'pitied the Serbs rather than helped them,' during the great Serbian retreat to the sea. He cannot forget the tiny piece of bacon that his mother gave to the starving Serbian soldier and the big slabs that were stored away for the family in the attic.

His nostalgia is not for the past but for that imagined world that we create when we are young, in which the injustices of the actual world are redressed. For as we grow older even that visionary world ceases to be credible.

'Old Montenegro,' writes Djilas, 'faded away with its men and customs, while the new order failed to bring peace and liberty even to those who hoped for these and fought for them.'

This book is full of gloomy prognostications and yet is fundamentally cheerful. Djilas has, I think, the sort of mind that in a more prosperous community might have been strongly introverted and might have harvested misery out of disillusionment and intellectual frustration. But it would be hard to be an introvert in Montenegro, where thinking has little status except as a dim prelude to violent action.

Djilas chronicles the poverty and disorder of his native land with a tenderness of feeling that sometimes seems to run counter to his indignation. It is clear that he loves Montenegro almost as much as he loves truth, and that he has never been affected by that weariness of living on which genuine pessimism must be founded.

[1958]

15

IRELAND AND NEUTRALITY

I

The old south Leinster town of Kilkenny is establishing the custom of an annual debate or symposium during the Tostal Festival, at which matters of moment to Ireland are discussed with much greater freedom and candour than is usual in Irish politics.

Last year, as reported in the *Manchester Guardian*, two Orange leaders, Colonel Topping, the Stormont Chief Whip, and Mr Douglas, the Secretary of the Unionist Party, travelled to Kilkenny and presented the Ulster case in uncompromising terms to an audience that was Nationalist, Roman Catholic and Anti-Partitionist almost to a man. The citizens of Kilkenny listened to a great many home-truths from the Ulstermen with the same polite attention that they gave to their own speakers, Mr MacBride, a former Minister of External Affairs and Mr Eoin O'Mahony.

This year the subject of the symposium was 'Can a small nation stand alone in the atomic age?' and Ireland's relationship to NATO and the Western bloc was debated with unusual force and frankness. Captain Liddell Hart, the well-known expert on military strategy, was the most eminent and authoritative of the speakers, but they were all of them well-known personalities and therefore the views they expressed have had wide publicity in the Irish press and are being broadcast on Radio Éireann.

They seemed to show that, despite the strong anti-Communist feelings of the majority, there is an undeniable trend towards neutrality in Ireland. It is not as closely linked with the question of Partition as many Irish political leaders have hinted, and it might show itself as an active movement for peace and not merely a passive drift from danger as it was in the last war.

Captain Liddell Hart dealt in an admirably objective way with the realities of atomic warfare and the new concepts of attack and defence that it had introduced. Despite the failure of many small nations to preserve their neutrality during the last war, others, like Ireland, Switzerland and Sweden, had, through luck or cunning, contrived to survive. In the atomic age decisive blows would be struck with incredible speed and violence at the large centres of population and the position of the small nation standing alone had not been made more untenable. Neutrality might, indeed, be more feasible, less hazardous, for a small nation than a scheme of joint defence with one of the great atomic-armed powers.

Against this, touching lightly on the Partition issue, Captain Liddell Hart explained how in 1941 a plan, of which he had himself seen the draft, for the invasion of Northern Ireland, had been presented to Hitler by a leading German general and it had been rejected principally because of the difficulty of retaining a foothold in Ulster against the strong British forces there. In a unified, independent Ireland it would be a much more costly business for Ireland to provide equivalent security.

The Irish team included those three stormy petrels of Irish politics, Major General Dorman O'Gowan, who has headed many campaigns against the Stormont parliament in the interests of Irish unity, Senator Sheehy Skeffington, who is tireless in tilting against established institutions in the cause of social justice, and Doctor Noel Browne, who was Minister of Health when the famous clash with the Hierarchy over the Health Bill occurred. Deputy Declan Costello, the son of the Taoiseach (Prime Minister), opposing these political heretics, advocated the crusading Christian ideals to which the great mass of the Irish public outwardly subscribes.

These ideals, contended Dr Browne, bore no relation to the hideous realities of atomic war or to our real feelings. 'We will talk and talk,' he said, 'but if war comes, we will stay neutral as we did the last time.'

And Senator Skeffington asked what the great powers had done for the small ones in the past. Had they not abandoned Manchuria and Abyssinia, and more recently Poland? Had not the Big Five introduced the Veto into UNO, lest the small nations should force some action on a point of principle? For an Irishman the real war against Communism must be waged at home against the miserable social conditions in which Communism is bred. You could not fight an idea with a bomb, but only with a better idea.

General Dorman O'Gowan said that as Ireland was a mutilated nation, she could not yet speak with a national voice. Therefore a special responsibility rested on the individual Irishman to make himself heard. Since 1939 there had been an appalling deterioration in the morality of war. With nuclear warfare we had reached the very bottom of civilization. We were not justified in using such a form of defence. Nehru was right. It might be possible to form a neutral belt across the centre of Europe to include the present satellites of Russia.

The symposium was recorded by Radio Éireann for broadcasting on 8 June, and the chairman, Mr Terence de Vere White, showed extraordinary skill in keeping his very voluble team within the prescribed time limits. 'War in the past,' he ended, 'has been associated with gallantry, but where is the gallantry now? Have not all our ideas of chivalry to be changed, and could not small countries help towards this ideological revolution?'

It may be said of this Kilkenny symposium that the Irish participants were unorthodox, and except for Deputy Declan Costello, the official militantly Christian view was not effectively represented. Against this it can be urged that none of the speakers were themselves pacifists. In advocating neutrality they were arguing from the evidence of past wars, and their arguments received powerful support from Captain Liddell Hart's masterly analysis of the probable course of a future one.

Though the presence of the British army in Ulster may have saved Ireland at some point in the war from a German invasion, in atomic warfare no army could shield them from disaster once an attack was launched. Others argued that an H-bomb on Liverpool or Belfast would, if the winds were appropriate, involve Dublin in its lethal effects. There was no small country whose collapse might not be engineered by the mere threat of an H-bomb. So it is on the moral plane only that a small nation can contribute to the maintenance of peace.

[1955]

II

Decisions about peace and war are always made in capitals, so comments from the provinces can only deal with the temper of mind, which, at long remove, influences such decisions.

Yet the very fact that Ireland's attitude to peace and war is a discussion at all, and cannot be inferred from England's, as can that of Scotland and Wales, is proof of an unquenchable thirst for independence.

This independence was not won by peaceful or wholly honourable methods. As with every small nation struggling to be free, the goal has been reached by a mixture of noble self-sacrifice and vulgar trickery.

Ulysses figures as prominently as Sir Galahad in our fight for freedom.

De Valera took the oath of fealty to King George in order to qualify for Parliament and get the oath abolished. His political rival — outbidding him for popular favour, got into power by the votes of those who favoured the British connection, and then declared an Irish Republic, outside the British Commonwealth. Maybe that is the way small nations must of necessity behave.

By a variety of subterfuges and equivocations and an odd flash of inspiration, I believe a small and powerless nation, which had always valued its freedom, would contrive to retain it.

The Romans were the first to realize the importance of Irish freedom. We read in the *Agricola* of Tacitus: 'I have often heard Agricola say that Ireland could be reduced and held by a single legion and a few auxiliaries, and that the conquest would also pay from the point of view of Britain, if Roman arms were in evidence on every side and liberty vanished off the map.' Yet Irish liberty did not vanish off the map, and perhaps Ireland's example encouraged stronger nations to resist absorption.

Somehow the Irish eluded for a thousand years after Agricola what looked like inevitable conquest. They were not years of peace or prosperity, and they may be said to have dodged conquest rather than repelled it. They succeeded partly because they were intractable, partly because they were remote and insignificant.

Even their conquest by the Anglo-Normans brought neither England nor Ireland any lasting profit; and a generation ago that conquest, in its main features, had to be reversed. And not only the English and the Romans, but also Napoleon, the Kaiser and Hitler, in their turn, seem to have found we would not really repay the tedious labour of subjugation.

History has given us a deep-seated conviction, blended of modesty and arrogance, that we are not really worth the bother of annexation.

Thus, our devotion to peace has had little idealism behind it, but is based on the sordid facts of history.

If the Irish had ever once fought a successful war or ever been successfully subdued, we should look at the whole matter quite differently. As it is, we shall – if it is anyway possible – be neutral in the next war as in the last.

Our pulpits and platforms will resound, of course, with denunciations of Communism and appeals to rally to the defence of Christianity and the Free World. But we've heard all this before, and we are sceptical.

Phrases like 'The Collapse of Civilization', 'Abolition of Free Speech', etc., have little magnetism among simple conservative country folk. They realize that even if London burns and skyscrapers totter, cows have to be milked and potatoes sown (in fact, rather more than usual, at an enhanced profit).

There are, of course, peace meetings in Dublin, but they are attended principally by middle-aged Quakers, by foreigners, by two or three Protestant clergy who are by no means in favour with the more orthodox members of the flock. Then there is perhaps a handful of young radicals, who give to the respectable a pretext for saying that the gathering is Communist-inspired.

In this hypothetical crusade it is the Border, of course, that will furnish us with the most satisfactory excuse for abstention. How, we ask, can a country engage in war when it is unjustly divided?

Just as a festering sore attracts bluebottles, so all who are predatory, pugnacious or vaguely discontented, gather greedily around this grave wound in our society.

There are the Patriotic Bluebottles, who say that those of English blood and sympathies have no right to be in Ireland, yet choose to ignore those 40,000 Irishmen who are emigrating annually and permanently to England.

There are the Holy Bluebottles, who complain that there is discrimination against Roman Catholics in the Six Counties, but who regard as a 'peaceful and moderate protest' (I am quoting an eminent Catholic bishop) the ecclesiastically organized boycott of all the Protestants of an area in County Wexford, because one of them infringed the *Ne Temere* marriage regulations [Fethard-on-Sea: see the author's 'Boycott Village' (*The Twentieth Century*, January 1958), gathered in *Escape from the Anthill*, 1985)].

To conclude, if war threatens, we shall certainly practise peace, even if we don't preach it. And though I do not anticipate from Ireland any bold stand for truth or freedom, it might happen, all the same, that our contribution to human freedom would be considerable.

Is it not something that almost alone of the countries of Europe, Ireland has never yet had military conscription?

[1958]

PART THREE

Autobiographies

16

HOME AND BIGSHOTTE RAYLES

When I went to school in England, my mother gave me as a rule of life: 'Do that which is nearer to thee.' I was nine and I knew of course that when people say Thee and Thou instead of You, they are talking generally and do not expect to be literally followed. Indeed the rule is impossible to observe, though I saw that my father and mother came reasonably close to doing so.

My mother was always bicycling to Bennettsbridge, where she organized a Boot and Coal Fund for the needy. There was later a branch of the Women's National Health that had something to do with Lady Aberdeen and tuberculosis. She got up concerts and jumble sales to pay for them, and when the war broke out the dining-room table was covered once a week with brown paper and string, and six or seven wives sat round it doing up parcels for Bennettsbridge men in Ruhleben camp in Germany.

I remember being told that all the Bennettsbridge men had taken the wrong turn when they got to France and that is why they all landed together in Ruhleben. They all came back safely. Johnny Whelan our groom had been in Salonika but he thought it was in France. Percy Upfold, the cowman, because of his agricultural appearance had been drafted to a German farm and asked to milk the cows, but he told me proudly he had pretended not to know how. He had told the farmer he could not get the cow to sit down on the pail.

My father was as active as my mother. As well as farming 600 acres and being hunt secretary, he had helped in bringing a co-operative creamery to Bennettsbridge, and was chairman of the committee. He had made the Maidenhall Cricket Club, which later turned into a tennis club in our inches (the fields by the river). He had carpentry classes in the barn at our main farm at Burnchurch, where my brother lives now, and as a magistrate he was always bicycling into Kilkenny in connection with assizes and gaols.

I was his eldest son so I went with him to the Kilkenny fair and to his other farm at Drumherin in the Ballyfoyle hills, which was some sixteen miles away, and I went out hunting with him, and helped him prune and spray the large orchard that he had planted at Burnchurch farm. But though I was adequately healthy and strong and considered highly intelligent in an academic way, I looked at cattle and sheep and horses with all the ignorant and uncomprehending indifference that Percy Upfold only pretended to have. There must be some not obvious explanation for this antipathy, because I have inherited from him his love of growing things, which I could not share with him. Often now I wish he was there to tell me how he grew nectarines and peaches and apricots on our garden wall, where I can only manage inferior peaches. And how did he make the sea kale so tall and straight and have arum lilies in time for Easter, unstained by greenfly.

He had been to Cambridge just as my mother had been to Cheltenham College for their educations but they did what was nearest to them without so much strain as most people would find today, and as we hacked home from the hunt he told me stories about all the places we passed, so that they seemed to belong to me and I judged what was 'nearest to me' by the distance a horse could travel: a circle of ten miles radius closely packed with oddity and episode. There was also a skim of responsibility over it; occasionally my father would get off his horse and explain to a cottager how he ought to prune his apples: 'Leave one fruit bud above the old wood, but careful with the Worcesters, as they fruit on the tips'; and sometimes he would tell them about a swarm of bees in the hedge and advise about securing it. Sometimes he'd brush it off into a box himself (they seldom had straw skeps) and tell them not to move it into a hive till after six, when all the bees had gone in.

As well as geographical nearness there was of course the nearness of kinship and here my mother was the arbiter, measuring in the traditional way. The 'nuclear family' as it is now called came of course first, after that came first cousins, second cousins, then third. These gradations had more to do with responsibility than with affection, though the two were usually fastened together. When I was growing up and talked of 'compulsory affection', my mother said angrily, 'You got that off Samuel Butler! I hate him.' And my father, who was not an irascible man, wanted to burn *The Way of All Flesh*.

Now, sixty years later, when the nuclear family seems to be disintegrating, I am glad that I belong to a kinship group that is neither too loose nor too closely knit, and to a neighbourhood group that has not yet entirely disintegrated. When my great-uncle Whitwell Butler came back from Waterloo, he sold his commission and with the proceeds bought the little property of Cooltrand, where my nephew now lives, and there are two other family houses where we have lived for three generations and five. And on Whitwell's 1825 map of his new farm, which was near my great-grandfather's farm of Burnchurch, I see that he had the same neighbours as my nephew still has, Macdonalds, Murphys, Mahers. We have been tethered to the same post for nearly two centuries, and if we were cattle we would by now have grazed down all the coarse grass so that it came up sweet and clean.

But we have not done this. Our affections are not really tethered to our neighbourhood. We have not found it possible to co-ordinate our loyalties, which stray away in contrary directions. A thousand inhibitions whose source is in history, in education, in religion, and the temperament that they shape, keep us apart. How rich we could be if we could pool our experiences and the wisdom we derived from them, but we never do. And now the consumer society is sweeping us all aside, preaching the mobility of labour, the mechanization and rationalization of agriculture. The properties that the landlords owned that were thought too large are now considered too small to be viable. A generation or two from now all the names on that 1825 map may have disappeared.

On the opposite bank of the river, Quigley Magnesite, a subsidiary company of Pfizer of New York, are mining the broad band of magnesium-limestone that stretches southward to the bridge and there crosses over to the west bank and past Mosse's mill to Maidenhall, where I have gravelled the avenue and the garden paths with buff-coloured dolomite waste. Our two nearest Anglo-Irish neighbours at Sheestown and Kilfera have sold their land to members of these great American firms, and beyond them on the east bank Fieldcrest Towels from Virginia are swallowing up another neighbour's home and advancing on my sister's house at

Lavistown. The whole picture of life is changing and to do 'what is nearest to thee' has become more obviously complex than it ever was before.

It is harder to love one's neighbours but it is also harder to hate him. One could burn a landlord's house or evict a tenant but how does one damage a great international consortium, which from some distant base tentatively stretches out a claw and can withdraw it again as easily as possible? I do not know and the odd thing is that it does not matter. We still love and hate and kill and kidnap according to ancient tradition, English and Irish, Protestant and Catholic. And if I am out of date in what I write so is everybody else. And I like it so.

I am an English-Protestant Irishman and though my family is of Norman descent and settled in Ireland for eight centuries and though its head lived till recently in Kilkenny, it would be an affectation to make much of that. My mother was half-English and I was educated entirely in England from the time I was nine. It would be an affectation too to make too much of the fact that when I was thirteen I 'lost my faith', as people still said, and never found it and became an Irish nationalist hating England. That is perfectly true but irrelevant.

A Frenchman cannot suddenly decide that he is no longer French nor can an Irish Protestant decide by an act of will that he is no longer Protestant. Basically I am still what my forebears and Anglo-Irish neighbours were and are. And to pretend anything else is not to forward this dream of loving our neighbours or, as I see it, doing that which is nearest to thee, but to delay it. Since I still live in the house where I and my father were born I should be something of an expert on this belief which I have inherited that we should do that which is nearest to us, though, being of an introverted frame of mind I do this less well than most people similarly situated would do.

My failure is only just a local and personal reflection of everybody's failure but it is the one I am best qualified to speak of. This is the story of one grain of pollen out of many a thousand grains, all of which were sterile, so that the tree nearby, not being self-fertile, failed to bear fruit.

This is a prouder statement than it sounds, for I think that nature intended the Anglo-Irish to be mediators between the English and the Irish, acting as a filter through which only so much Anglo-Saxon culture could pass as the Irish genius could assimilate without destroying itself. Instead they preferred to be *Kulturträger* in the arrogant German way, to exasperate a proud and sensitive people and to be thrown out. Without them, Anglo-Saxon vulgarity flowed in unchecked and anything that was distinctive in it has been submerged.

[1970]

* * *

The following headnote was furnished from an offprint of 75: Bigshotte *1895–1970, a magazine celebrating the seventy-fifth anniversary of this preparatory boarding school in Berkshire, England, where Hubert was sent at the age of nine. (His comment on its cover reads: 'My contribution, enormously abbreviated and bowdlerized, is on page 19.') A contemporary, G.L. Braidwood, wrote of his Bigshotte days: 'Our daily routine started with a cold bath each morning supervised by Mr Reeve ... My brother says in his time Mr Reeve shot rabbits on Saturday for Sunday consumption; this, no doubt, helped with wartime rationing.' (Ed.)*

[Hubert Butler came from Ireland to Bigshotte in 1910 and in 1915 won the Second Scholarship to Charterhouse. From there he was Top Open Scholar to St John's College, Oxford. After Oxford he joined the staff of the Irish County Libraries. Then he went to Russia where he taught English in Leningrad. Later he studied in Yugoslavia. Then he worked in Vienna with the Quakers for the refugees, returning to Ireland in 1941. He founded the Kilkenny Archaeological Society. He writes for newspapers and has translated some Russian works and has broadcast on English and Irish radio. Mr Butler still lives in Ireland, at Bennettsbridge in County Kilkenny.]

My headmaster was W.G. Reeve. He was a very remarkable man. He inspired me, for example, with an absolute passion for trigonometry, which faded as soon as I got to Charterhouse, where, though I had gone with the top Mathematical scholarship, I took Greek instead. Maths had become a deadly bore.

When I first came to Bigshotte, Reeve had a kind, fat sister, Miss Reeve, and a fat wheezy dog called Rex. Both of them died before I left and he married a very nice woman, Elsie Bowering, from Surbiton. There were only twenty-five boys but Mr Reeve was a brilliant teacher and games teacher and, though such a small school,

we used to win all our matches. He was personally very kind to
me and made me head boy before I deserved to be. (I was a very
silly one.) I think that Bigshotte must be a very different place now
as none of the masters would then have had the idea of asking the
boys to find out about the school. We were very traditional.

I really hated Bigshotte, despite the fact that everybody was
very kind and the food was good and there was only a little bullying when one was rather young or if one was in any way odd.
Perhaps I hated it because I was Irish, or perhaps because I was
very futile at all the games they played.

We used to go for Sunday walks to Caesar's Camp. In our day
the swimming pool was behind the laurels in front of the front
door, and a path led past the Changing Room and a prickly shrub
with purple berries on it to the 'pavvy' and the playing fields.
There was a golf course all round it as Mr Reeve was very fond
of golf. The boys had their own gardens under the classroom
window that faces the drive.

[1975]

*This seat of learning in Wokingham near Reading changed its name to Bigshotte
School in 1918, until its closure in 1977 when it merged with Eagle House, a
feeder for Wellington College. Among its more distinguished alumni is the writer,
gardener and broadcaster Monty Don, who was there in the mid-1960s. (Ed.)*

17

CHARTERHOUSE

How does one write interestingly about being bored? Real boredom is an affliction seldom known to the physically oppressed or the frightened. The victims of *taedium vitae* usually have three good meals a day, and an unexacting occupation. Occasionally some dream of ecstasy flashes upon the dreary scene only to show that all the doors that lead to it are locked.

Fortunately there is little necessity to write about Charterhouse. Robert Graves, who was a few years older than I was, has said all that needs to be said. He and Neville Barbour, later a friend of mine at Oxford, decided that the tradition of the school was so strong that it would not be sufficient to dismiss all the staff and begin again. One would have to demolish the school buildings, which were so impregnated with the public-school spirit that no disinfectant could purge them. One would have to rebuild somewhere else. Robert mentions an oppression of spirit that even as an adult it is painful to recall. He relates how schoolwork was despised and the fifty scholars scattered through the ten houses were plagued as 'swots', unless they pretended to hate their accomplishments as much as their persecutors did.

I do not remember being bullied as Robert was, or, if I were, I have forgotten the details, but in my house, Verites, I had to sit at every meal with two other swots. We had nothing in common with each other except an aptitude for school subjects and the consequent pariahdom it forced on us. It was impossible to turn on the overwhelming majority so we turned upon each other, and I came to loath Wallace-Edward's damp beaky nose and Dupont's whole body and soul. Nature had speckled his face with cozy pustules and if he dropped a handkerchief or an undergarment in the changing-room it was thought amusing to hand it back to him with a poker or a tongs. His sole defence was a blistering tongue, which he only dared to use upon his comrades in misfortune.

Wallace-Edwards did not feel quite so oppressed as Dupont and I did, so he did not have to bury his head so deeply in the sand of academic achievement. Now that I have come to terms with my feebly self-depreciating character, my aimiable insincerities, I can acknowledge without conceit that there was no branch of polite learning, as it was interpreted at Charterhouse, at which I could not excel, but nobody valued these excellences much so I did not value them myself. Indeed they have never done anything for me except open doors through which I did not wish to pass, and when I got to Oxford and found that they in no way qualified me to promote what seemed to me the most urgent thing in life, the demolition of Charterhouse, I relaxed my efforts. Were they really efforts though? It was more like a mechanical process. An active mind, compressed in a box, flowed through the only exit, a small-bore cast-iron pipe, which led into a vacuum. When the pipe was enlarged, the pressure was reduced and the flow decreased.

I have always had a good *ad hoc* memory for the unimportant, evacuating unwanted knowledge almost as quickly as I absorb it. I easily passed my New Bugs Exam. 'What are the colours of Hodgsonites? Who won the match against Winchester? Who walked backwards into the fountain when reviewing the Officers Training Corps?' A fortnight later I had forgotten all the house colours and even the school colours. I do not know what an Old Carthusian tie looks like. But it was A.H. Todd who fell into the fountain. He was my housemaster and every memory of him is durably coated in loathing.

I had gone to Charterhouse with the top mathematical scholarship, but the magic of algebra, geometry, trigonometry was linked irrevocably with those dreamy privileged hours I spent with Bertie by the dying fire, when all the other boys had had their cocoa and gone to bed. As our pens scratched in unison, express trains overtook slow trains, cisterns were filled with water by big pipes and small pipes, and beyond them sines, cosines and tangents beckoned us on like the sacred words of Hindu meditation to deeper mysteries. They promised to show us that life below its troubled, often hateful, surface has a calm regular pattern to which even Mr Reeve and all the boys were bound to conform.

I do not recall if what I did when I reached Charterhouse was called pure mathematics, anyway it was purged of all the human impurities that I liked, the hints of triumph over the obvious and pedestrian. I realized I was not a real mathematician at all but a solver of riddles with a human content. I found myself on the low rung of a ladder that led to the construction of mechanical marvels, like the Irish mailboat, which only fortified what I wished to destroy.

Somehow or other I sidled out of mathematics onto the classical side and found myself learning Greek, which those with classical scholarships already knew, and very soon I caught them up and passed them and for my last year at Charterhouse I was head of the classical sixth and had I shown the faintest aptitude or desire for 'leadership' would have been head boy. It was not till years later that I understood what relevance to me and my life Greek and Latin could possibly have. The war was on and I was painfully conscious that I had none of the practical accomplishments that were in demand. At home rectors' daughters had left Ireland to drive lorries in France or make bombs in Bristol. Who could possibly want Latin and Greek? So I used to get up at four or five in the morning and sitting at my wash-hand stand study *Pitman's Shorthand*. I devoted to it the same application that I gave to the classics, and I can still write it as well as I write Greek but I cannot read what I have written.

Many years later this heavily cultivated soil began to bear a little fruit for me. I understood how the experience of the Greeks can still illuminate everything we do and suffer but that the academic knowledge I had acquired was a barrier to understanding this. As I still feel savage about the teaching of Greek, I shall refer to what I wrote about it in my middle age ('Return to Hellas' in *Escape from the the Anthill*, 1985).

A.H. Todd, my housemaster, was a hideous old man with one eye, who had because of the war stayed on beyond the retiring age. He and another classical master, Dames-Longworth, had together compiled a fat coffee-coloured anthology of 'passages for unseen translation', from Greek and Roman writers. Dames-Longworth, a showy Irish gentleman with a splendid moustache and baggy check suits, used to swagger around the classroom, declaiming sonorously some 'passage' or some 'superb rendering' into Greek iambics of Herrick or Landor. He was a racquets champion and had I believe built the school racquets court at his own expense. Some boys took art or music instead of the OTC, which followed on his class, and he would bay out, 'Any old crocks for Studio? Off with you now!'

A portion of my mind is soft and unresisting as blotting-paper and though the active part of it was far away I soaked up most of this stuff effectively and usually won the Form Prize. As the war was on, the prize money went to the Red Cross and we were given Carthusian bookplates '*Deo Dante Dedi*' to stick into books of our own. Whatever God had given me, Charterhouse gave me nothing, indeed it took something away, for at sixteen I had visions of intense happiness and freedom almost within reach of my hand if I only dared to stretch it out. But I never seriously considered running away. I was bound to the school by a thousand Lilliputian threads, of which physical cowardice was the weakest and most easily snapped and my affection for my parents the strongest. Once released I could, I knew, find my way through the jungle, for every now and then I met signposts to happiness and truth, pointing down paths that I could not follow.

One holidays I found *Robert Elsmere* by Mrs Humphrey Ward among my mother's books and I read it with astonishment and joy and pride. So I was right after all, and Mr Reeve and Mr Carr and all the masters at Charterhouse and my parents were wrong. No sensible person could really believe all that. I had never before heard a whisper of unbelief and here I was having thought it all out for myself at the age of thirteen, whereas Elsmere, a middle-aged clergyman, had to have those long conversations with Langham, the frigid melancholy sceptic from Oxford, and Squire Wendover, who had discussed it all with Strauss and Baur at Tubingen and had on his shelves autographed copies of the works of Schelling, Boeckh and Von Humboldt. Elsmere and his friends, before he gave up his rectory and all but broke his wife's heart and founded The Brotherhood of Christ, had felt like a 'castaway on a shoreless sea', 'black devils had gnawed at their hearts'. They had felt themselves to be 'aliens from the household of faith, enemies to the Cross of Christ', but yet there was no alternative.

'Imagine', cried Elsmere to one of his Oxford friends and tutor Henry Grey, 'standing up Sunday after Sunday to say the things you do not believe' ... and Henry Grey had felt for him deeply. 'The parting with the Christian mythology is the rending asunder of bones and marrow. It means parting with half the confidence, half the joy of life … but have trust. Reason is God's like all the rest. Trust it! Trust him. The fading strings of the past are dropping from you; they are dropping from all the world.'

I found all this intoxicating, but to whom was I to talk about it? The book had been written about thirty years before, but I had never met anybody or heard anyone talk of dropping those leading strings who looked as if black devils were gnawing at his heart. I had to go to confirmation classes with Mr Todd, accompanied by the other two 'clever' boys, Dupont and Wallace-Edwards, and my eyes roved round the room as he told us that, 'Prevent us, O Lord …' didn't really mean 'prevent', but I had never thought it did or indeed wasted any thinking on it. Now of course was the moment to say that I parted with Christian mythology but it would have been a half truth if I had not added that the parting was a source of joy and satisfaction to feel no black devils, shoreless seas, rending of marrows. But I felt blameworthy too. I had, I thought, been given 'a message' at Bigshotte. I was obviously obliged to deliver it but when, where, to whom? Should I break in suddenly and tell them that I did not believe that Jesus was born of a Virgin or was the Son of God (what could that possibly mean?) or rose from the dead or ascended into Heaven? And that it would be hypocrisy for me to be confirmed?

The fireplace wall of the housemaster's room was covered with ornamental brass plates, such as were then worn by carthorses in various parts of agricultural England. Another wall had photographs of boys at the swimming bath with towels round their middles. Mr Todd used often to turn up among the bathers with his camera and its portable stand and pose the boys in different ways. In those pre-Freudian days no one thought this at all odd, and, in fact, I suspect that Mr Todd was a very ordinary old person and that these now fashionable speculations distract us from the important ones. If he had erotic thoughts – and this never occurred to us – he suppressed them. Possibly this act of suppression caused him for safety's sake to see us all in one dimension, as the camera does, and never to wonder what we thought or desired or hoped or hated.

For this dreadful old man in the armchair, we perhaps all of us had the thickness of cardboard. He diminished us by his incuriosity. How could I tell him that I did not wish to be confirmed? How could I talk to him about my Bigshotte doubts and about

Robert Elsmere? So the Bishop of Winchester laid his hands upon my head and asked God that I should daily increase in His Holy Spirit more and more.

And in the holidays I talked to my mother about *Robert Elsmere*. She told me it was a very old-fashioned book and that even Edward Gresy, who was a free-thinker, did not care about it. I was more interested to know that this important relation was a free-thinker than that he did not respect Mrs Humphrey Ward. I asked my grandmother about him and about Mrs Ward. She wouldn't admit that he was a free-thinker and spoke of his friendship with Mandell Creighton, the rector of the parish in which Fallodon lay, who had become Bishop of London. Yet in retrospect I think that from the family point of view he was a free-thinker, though he wrote to his wife, who was more hostile to orthodoxy: 'At the present time Christianity is not all bad, it is not even all dead amongst the sparks of good which are flitting about the world, it strikes out not a few itself, and some of these real large ones for everyone to see.'

As for Mrs Humphrey Ward, Granny did not at all approve of her and regretted that her sister, Harriet Grey, had had to sell to Stocks, an old house near Berkhamstead she had inherited.

[1970]

18

ON SEX

I am at a New England bus terminal on my way to Albany and like several hundred other people in this huge hall, I would guess, I am thinking about sex. How can we avoid it, because in the middle and at the side there are two large racks of sexy papers and paperbacks. The former sweeps in a semi-circle around the counter, where coffee and Coca-Cola are dispensed, so one can investigate as one sips. Most of the books have stimulating titles about beds and bedclothes, flesh and passion, and there are variants like *I Was a Lesbian for the FBI* and a real-life biography, *The Richest Call-Girl in Nevada*. The paper covers correspond. There is a revolving wire bookcase so thickly layered with pictures of flesh that when you push it smartly it turns into a rose-pink cylinder. But, even when the assailant has not a knife in his hands or teeth, all the nudes seem to be recoiling frantically from what is about to happen. None of these were happy occasions.

Yet I must admit that the crowds queuing up at the various gateways for New Haven, Providence, Syracuse, Albany, Cincinnati, seem too anxious to look lecherous. It has been raining outside and those with most regard for their appearance have put on over their hats very anti-aphrodisiacal mackintosh bags. And still, I argue, travelling fuss can nowadays be stored in a small subordinate lobe of the brain, only temporarily and partially restricting the realm of fantasy. Up to a point those bookstalls must mirror these peoples' minds. If not, why are they there? Supposing for example there were nothing but Bibles and hymnals and the works of Dr Norman Peale on the bookstalls and texts on the walls, very few travellers would be able to disengage their mind completely from religion. For example, every time I pass the rack where free back-numbers of the *Christian Science Monitor* are exposed I think of Mrs Eddy and my aunt Harriet and as they are free I sometimes take one. It is obvious therefore that, like roses on a cast-iron trellis, sexy thoughts are winding in and out of even the most inflexible preoccupation with the journey ahead. It would be very hard to exclude them. Also at places like this, where men and women congregate fortuitously and impersonally, one thinks first of bodies, only secondarily of minds, opinions, experiences, sympathies.

Half these people – no, that's an exaggeration, let us say a third of these people, of the males anyway, a third of the time, with a third of their minds, are indulging in visionary ecstasies of sex. As they edge along with their bags towards the exits, some are thinking of pleasures that are more or less ordinary, however impossible or improbable they may be. For others, monstrous and delightful things are happening along the edges of consciousness. Whips and knives are flashing through the air, there is a rending of garments, lustful snarls and scared gratified squeals. Only a tiny exposed portion of this irridescent iceberg of cerebral bliss is left in the real world to grip the bags with both hands and, planting the ticket between the teeth, to push through towards the long hump-backed bus.

I have ten minutes still to wait. There are a few people, who do not seem to be travelling but have come to enjoy the crowds. A male prostitute in a bright scarlet jacket flits by like a bright Burnet-moth; he hovers agreeably now and again over select solitaries, the odd, the desultory, the rich; only once does it seem worth his while to ask the time. All the orgies here are cerebral and he would have glided out again into the street if he had not observed a refined person, who has just bought a serious anthropological paperback about puberty among the pygmies. I conjecture that as soon as he saw the place-names over the exit doors, Athens, Syracuse, Ithaca, the refined person began to hellenize the pygmies rapidly in his mind, and that at present he is chasing Maenads on a mountain in Thessaly (in a routine way because he has done it so often before – I am guessing again of course), his eye lingers on the word Syracuse and he begins to pipe rather uncertainly to shepherd boys on the slopes of Etna and, though the switch to Etna has occurred before the Burnet-moth asks him the time, he answers very coldly indeed. The moth is thin and tired and his image, suddenly intruding itself into the Etnaean pastures, which have just with the help of a recent Sail-into-the-Springtime Package Tour been furnished with prickly pear and almond trees breaking through the cracks in the lava, seems drab and dangerous. Obviously imagination works here with the speed of light. It is far richer in colours and resonances than among the pygmies or among any of those spontaneous, dark-skinned people, who snatch at some meagre ecstasy almost as soon as it has been conceived. And when fancy appears to have burnt itself out, there is always within reach some literature or art to refuel it.

But what keeps the fruits of fancy so perennially fresh is that they have been scientifically processed and are well sealed in. A breath of air from the real world would turn them bad. Everyone is aware of that. For example, supposing someone were to take out a real whip from his overcoat pocket and sketch out on real female flesh the faintest adumbration of a real weal; though the general reaction might be one of interest and excitement, all the fantasy whips and knives would be dropped, the tall man would scramble down from Etna and everybody would unite in expressing disapproval. Fancy is allowed all this licence just because it is sealed off from fulfillment, very rigorously indeed.

At the same moment the situation presents itself to me vividly in all its insoluble complexities, a stuffy-looking man beside me is handling *Sons and Lovers,* which the salesman has advertised by the legend, 'By the author of *Lady Chatterley.*' If the enemy is the commercial exploitation of sex, and that is one of them certainly, I should explain to him that it is not the dirty kind of book he thinks it is, but a masterpiece, which very likely he wouldn't appreciate. But before I can think how to put this politely the Albany bus is announced and I see him buy the book.

As I go away I formulate excuses for myself but most of them I reject.

A. It would be intrusive and he'd misunderstand you.
   Answer. You'll never see him again and it doesn't matter.
B. It will punish him for wanting to read a smutty book.
   Answer. Smut is not so bad as the commercial exploitation of smut.
C. It may lead him to appreciate good literature.
D. It'll help D.H. Lawrence's reputation to have his books bought.

I just don't know what the answer to C and D are, but I suspect them. The fact is that, if only I knew how, I would repudiate utterly this megalopolitan civilization, which has learnt how to put its treacherous questions so plausibly, which reduces all sensible answers to futility, turns good books into bad ones and earnest strivings into obscenity, which has made all of us its accomplices.

When I got into the bus, I took out a battered copy of the Sunday *Observer*, which had arrived by sea-mail, weeks old. It contained an article by Kenneth Tynan rejoicing over the decision in the *Lady Chatterley* case. Most of England's most distinguished writers had testified to Lawrence's sincerity and to the purity of his intentions. The sexual impulse was beautiful and creative. It was not to be feared and suppressed. The Bishop of Woolwich, who is one of my heroes, for he is trying to preserve the continuity of the Christian tradition without doing outrage to contemporary integrity, gave support to the publishers in their claim to publish *Lady Chatterley*. So I suppose that he and all the other upright men are in a sense responsible for the American backwash from an English trial, which has planted *Lady Chatterley* plum in the middle of all the obscene books on all these myriad bookstalls of America.

Kenneth Tynan's article in the *Observer* is witty and brave and just, but, like all the other liberal opinions, it is a minority view addressed to a vast majority. What is the use of a few grains of red pepper in an ocean of soup? Would it not be better to keep them to flavour a small cup? Tynan's enemies push their way into the very heart of his article, for to read him I have on the left-hand side to work around the picture of a handsome young priest offering Mass on behalf of the Catholic Enquiry Association, and on the right I have to read down both sides of a lady wearing a 7.5-guinea frock from Debenham & Freebody.

Between the two of them Tynan's article has been pushed onto page 25, and perusing him there I am aware how tortuous and complex his argument is, and how helpless and foolish humanists often are. While Tynan winds his way expertly through compromise and qualification, the young priest, plonk in the middle of it all, looks ahead with steadfast faith, clear candid eyes and spotless linen. He has not a doubt and his calm conviction must surely carry the day with the lady from Debenham & Freebody, who beyond the fact that her frock is cheap and pretty, has not an idea in her head. He knows that Lady Chatterley must return to her husband

and Mellowes to his wife, and that though there will through the grace of God be forgiveness for those furtive and squalid ecstasies in the gamekeeper's hut, there is no future in them.

He is of course perfectly right about that. These ecstasies are things to read about but not to imitate. Perhaps some of those people at the bus terminus would find some of the ideas helpful on a legitimate or a much more discreet occasion – wasn't there a daisy-chain used as a very original decoration? Now that would be practicable, even for somebody who got her frocks at Debenham & Freebody. But that passage about them chasing each other naked round the house, delightful as this might be and showing, as the bishop would agree, a consciousness of the beauty of sex, has to be sealed away in the subconscious and only used furtively to stimulate legitimate or solitary ecstasies. Whether in Providence R.I. or Bishops Stortford, it would be hopelessly unwise ... [illegible last para of ms.].

[1962]

19

ABOUT DEAFNESS

Compared to blindness, deafness is not a very serious affliction to the victim but terrible to his family and friends. I am now very deaf myself so I remember with shame our exasperation when my father was deaf and we had to say everything louder and louder and over and over again. My father, when he was younger, was a great storyteller and his stories were not all about the comic things that happened from day to day. He told us about the strange things that happened in his childhood, his youth and manhood, but I don't think he heard himself speaking or knew that he often told the same story five or six times.

When we were very young children we enjoyed this and encouraged him. We would leave our own beds when the maid brought morning tea to our parents and we'd snuggle in beside them. We knew all his stories by heart and we'd say: 'Tell us the one about Mrs Mollan,' because we liked to hear it over and over again. Mrs Mollan must have died in the 1880s. She lived in Thomastown and was enormously fat and she sat behind the coachman in a carriage with a box-shaped top called a wagonette. One day she was going to a party when the bottom of the carriage fell out. She caught at the bar below the carriage floor and shouted at the coachman to stop. But he was deaf and thought she meant him to go faster, so he whipped the horses, and though she was fat her feet moved rapidly. She screamed but nobody heard her. Her feet tumbled faster and faster till the coachman got out to open the avenue gate and saw her puffing and panting behind the wagonnette.

We loved to hear this story repeated. 'Tell the one about Mrs Mollan, please, please.' But a few years passed and we didn't get into his bed so he told his stories at breakfast or lunch. And we were ashamed of him before visitors when he told them over and over again.

My father never discovered a cure for deafness. Is there one? I heard there was, and paid a large sum of money to be told the secret. Great pains were taken, my ears were precisely measured and a plaster model made of their insides. Sometimes I wear them hopefully in the daytime but I've never fully learnt how to put them in, though it's nearly two months.

[1989]

20

THE APPLEMAN AND THE POET

A Limerick doctor with a German name has lately been urging the government to import German apples that could be sold at Christmas at 2d each. And he says that the housewives of Ireland should march to Dublin on behalf of their apple-starved children.

I have been waiting eagerly for some eminent Irish apple grower to answer him and to organize a countermarch and an apple-battle in Stephen's Green, but there has not been a squeak of protest. I can think of several reasons for this.

Firstly, most of those who know how to grow things and also to write about them have by now become government instructors and their livelihood only depends indirectly on apples. And even if the tabu that ties the tongues of other government servants does not affect them, they are probably organized heirarchically, and the middle-sized bear must hold his tongue if the big bear is silent.

Secondly, the biggest Irish apple growers are going over to mass production and factory methods. Distribution is as important as production and in a good apple year their buses can travel all over Ireland with cheap apples and kill our small and struggling local enterprises at the drop of a hat. German apples might not disturb these magnates much. Their ideas are nationwide and might become global. Maybe they will soon be worrying themselves about the poor apple-starved kiddies of Dortmund and Essen.

Anyway their problems are very different from those of the average apple grower, average in acreage, income and knowledge, and it is on behalf of this person that I force myself into print. Some years ago we did have a champion, a neighbour with twice my knowledge and five times my apple trees. He battled for us in the press but then he gave up hope. He left for Dublin and the trees were bulldozed and sold as firewood.

Yet the government does not, at least in theory, share this despondency, for every country has its instructor. They are intelligent, hard-working and helpful men. *But* they are too good for us. They should be growing apples in Avalon or in the Garden of the Hesperides, where no worldling ever murmurs, 'Does it pay?' They tell us always that if our apples are clean, nicely coloured and well packed, they will be profitable. And this just is not true.

I found this out twenty years ago and sadly gave up spraying and manuring some two or three acres that I had planted with a government grant. I could not bring myself to bulldoze them, but they were a heartbreaking sight in the autumn; the Worcesters were sticky and tunnelled with Codlin moth, the Laxtons had Botrytis on their tops and Scab on their sides, the Charles Ross had been devoured by greenfly and the fruit hung in clusters like snub-nosed grapes. I had some dark grey Irish Beach with every disease known to Rothamstead and Reading. It was shame rather than hope that led me to the County Instructor once more. He was as clever as they always are and I was obedient, and in two years I had the most beautiful apples in the county. My Charles Ross were rosy-gold and so large no one could face them as eaters. And I got from some society a small and hideous silver cup.

I sold all the apples, but when April came round again and I totted up the bills for Captan, Melprex, Potash, Superphosphate, Nitrogen, I realized I had done better in the days of Botrytis and Scab. The wages bill was huge, for my orchard was not big enough to justify big machines and the apples had to be sprayed from an ancient contraption on a donkey, that turned the donkey and all that tended it a bright orange colour. Since the spray was poisonous we dressed for three days like Arctic explorers.

I went once more to the County Instructor and said, 'How can I make them pay?' And he gave me a most memorable reply: 'I am an appleman,' he said. 'I am not a poet.'

This has helped me to construct a new definition of poetry and to understand why our creamery system, the most satisfactory and enduring branch of Irish agriculture, owes so much to Æ and to Horace Plunkett, the patron of poets. A poet is perhaps the man who can see a little beyond the narrow craft in which he excels, who asks 'Why?' as well as 'How?' We are mostly nowadays stunned by the crass ignorance of those who do not specialize in the same field as we do. And sometimes also we preen ourselves on it. A poet's reaction, on the other hand, would be anguish. He would grieve for the uselessness of knowledge, the sterility of skill, the vanity of abundance. He would be able to answer that Limerick doctor.

My later experiences are relevant, I think, for five years ago the tide turned. I was just about finally to bulldoze the trees, when the man who had done most of the work on them said to me, 'I can't bear to pull them up. What about this? I'll do all the work on them free and we'll share costs of manure and sprays and also the profits.' This was the sort of partnership that Æ would have applauded and it has worked splendidly. And this year, just because there has been an apple shortage, we have each of us earned nearly half as much as a Dublin bus-driver and almost a quarter of what a Limerick doctor should expect.

A couple of things beside the apple scarcity have helped us. A neighbour now has a huge spraying machine and we hire him for a few hours to do the work that the donkey, who is out at grass (his coat turned from yellow to grey), did in three days. Then there is the Country market on Saturday morning in the market square, and we sometimes go to Athy, whose market has survived better than that in Kilkenny. At least it has not been turned officially into a carpark and every Tuesday the carrots still outnumber the cars. If you get there early you can arrange your produce on the steps around the central monument and there is usually at least one stall-holder who has grown a proportion of what he sells in a garden near Athy, though of course most of his stock comes from Dublin. We are very backward and I do not think that as yet much of it comes from Dortmund; it mostly goes up to Dublin from places like Athy and Kilkenny and then comes back again a couple of days later. If you object to the stupidity of this, that means you are still living in those dark ages when country people still ate their peas out of pods and not out of nice tins. In fact if mass production is to succeed you have simply got to be stupid. If you doubt me ask that nice young lady who sells you plants across the supermarket counter how to grow mustard and cress. Be gentle with her because if she had any interest in the world of Nature, she would have wasted away.

The apple-marketing system is a man-made mechanical monster whose flounderings one can anticipate but not control. It is helpful to recall what tiny brains the vast prehistoric reptiles had, for surely the only way to survive is to become a reptile oneself. Last year we did quite well with our Worcester Pearmains by picking them green and in this way getting them to Dublin before the huge consignment of English 'seconds' had knocked the bottom out of the market. They must have been horrible but they were exceedingly profitable.

What else is one to do? Once many years ago I took some beautiful Conference pears to the man from whom we bought our groceries and he said, 'No thank you, we get our pears from Italy.' I snapped back, 'In that case I'm going to get my groceries from Italy.'

But this would be very complicated. Could not some poet (in the appleman's sense of the word) think out the proper retaliation? The small grower is the image of Ireland, a country with small demand and small supply. It will kill us to impose an economy that would be suitable for Clydeside or the Ruhr or the industrial Ukraine.

And as for these apple-starved Dublin children, are they not mostly country people who have recently emigrated to the city because country crafts such as apple growing have been strangled by the brainless, faceless Reptile, to whom the Limerick doctor would like to sacrifice the few small growers who remain. He would be doing us a good turn if he would explain to us if and why German country children have more and cheaper apples than we do. Has it for instance anything to do with those country roads bordered with apple trees belonging to the Gemeinde? And if so, will someone tell us the story of the apple trees that still line some of the roads in Co. Wexford. Who planned them, what was his plan, and was it carried out?

In the meantime let the government encourage the regional marketing of regional products. What our grandfathers did naturally when they laid out those vast market squares, which have turned into carparks, they will have to do artificially. How? That is up to them.

The basic facts are these. Our climate and soil are as suitable as those of England and Germany for the growing of apples. Each county could grow enough to supply its own needs and to send its surplus to the large cities. Apples are good to eat and wholesome, and apple-growing is a pleasant occupation. It requires intelligence and skill and yet leaves the mind free for other things.

If the small man can stay at home growing fruits and vegetables, the roads will be less crowded, the fruit will be fresher and the apple-starved Dublin children will get their fill.

[1977]

PART FOUR

Musings of an Irish Protestant

21

STOCK-TAKING IN THE
IRISH PROVINCES

On the principle of '*ex pede Hercules*', a small Irish town of 10,000 inhabitants is quite a good place to study the tangled loyalties of our country. For Ireland is run by countrymen who reveal themselves with fewest inhibitions in rural surroundings. The revelation is of more than Irish importance, for our emigrants never quite forget the domestic pattern. Senator McCarthy does not really surprise us, and Jimmy Walker, the famous Tammany mayor of New York, was one of our own, returning once or twice to Kilkenny, the town of his childhood. Men very much like these world figures, reduced in size, still walk our streets. Perhaps Providence tries them out as small-scale models in tiny towns. Will they work? Yes, they do! And then they are recast in a gigantic, transatlantic mould.

Our town, which has been admirably described by the novelist Francis Hackett, was built by the Normans. It is dominated by the now empty castle of the Dukes of Ormonde, by the thirteenth-century Protestant cathedral, by two other large Protestant churches, St Mary's and St John's, and a number of modern Roman Catholic churches, convents and monasteries. It is, as one would assume, a stronghold of institutional Christianity and it is not surprising that ecclesiastical considerations often intrude into the deliberations of our public bodies.

For example, not long ago the residents of Asylum Road informed the Corporation that they would like the name of their street changed. The Corporation discussed it at great length and two names were suggested, Nuncio Street and Berkeley Street. For the Papal Nuncio had recently visited the town and his name had been inscribed on the Roll of Freemen; Bishop Berkeley, the philosopher, had been born near the town and, like Swift and Congreve, educated at Kilkenny College.

The principal champion of Berkeley was a councillor who goes as near Communist views as it is wise for an Irish official, and that is not far at all. A great deal of middle-aged unorthodoxy in Kilkenny is aristocratic in origin, for the old Countess of Desart, who was wealthy and philanthropic, started, some forty years ago, political economy classes. Before the classes were taken over by the local seminary and safely harnessed to the Papal Encyclicals, some disturbing, though ancient, books were handled, and the views of Robert Owen are not unknown to our citizens.

Anyway the councillor's suggestion, because of his 'Red' associations, was regarded with suspicion; it was privately whispered that Berkeley himself was a 'kind of Communist' (and in fact *The Querist* is full of subversive and even equalitarian suggestions); there were outraged letters in the local press and a hasty retreat by the Berkeleyites; a prominent citizen who had seconded the proposal hurriedly explained that he had only done so 'to start a discussion'. The liveliest of the letter-writers argued:

Philosophy is all very well for the gentry, but for the working-class people of Upper Patrick Street the Faith of Our Fathers and a reasonable rent for the new council houses are more to the purpose. And why should a Protestant bishop be commemorated in Kilkenny when the Blessed Oliver Plunkett would certainly not get a street named after him in Belfast?

The street was without more ado called 'Nuncio Street'.

It is sadly characteristic that our local Protestants held aloof from the controversy, although a couple of years ago they had canvassed the academies of Europe and America in the name of Berkeley for funds to build a new hall at Kilkenny College. Though they are influential, they are cautious and do not believe in 'getting mixed up in things', and they chose to forget that Berkeley had expressly stated that 'the Protestant gentry' could not flourish 'exclusive of the bulk of the natives' and that he would have relished a purely sectarian homage.

Only one eccentric Protestant, suspected like the councillor and the great Bishop of Cloyne of being Communist, took up the cudgels for Berkeley and said that it was a disgrace that in the States a town of a quarter of a million had been called after him, though he had never lived there, while the town where he had been born and bred grudged him a single street. 'Also the Blessed Oliver had no connection with Belfast, while Berkeley had the closest with Kilkenny.'

The councillor who had first proposed Berkeley saw he was getting into bad company, but a lucky chance soon gave him an opportunity of restoring his reputation. Something was said at a Dublin meeting by the eccentric Protestant at which the Papal Nuncio took offence, a special meeting of the corporation was held to denounce him, and the 'Red' Berkeleyite joined cordially in the denunciations.

But the Berkeleyites had underestimated their strength. A few weeks later Mr de Valera was addressing an election meeting at Cloyne, at which he bestowed the highest of praise upon Bishop Berkeley. 'He was', he said, 'the first economic Sinn Féiner ... a wonderfully cultured, enlightened and kindly gentleman, who rose high above the prejudices of his class, and loved his country and his people.' He quoted a series of observations from *The Querist*, which do, in fact, justify Mr de Valera's claim to be a practical exponent of Berkeleyism. Berkeley was, like de Valera, a strong believer in economic self-sufficiency and had asked for 'a wall of brass a thousand cubits high round Ireland'. He would have supported de Valera in his demands for native wheat and sugar, bacon and boots, which have for many years drawn upon de Valera the hostility of the majority of the bishop's co-religionists.

I do not know whether, after all this, the Protestants of Cloyne gave their vote to Mr de Valera's candidate (he was unsuccessful), but I think that the Taoiseach spoke from his heart and that Irish nationalists, even extreme ones, are usually ready to acknowledge the part played by Protestants in the building up of the Irish nation. It is our trump card, but we usually play it shamefacedly and without conviction. Alternately, we betray the Protestant nationalists, who were all, to a man, minority-minded people, by being too ingratiating and sycophantic. Protestants who think that to be respected in Ireland they have to suppress their Protestantism or qualify its demands are very blameworthy. If occasionally our liberties have been slighted, it is more often due to our failure to stand up for them than to any intolerance of the majority. For the re-christening of Asylum Street only a tiny gesture towards Berkeley and towards Ireland was needed, but we could not give it and this infinitesimal defeat was symbolic of the larger ones we meet, and have still to meet, on the national scale.

But I think it is easiest to continue our investigations on the parochial scale.

The Kilkenny of Francis Hackett's novel vanished a generation ago. In those days he described it as 'an invalid community, a poor emaciated creature with two big bulges on it that ate up its strength'. One of these bulges, the British garrison, has now gone. The bugles no longer ring through the valley; the well-groomed officers and men from Berks and Notts and the Buffs no longer fill the empty pews of St Canice's, St Mary's and St John's. The Protestant Ascendancy still thrived in those days, and the well-drilled Sabbath observance of the military perhaps gave to the Reformed Churches a spurious illusion of immortality. A new Presbyterian church was built and St Mary's was entirely re-roofed.

Hackett would no doubt say that we ought to be spiritually healthier for the removal of Bulge No. I, and perhaps we are, but the operation has shaken us terribly and no new tissue has grown yet over the scars. The Presbyterian church has been closed for many years. So, too, is St Mary's and our Church has not the money to cut the ivy from the collapsing Tudor tombs of the merchant families in the graveyard, or the energy to organize a gang of parishioners with slashers, hoes and mowing machines. Yet St Mary's is in its way famous and contains much of beauty and interest. Seven years ago Mr O.G.S. Crawford, the Editor of *Antiquity*, made a series of photographs of St Mary's and the other antiquities of our town. The photographs are carefully preserved and it may soon happen that these will be the only records of a beauty that has ceased to exist.

The literary records of local Protestantism are also disappearing. I think you would have to go to Dublin, for example, to reconstruct the story of the Reverend Peter Roe, who was rector of St Mary's in the Napoleonic days. He was famous for his war with the Kilkenny Players and their supporter, the bishop, a more literary, less puritanical figure. What denunciations against the theatre, 'that gilded bait to lure souls into Satan's net', once poured from that now crumbling pulpit! You can only find them in the National Library today, and there too I was glad to find the Kilkenny Players' reply, delivered from the stage by Sir Robert Langrishe, in a prologue to one of Otway's plays; here are four lines of it put into the mouth of an imaginary Dr Cantwell, who is none other than the rector of St Mary's (Cantwell, suitably enough, formerly de Canteville, is still a common Kilkenny name):

> 'When alms are given, let *me* dispense the boon!
> Heaven smiles upon my works and mine alone.'
> (As if the canting hypocrite would say,
> 'There's but one gate to Heaven and *I*'ve the key!')

And two lines from the players' answer:

> ''Tis *yours*, grave sirs, to preach, 'tis ours to play,
> Heedless of what a meddling priest may say.'

The Players, of course, won, and for twenty years during their two annual seasons Kilkenny was the rendezvous for the fashion and intelligence of Ireland. It was said that mothers of marriage-able daughters found Kilkenny next best after Bath for finding suitors. There were many English visitors. For example, William Lamb, the future Lord Melbourne, brought Lady Caroline there to distract her from her fatal passion for Byron, and despite the rector of St Mary's huge sums were handed over every year to the charities, Roman Catholic as well as Protestant, of the town.

The material decay of St Mary's is not half so sad as the decay of that lively spirit of intellectual independence that once alarmed its rector. The Kilkenny gentry who supported the Players could not be called anti-clerical or disloyal to their Church, for the bishop was on their side, but their solidarity did not depend on sheepishness. Were they so easy and confident because of their broad acres still untouched by Land Acts, or because less was expected of them in the way of acquiescence when the pews of St Mary's were still filled with disciplined young worshippers from Berks and Notts and the Buffs? Anyway they did not toler-ate 'meddling priests' and 'canting hypocrites' in their own ranks and they would have endured them even less outside. But nowa-days Rev. Father Cantwell, PP, has it all his own way. At a mere nod from him Little Theatres (the famous one at Birr for example) close their doors and struggling rural cultural societies begin to quake; no Langrishe rises from the meekly resentful ranks to say:

'Let us with mirth put by their weak attack,
Retort in rhyme and laugh their follies back!'

But sadder, stranger than St Mary's, are the derelict country churches. A few months ago I climbed on the cemetery wall of an empty Protestant church in North Kilkenny and looked in through the broken panes. It had been closed for eighteen years, but the hassocks, the coconut matting, the plum-coloured pew cushions, still looked and smelt as those things always do. The hymn numbers for the last service still hung in the rack. Plainly it had died undramatically and by easy stages. The services had grown rarer and rarer, and the last still-enduring interval had never been certified as death. It was not exactly optimism that had kept the hassocks there till they were unsalable, but some embarrassment about writing '*Finis*' to a story whose ending seems so inadequate. At the least it still registered an unaggressive protest in a land of conformity, like that other Kilkenny church of Graignamanagh, where the poachers used to hide their salmon under the heating apparatus till lately the caretaker betrayed them.

At this point I can hear some 'broadminded' Englishman, like Shaw's Tom Broadbent, probably a Liberal and agnostic, saying: 'Don't be a dog in a manger! Make a generous gesture towards the Roman Catholics whose churches are overcrowded and give them your empty St Mary's and the rest. Aren't they Christians too? Or sell them to the Romans and get a little cash in hand to pay your curates a living wage.'

How hard it is to reply except by suggesting that often broadmindedness in England is the result of imperial expansion, as it was in the Rome of Juvenal, and there can be no counterpart to it in our contracting community here. Long ago, like the Syrian Orontes, the Liffey and the Ganges and the Jordan flowed into the Thames. In a short walk around Holborn you can see the premises of a dozen different sects. You can read in the Coronation Number of the *Psychic News* that Queen Victoria herself subscribed to their beliefs. For an Irishman it is all very exhilarating, but very alien. The pattern of life here is less exciting but less confused. The only cleavage that really counts is the schism of the Reformation. And that gulf will never be bridged if we underestimate its depth and vastness.

Yet many Church of Ireland people, and also urbane unbelievers among the Anglo-Irish, are now anxious to repudiate all kinship with the more vulgar, esoteric or intolerant of the Reformation's children. Yet we cannot do this without falsifying our pedigrees and invalidating the title-deeds of Irish Protestantism, and of its embarrassing offspring, Urbane Unbelief.

Sir Christopher Lynch-Robinson, whose revealing and attractive book on Ireland, *The Last of the Irish R.M.s,* was recently published, expresses a prevalent mood of cultivated Anglo-Ireland better than anyone I know. He is an Urbane Unbeliever (the sect is now so well established that they deserve capitals). He says that while he believes in contraceptives and divorce and considers Catholic dogma 'an elaboration of superstition and speculation', one must admit it is 'the chief bulwark between civilization and Russian Communism' and 'it works'. He generalizes like this: 'Irish Catholics do not think about their religion but accept it blandly, which is not so unreasonable, for after all one's supernatural beliefs are entirely a matter of personal taste.' And he explains that when he visited his old home in Co. Mayo, now a convent, it was only from loyalty to his dead grandfather that he shuddered when he found an altar in the drawing-room and a stained-glass window pierced through the wall. 'I am no bigot, and the difference between a man who likes marmalade and a man who likes jam, but, etc.' The reference to marmalade reminds me of an old Russian verse in which a young lady argues in the same way: 'Sasha loves chocolate, Masha love jam. Why am I to blame because I love a soldier?'

Sir Christopher's amiable Protestantism, smiling its rueful goodbyes, is not, I am sure, a native product, though it has a wide vogue among our post-war immigrants, our returned natives, and more rootless Dublin intellectuals. It is not so much their disbelief in dogma that is un-Irish, as their delusion that dogma doesn't matter. Sir Christopher's is the adjustable, all-purposes Christianity of empire builders and constitutional monarchs, as wide as their horizons and as deep as their ankles. Religion is valued not for its truth, but for its function as a social cement, a 'steadying influence' (that is one of Sir Christopher's phrases).

Some of our Dublin Protestants apostasize in a more sophisticated way. They would like to lean out across the strife-torn centuries, across the disputatious rabble of Baptists, Marxists and Vegetarians, and touch the cool finger-tips of Rome, the Eternal Mother – provided they are under no obligation to believe a word She says.

These ideas might be a mild stimulant to religiosity in what our Catholic bishops describe as 'Pagan England'; in a small Protestant community struggling for survival they plainly act as a deadly narcotic.

Obviously, if we are to reach any real moral unity in Ireland, it will not be by repudiating our past, whether we belong to the Roman or Reformed Churches, or by reinterpreting it in terms of contemporary politics. The Moderator of the Presbyterian Church of Ireland, Dr Davey, has stated the problem well:

The unity of the Church will come quickly enough once men have become independent enough to think for themselves and humble enough to let others do the same; and it will be a unity, not of intellectual or aesthetic standpoints but a moral unity of brotherhood, tolerance and sympathy — in short of love.

Substitute 'Ireland' for 'the Church', and this statement will be equally true. But I should explain that Dr Davey's books were recently burnt in a main square in Belfast by a crowd of angry Presbyterians shouting, 'Hallelujah!' Today in Ireland it is by no means easy to be independent and to think for oneself.

[1953]

22

NO PETTY PEOPLE?

I. ROSSCULLEN AND THE REFORMATION

In the last few years Southern Irish Protestants, once renowned for their eloquence and intellectual daring, have become one of the most inarticulate minorities in the world. When, at very rare intervals, one of our spokesmen on health committees or county councils or the like in the provinces makes a remark that reaches the Dublin press, it is usually of staggering ineptitude. It was a crescendo, or rather a diminuendo, of such remarks that started the recent controversy on 'Toleration'. It appeared that the nadir had been reached when, at a meeting of the Rosscullen Town Commissioners, Mr O'Connor-Jones (names and details are all imaginary, and could be adapted to twenty different episodes), speaking on behalf of the Protestant community of Rosscullen, warmly supported the resolution deploring the Keady shooting, when an innocent man had accidentally been shot by B Specials. 'I would like to say,' he added, 'what a very fair deal we of the minority faith in Rosscullen have always had. And I shall certainly tell my friends in the North that we down here enjoy complete toleration.' This remark was very well received; for the resolution was a logical sequel to one which the Town Commissioners had passed shortly before, congratulating those who had taken part in the raid on Armagh Barracks. Mr O'Connor-Jones had on that occasion not been present. He had had a bad cold.

The episode reveals that either the traditions of centuries have been completely reversed, or else those who adhere to those traditions have renounced all right to defend them in public, and simply cling to them as one clings to old pieces of furniture. 'If

I am careful,' they might say, 'they'll see me out. What does it matter what happens to them after I am dead? I shan't be at the auction to grieve.'

It is barely forty years since many of the heads of the Protestant Churches gave their blessing to the Ulster rebellion against Home Rule. The Primate, Dr Crozier, stood on the platform with Carson, and the future Primate, Dr D'Arcy, a mild, scholarly man, was reputed to have consecrated machine-guns in his diocese of Down. To many far-seeing Protestants all this was tragic. It is not until every possible means of passive or peaceful resistance to injustice has been tried that clergy should start blessing machine-guns. But Mr O'Connor-Jones' father, a prudent man also with a proper respect for *force majeure*, praised the Orangemen as cordially as his son now denounces them. He was as unwilling to express his abhorrence of civil war as are today the dumb Catholic masses, and their obsequious Protestant satellites who deplore the Armagh and Omagh raids and their inevitable consequences, but are frightened to say so. Protestants and Catholics alike, we are not now distinguished for moral courage.

The O'Connor-Jones family – which is, in my view, a very stupid and untypical one – can see no *via media* between machine-guns and grovelling capitulation. I had hoped that the correspondence in *The Irish Times* would indicate some way in which the minority in the South, without betraying its principles or its posterity, might work with our Catholic countrymen for the unity of Ireland. It did not do this. But a great many old arguments were taken down from their shelves, dusted and put back again. At least the problem was stated clearly once more and that was a stage, though a short one on the way to a solution.

I have said provocatively 'the unity of Ireland' because, if the likes of Mr O'Connor-Jones are permitted to act uncontradicted as our spokesmen, it is plain that our Protestant community is almost moribund. The paralysis that has started in the brain will soon extend to all the members. Cut off from our brothers in the North we cannot survive for more than a generation longer. If we are really dying, we had better die. There would be no sense in clutching at the Ulstermen as a drowning man in his last paroxysms clutches at his friend, dragging him down too. But we are surely not dead. There are a few grounds for an optimistic belief that in a United Ireland, though nowhere else, we could once more play a vigorous part.

In what follows, I am using the terms 'Protestant' and 'Catholic' in a loose, layman's way. There is no significance beyond brevity in saying 'Catholic' rather than 'Roman Catholic' and by Protestant I mean what Catholics sometimes call 'Dissidents,' a negative term for which I know no positive equivalent, except a clumsy one like 'Children of the Reformation'.

Mr Gray-Stack (29 March) was perfectly within his rights in objecting, as a clergyman, to Mr Ewart Milne's claim (25 March) to be a Protestant on the grounds of 'affectionate memories' of a Protestant upbringing; but it was an ecclesiastical objection, not a lay one. A lay objection would be different. The Reformation in our eyes liberated the human mind from the shackles of medievalism, and a Communist, by imposing new shackles, surely repudiates it as vehemently as does a Catholic. But, with these reservations, a layman can use the word 'Protestant' loosely, as he uses the words 'Frenchman' or 'Etonian,' for men who cannot alter the early conditioning of their minds by a new passport or a new critical attitude to their upbringing.

The Protestant community, in fact, in Ireland as in England, can make no claim to homogeneity. It is divided into many sects, and within each sect you will find a wide range of belief, extending from the extremes of credulity to the extremes of scepticism. The Catholic community may well be equally diversified, but it presents a façade of uniformity to the world that Protestants have seldom attempted to imitate. Protestants are often curiously apologetic about the rather broken front we present to theological attack. I cannot see why. When some fundamental liberty cherished by all alike appears to be attacked, the ranks are quickly closed. I am not defending the Ulster rebellion when I quote it in illustration of this rapid power of mobilization.

Our greatest age was one of extreme heterodoxy. In the eighteenth century a Bishop of Derry was a deist, a Bishop of Cork was an Arian, and there was an equal irregularity among their congregations; yet it was the age of Berkeley and Swift, of Flood and Grattan, and towards its close it was marked by tolerance to all rather than by bigotry. And in the twentieth century we would have to disown almost all the Irish Protestants of European stature if we were to judge them by the Thirty-Nine Articles or any other inflexible criterion of theology. Lecky, our greatest historian, was a rationalist; so was Tyndall; so was Bury, the biographer of St Patrick. Yeats, Shaw and Æ were all highly unorthodox, yet it has never been disputed that they were Irish Protestants. In Sean O'Casey it seems to me that his Protestantism has far deeper roots than his Communism, and our community would impoverish itself to little purpose by disowning him.

It is necessary to emphasize this, because opponents of certain Protestant claims often attempt to discredit them by saying: 'Even your own bishops reject them.' When Yeats, for example, in 1925 made his famous 'We are no petty people' speech on divorce, he was opposed by a Protestant bishop. But this disagreement reflected discredit on neither of them, since our bishops neither exact servility nor receive it.

Yeats made the position clear in this speech, which Mr Montgomery rightly said was the most notable defence of democratic rights made in Dáil or Senate by a Protestant since the Free State was established. For an Irish Protestant, this speech should rank with Milton's 'Areopagitica' and the 'Doctrine of Divorce'. It was a noble, earnest and well-argued defence of personal freedom; but it was an isolated layman's speech, and when he made it, Yeats knew that in this land of careful conformities he would never again be elected to the Senate.

Once you attempt legislation upon religious grounds you open the way for every kind of intolerance and for every kind of religious persecution. It is one of the glories of the Church in which I was born that we have put our bishops in their places in discussions requiring legislation. Even in those discussions involving legislation on matters of religion, they count only according to their intelligence and knowledge. The rights of divorce and many other rights were won by the Protestant communities in the teeth of the most bitter opposition from their clergy.

But obviously Yeats was less concerned with divorce than with the defence of the Protestant minority. 'You have no right,' he told the Senate, 'to force your theology on persons who are not of your religion.' To capitulate was to concede such a right.

II. KING OR REPUBLIC?

In this question it was Henry Grattan who gave the clearest direction to those Irish Protestants, who venerated, as he did, the Crown and the Empire:

Regard, I acknowledge, should be constantly had to the general welfare of the whole empire, whenever it is really concerned, but let me add that general welfare should never be made a pretence nor be artificially and wantonly introduced ... I laugh at those Irish gentlemen who talk as if they were the representatives of something higher than their native land, the representatives of empire, not of Ireland; but so talking and acting, they will be in fact the representatives of their salary. Let me tell these gentlemen, if they are not Irishmen, they are nothing.

Grattan might well have agreed with Mrs Byrne that the young Irish Protestants in the dancehall were mere Irish mercenaries of England. It is impossible to tell. Yet in the last thirty years beyond all question, both Anglo-Irish culture and Irish Protestantism have been far more vigorously and successfully defended by those who put Ireland first than by God-Save-the-Queeners, who have often regarded our Irish struggles as too provincial for their attention. Mr O'Connor-Jones, for example, is a crypto-God-Save-the-Queener, despite the fact that he associated himself with that resolution against the Northerners. He and his wife went over to the Coronation and he sends Christmas cards of little Prince Charles to all his Protestant clients. On the other hand, he advised most earnestly against the exhibition of the Coronation film at Rosscullen, either in the cinema or the Diocesan Hall. It would, he said, 'only cause unpleasantness'. And the avoidance of 'unpleasantness' has become, for Mr O'Connor-Jones the fortieth article of his religion.

Mr Truell would be disconcerted to find how much Mr O'Connor-Jones agrees with him about the advantage of 'belonging to a great family of nations stretching to the Antipodes'. One advantage is that, if there was serious danger of 'unpleasantness' in Rosscullen, one would just go to the Antipodes. He is going to go there anyway when he has retired and sold his hotel because his daughter Maureen is very well married in Sydney and has offered him a home there, and he has a son in the Singapore police.

As for Yeats, Mr O'Connor-Jones has never heard of him (Dr Gogarty once said that most of the Anglo-Irish thought that Yeats was an optician in Nassau Steet), and in any case he does not approve of 'all this trouble-making about divorce and dirty books' as he calls it. He gets his banned books through a circulating library, but it must be admitted he is a bit muddled about divorce. He thinks Princess Margaret should be allowed to marry whom she pleases, poor girl, and he was very indignant when someone suggested that the Prime Minister of England was 'living in a state of public legalized adultery'. (That was the way Father Peter Finlay, opposing Yeats, described the marriage of divorced persons.) In fact Mr O'Connor-Jones approves of, and will, if it suits him, exercise all the liberties for which Yeats and his predecessors in England fought; but he does not want to be involved in the squabble personally, and he reserves to himself the right to sneer at those who are. He wants to pass his last years in Rosscullen at peace with his neighbours, who are going to give him a handsome presentation dining-room clock when he finally sets off for Sydney.

Thus I do not think that an Irishman can commend imperialism, when it is used – and it very often is – as a loophole through which our first loyalty, which is to Ireland, can be dodged. The English respect this attitude, or Grattan, who fought them so relentlessly on Ireland's behalf, would never have been buried in Westminster Abbey. The Empire can give us 'jobs', but it cannot direct us to any need more pressing or any duty more urgent than confronts us at home. But Ireland today, because of the Empire, is flooded with 'spiritual' absentees, almost as useless as the physical absentees of Maria Edgeworth's day. Despite the material evidence of faces, hats, cars, television sets, bank balances, they are for us only shadows of men, whose substance is somewhere else. They have never heard of Grattan, Flood, Parnell. They are shallow-rooted plants, and the first gust of an approaching storm will blow them across the Irish Sea.

I believe that even in Ulster the quarrel about the monarchy could be kept subordinate to far more vital disagreements. Hugh Shearman, the most intelligent of Six-County propagandists, has written:

Irishmen have something to which they are just as loyal as Englishmen, something that moves them just as deeply as an Englishman might be moved by his particular loyalties, but to focus that sentiment on the King seems to many of them embarrassing and, in the circumstances, dishonourable.

And I suspect that even some Orangemen were embarrassed by the English attempt, sponsored by the Archbishop of Canterbury, to find a mystical focus for Christianity in the Coronation. If it succeeded, it was because the Queen was young and charming. What success would the Christian royalists have had in the television age if Providence had given them some obese old *roué* like George IV as a symbol of their faith? King Billy dismissed his own Coronation as 'a silly Popish ceremony,' and if his Ulster followers had been susceptible to the royalist mystique, they would not have chased the Lord's Annointed across the Boyne

Catholic scholars who disapprove of nationalism are perfectly correct in tracing the republican and separatist spirit to Protestant origins, and in particular to Ulster. Five out of six of the United Irishmen were Protestants. The Protestant gentry, who in 1782 assembled in the church of Dungannon, Co. Tyrone, were fully prepared to make the Duke of Leinster King of Ireland, if the royal assent had been refused to their demand for an independent legislature. The American revolt was enthusiastically greeted in the north, whereas the southern Catholics were disapproving. Their leaders in 1775 sent an address to the king proclaiming 'their abhorrence of the unnatural rebellion,' and laying at His Majesty's feet 'two millions of loyal, faithful and affectionate hearts and hands ... zealous in defence of His Majesty's most sacred person and government'.

A few years later, after the French Revolution, a riot broke out in Belfast because dragoons tried to cut down the emblems of Washington and of Mirabeau and Dumouriz, which were hung along all the streets.

There is scarcely a Protestant in the south who has not among his forebears and ancestors a Cromwellian who would gladly have had Charles II decapitated, as well as Charles I, had any serious effort been made to restore to the royalists their expropriated lands. And many of them were republicans from principle and not merely from self-interest.

I am saying this not to decry royalism and praise the Republic, but merely to suggest that, north or south, there is no ancient and inviolable tradition in favour of one or the other, and that to associate Protestantism with monarchy and Catholicism with republicanism is a fantastic misreading of history. It serves only to obscure distinctions that are fundamental and vital. Mr Montgomery said rightly that it has led Ulster Protestants into 'the most un-Protestant error of mistaking the symbol for the spirit'.

III. THE RIGHT OF PRIVATE JUDGMENT

If, then, one excludes royalist or imperialist loyalties, how would an Irish Protestant, on the plane of everyday life, not of theology, define his most fundamental disagreement with the Irish majority? The best and most courteous expression of it comes from the Convention of Dungannon in 1782, which, far more than the '98 or any succeeding rebellion, Arthur Griffith considered to be the inspiration of Irish national independence. It is curious therefore that Mr Gilmore (4 April), quoting the proclamations of 1798 and 1916, did not refer to that of 1782 and to the important clause:

That we hold the right of private judgment in matters of religion to be equally sacred in others as in ourselves. Therefore, that as men, as Irishmen, as Christians and as Protestants, we rejoice in the relaxation of the Penal Laws against our Roman Catholic fellow-subjects, and that we conceive the measure to be fraught with the happiest consequences to the union and the prosperity of the inhabitants of Ireland.

This was the natural corollary to their other resolutions:

That the claim of any body of men, other than the King, Lords and Commons of Ireland, to make laws to bind this Kingdom is unconstitutional, illegal and a grievance.

The Bishop of Derry also advanced this Protestant belief in private judgment both as a reason for liberating Ireland, 'this high-mettled nation, from the petulant and rapacious oligarchy, which plunder and insult it,' and also for Catholic Emancipation. To the Presbyterians of Derry, who complimented him on the liberality of his religious sentiments, he described himself in reply as 'a Protestant bishop, who feels it his duty and therefore has made it his practice to venerate in others that inalienable exercise of private judgment, which he and his ancestors claimed for themselves.'

It is obvious what a large part this Protestant 'right of private judgment' played both in securing Grattan's Parliament for Ireland and in stimulating later generations of Irish Protestants to fight for self-government and the emancipation of their Catholic countrymen. They have used very freely this 'inalienable right' on behalf of others; it is inconceivable that they should now renounce it, when their own survival seems in a large measure to depend on its exercise.

It is certain that those Protestants who fought for Catholic Emancipation expected that the toleration that they asked for and the principles of which they disapproved should be reciprocated absolutely to themselves. Here and there, of course, there were doubters. Lord Charlemont, for example, who was in command of the Volunteers, and also Henry Flood, were not ready to endorse the Bishop of Derry's violent demands for complete emancipation for Catholics, though I think they were more genuinely concerned than he was for the miseries of their oppressed countrymen. But Charlemont believed that Catholicism was 'in its principles and tenets hostile to civil liberty,' and that the emancipated Catholics would ultimately trample on those liberal and democratic principles in whose name their emancipation had been secured. Had he some prophetic foreknowledge of Dr Lucey and his important dictum, 'The bishops are the final arbiters of right and wrong even in political matters'?

Charlemont hesitated, and Jonah Barrington and others believe that it was to this hesitation of Charlemont – who was ready to sacrifice everything to Ireland but his principles – that we must attribute the failure of the Volunteer attempt to force the Reform Bill through the Irish House of Commons. From that failure proceeded the '98 rebellion and the Union, and a chain of tragedies that led to the shattered, intellectually sterile Ireland of Mr O'Connor-Jones and the Stormont Partitionists. Barrington believed that Charlemont's mistrust was unfounded and that 'the Catholics of 1780 preferred their country to their claims to their country'. That may be so, but Charlemont was surely more wrong in underestimating the generous and impatient spirit of his own co-religionists, particularly those of Ulster, who were ready to stake their lives on the mere possibility of Tone's 'brotherhood of affection, communion of rights and union of power among Irishmen of every religious persuasion', and to precipitate a rebellion rather than endure any longer the continued disenfranchisement of their Catholic countrymen. Perhaps their impatience was more blameworthy than Charlemont's distrust, but neither were in the event ignoble or unjustifiable.

One cannot overestimate the tremendous importance of the famous sentence in the proclamation of Dungannon: 'We hold the right of private judgment in matters of religion to be equally sacred in others as in ourselves.' It animated all the Protestant opponents of the Union, whereas that measure acquired considerable support from the contrary doctrine, reiterated recently by Dr Lucey, which no Irish Protestant has ever tolerated from his own hierarchy. It was as 'a final arbiter of right and wrong in political matters' that Archbishop Troy sent pastoral letters to all his colleagues, instructing them to do propaganda for the Union, and that Dr Flood, the President of Maynooth, received commendation of Castlereagh for his zeal in the cause. Surely Barrington was right when he said: 'No body of men ever gave a more helping hand to their own degradation and misery.' Like 'the petulant and rapacious oligarchy', they had preferred their claims to their country and allowed themselves to be duped by the enemies of Grattan and Charlemont, so that, in fighting for the right of private judgment, Irish Protestants would be fighting not only for their own rights, but for the principles from which Irish self-government derived. This is not mere Protestant special pleading. It is the constant refrain of many English Catholic scholars who disapprove of Irish self-government as inspired by Protestantism, and wish to see Ireland once more under the British Crown.

So, though the secession of the Six Counties has enormously impoverished the independent spirit of the south, no southern Protestant, except those of the calibre of Mr O'Connor-Jones, could question the right of the Ulsterman to refuse allegiance to the Dáil or to 'the final arbiters' who stand above it.

Grattan, when he spoke against the Union, was surely speaking also against that coercion by civil war that the anti-Partitionists envisage. 'You cannot,' he said, 'identify or bind two people together by mere operation of parchment or paper; the will of the parties is essential to marriage, national or personal ... Without a union of hearts identification is extinction, is dishonour, is conquest.'

And in the domestic sphere it was because he saw a threat to this sacred right of private judgment that Yeats fought for the right of divorce in the Senate, and in press and pamphlet against the censorship. We are perfectly aware that that right can be abused, but its infringement is far more serious than its abuse, against which the law provides adequate penalties. And if Protestantism is to survive in the south, as an active co-operative and patriotic influence and not a snarling and revengeful one, the least encroachment upon that right has to be watched with the closest vigilance.

IV. THE ULSTER-SUSSEX AXIS

Almost as disturbing as what Dr Lucey told the Christus Rex Congress at Killarney was Mr Hanna's reply to it, when he addressed the Ulster Young Unionist Council in the North. He said:

I accept the view of Dr Lucey that in an overwhelmingly Roman Catholic country such as the Republic, the Hierarchy may exert its authority and intervene in political matters. What I do not accept is that the Hierarchy have any right to direct me.

What is sinister here is that Mr Hanna bases his counter-attack on Dr Lucey, not on the rights of private judgment or the claims of minorities (such as the Catholic minority in England has been granted), but on the *sacro egoismo* of the Ulster Protestant and his possibly transient ascendancy. He seems ready to propitiate Dr

Lucey not only with the souls of the southern Protestants, but with the souls of Ulster's posterity. For how long can the Protestant majority last in the north at the present rate of Catholic increase? Observers sympathetic to Stormont, basing their calculations on Northern government statistics, think that it might disappear in a few decades, seeing that it is only unemployment that stems the influx of Catholics from the south.

And what consolation will it be to a Ballymena Protestant of 1985 to reflect that a few years before Mr G.B. Hanna had succeeded in dodging the directives of the Hierarchy through death or retirement to Sussex? For Sussex figures with ominous frequency in Northern propaganda. The last to produce this unreal equation of Sussex and Ulster was Col. Montgomery Hyde, MP, who claimed that Ulster was every bit as much a part of the empire as Sussex. If an excellent historian like Col. Hyde can produce such false analogies, what hope has the ordinary Orangeman of thinking straight? For a Sussex man's loyalty to England overrides that purely regional loyalty to Sussex of which many a Brighton commuter is scarcely aware. If Ulstermen really only feel this vague regional loyalty to the land of their birth, then Dr Lucey is assured of victory. He will canter into Stormont easily ahead of the birthrate.

Anglo-Ireland, whose intellectual and spiritual centre was in the south and not the north, was crippled, and almost extinguished, because countless southern Irish Protestants persuaded themselves that they could do their duty in one part of the empire as well as in another. When the pressure upon them in Tipperary and Meath, where they had lived for generations, became uncomfortably strong, the Sussex-wards exodus began. Only a Grattan or a Charlemont, speaking in the name not of Ulster or of Leinster, but of Ireland, could have recalled them to their posts, and urged them to resist. But there was none to speak. Those who had the necessary gifts and force of character were exercising them on behalf of some other branch of 'that great family of nations which stretches to the Antipodes'.

Infallibly the same thing will happen in Ulster if the resistance of the Ulster Protestants is made not on Irish lines, but on imperial or Ulster-cum-Sussex lines. Sussex is no more interested in Ulster than it is in Munster, Leinster and Connaught, and it is probable that, if it suited imperial needs, the Six Counties would be handed over to the 'final arbiters' tomorrow. There is something hideously probable in some of the evidence given by the recent poll in Britain organized by the anti-Partitionists. It revealed that nearly one quarter of the inhabitants of Great Britain did not know that Ulster was not *already* subject to the Republic. There would be no drama of 'betrayal' about it, no deliberate cruelty, but the mighty monster of the British empire would absent-mindedly give an irritable frisk of its tail, and the tiny cart that the Ulstermen have hitched to it would be tossed aside with all its occupants. Against the vast panorama of empire, Mr Hanna and his prejudices would seem very parochial. Solely against a domestic Irish background could they carry weight.

It is only by an assiduous ironing out of history, ancient and modern, that Ulster memories can have become so blank, so receptive of the imperial rubber stamp. Obviously, dutiful citizens have forgotten Charlemont and the Volunteers, but they must also have forgotten how, because he was a Home Ruler, they nearly lynched Winston Churchill in Royal avenue in 1912, and how, if we are to believe General Gough, he planned to coerce Ulster with the British army into accepting Home Rule. How can they doubt but that any British statesman would automatically subordinate regional loyalties to imperial necessity?

I do not think the problem of reconciling remote loyalties with near ones was ever stated more clearly than by Charlemont himself, a great Ulster landlord. He never considered Ulster as anything but an integral and vital part of Ireland:

Let it not be said that Ireland can be served in England. It never was, it is the nature of man to assimilate himself to those with whom he lives ... The Irishman in London, long before he has lost his brogue, loses or casts away all Irish ideas, and from the natural wish to obtain the goodwill of those with whom he associates, becomes in effect a partial Englishman, perhaps more partial than the English themselves ... let us love our fellow-subjects as brethren, but let not the younger brother leave his family to riot with his wealthier elder. Let us at all times act in concert for the universal good of the empire, but let us consider that we are best enabled to perform that duty by contributing to the prosperity of our own country ... Where is the English party that is not more or less hostile to the constitutional and commercial interests of Ireland? But Ireland must be served in Ireland ... It is the unnatural son, who profusely assists in the luxurious maintenance of a beloved alien at the expense of his mother's jointure.

And how pertinent this is to the problems of Ulster and of Ireland!

Like the circles raised in the water by the impulse of a heavy body, our special duties, as they expand, grow fainter ... The love and service of our country is perhaps the widest circle in which we can hope to display an active benevolence ... If every man were to devote his powers to the service of his country, mankind would be universally served.

Reasoning like this – and Charlemont was the most reasonable Irishman of his day – we would argue that the Irish Protestant genius, in Ulster as in the south, was evaporating in very faint circles on the periphery of the empire, and that to their cost they are neglecting in the service of 'the beloved alien' their immediate first-circle duty to their Anglo-Irish brothers in the south, and their second-circle duty to all their Irish compatriots, Catholic as well as Protestant.

It is expedient to act like this, but where expediency alone is consulted, monstrous alliances of opposites take shape, as in the Nazi-Soviet Pact, or the understanding between Castlereagh and the Catholic Hierarchy at the time of the Union. Is there not today strong evidence of some similarly misbegotten collusion between the intransigence of Mr Hanna and the intransigence of Dr Lucey, of which the object is not union this time, but prolonged Partition? A student of the more ultramontane Catholic papers cannot have failed to detect a note of alarm at the possibility of a premature removal of the Border. 'Later, later, perhaps,' the unwritten warning can be inferred, 'when the advancing Catholic birthrate or the tide of Catholic immigration has broken the Ulster spirit, but not *now*, emphatically, no!'

Mr Hugh Montgomery showed clearly in his letter why the supporters of Dr Lucey must inevitably be only lukewarm anti-Partitionists. 'What a spirited debate,' he wrote, 'we might have seen in the Dáil on the Noel Browne health scheme, if the representatives of Protestant Ulster had been in their seats, and how much more honest the outcome would have been!'

But I do not think that Dr Lucey would appreciate 'a spirited debate,' or that his idea of an 'honest outcome' would be the same as ours.

V. DINGLE IRREDENTA

A few weeks ago I listened to the shortest, politest and most convincing anti-Partition speech I have ever heard. It was on the doorstep of a small hotel in the Dingle peninsula, and the little maid had just told us they were full up. And indeed they were, for behind her in the dining-room, through clouds of cigarette smoke and teapot steam, I could see a phalanx of young men and women, warmly debating in quick Ulster tones. They looked like a geological or a sociological reading party. 'Who are all those?' we asked in amazement. 'Oh, they are very nice,' said the little maid, swift to suspect disparagement and to defend them. 'They're English. They're from Londonderry.'

So Derry people are English! It has come to that. I wish she had dropped this bombshell in the dining-room instead of on the doorstep, so that I could have recorded the bomb-damage. My impression is that they would have been annoyed rather than flattered by the maid's polite assumption that they were nice foreigners. I think they would have felt that Dingle was theirs in some special way in which Sussex is not; that they were Irishmen, who had not shed all responsibility to Ireland, one and indivisible, simply because their fathers had pocketed their small northern dividend and walked away. Just as the glens of Antrim are ours, so Dingle is theirs. Charlemont would have put it in the second circle of their obligations, while Sussex would scarcely be in the tenth.

Have they really renounced all responsibility for this beautiful and fascinating region? Have they a right to do so? Dingle has the look of a property up for sale, with the shutters closed in half the windows, and the elderly caretakers suspecting a purchaser in every prosperous-looking stranger. Who knows what sort of a crook will take it if the relatives of the family renounce it? And cannot the same story be read all over the western seaboard? Arthur Griffith's Sinn Fein Ireland is as dead as Carson's Unionist Ireland, and the two epitaphs could appropriately be written in Kerry. The Kerry landlords have gone – leaving no traces but a few mouldering mansions and the lovely plantations of Ventry and Muckross and Derreen. And those who succeeded to the land are following them. Dingle was one of the centres of Irish-speaking Ireland; but you will find now that fully half the young people are emigrating to England and the empire. They are not becoming West Britons, as Griffith and Douglas Hyde feared they would – they are becoming plain, unhyphenated Britons. Twenty years ago an Irishman who still believed that an Irish-speaking Ireland was possible was an idealist; ten years ago he was an amiable self-deceiver; today he is a crook or a dangerous paranoiac, whose judgment on no single subject could be trusted.

But the problem of an empty countryside is a universal one, and belongs to the north as well as to the south. Some attribute it to the craving for nylons and movies, which has devastated the agricultural regions of Europe more irrevocably than an invasion of Huns and Avars, and filled the cities with unemployed. It is more sensible to attribute it to the twentieth-century spirit of adventure, intellectual and material, for which there is no outlet at home.

Often the only way to prevent a restless beast from straying over a cliff is to hobble it, and, if the Gaelic revivalists had managed to keep the Irish at home by shackling them with an ancient language, much could have been forgiven them. But they have failed, and the ceaseless and small-minded Anglo-Irish gibes at the Irish language and its cult have made the admission of failure psychologically impossible. These gibes are based on an ignorance of a strong strand in the Irish Protestant tradition. Henry Flood and many of his colleagues felt for the Irish past a reverence and a curiosity that the O'Connellites seldom showed. They realized that our civilization would probably have been richer, as well as more stable, had it been possible to preserve the old language and the old ways.

Moreover, to a certain extent we are all equally involved in the Irish-Ireland experiment, and the problem of divided allegiance to which it is allied. Griffith's Sinn Féin Ireland was modelled, as Griffith himself makes clear, not on the tactics of O'Connell's Catholic agitation, but on those of Charelemont's Protestant revolt. Griffith's Sinn Féin did not unite Ireland, as the Volunteer movement had done, because it was a hundred years too late and had little support or leadership from the Protestant people whose ancestors had successfully challenged the British government at Dungannon. By the twentieth century the Anglo-Irish were no longer capable of thinking as a body, and had little to offer towards the problems of Irish unity and of their own survival except slogans from the English press and political platforms and a few verses of anti-Catholic doggerel from Kipling.

Are the Charlemont Papers textbooks in all the schools of Northern Ireland? They ought to be, for Charlemont confronted all his life the problem that faces every Anglo-Irish Protestant; how can one be a good Irishman, without servility, condescension or play-acting, or any sort of cultural or spiritual apostasy? He wrote: 'In acting as an Irishman, I may always hope to perform the part of a true Englishman also,' and he showed his contempt for those who inverted this principle of action, setting English loyalties first. He would have been equally puzzled by the Anglo-Irish nationalists of thirty years ago, who often felt they had to wear kilts, write their names in Irish, and become Catholics in order to show their devotion to their country.

Charlemont was of course an Ulster aristocrat, but the aristocratic tinge of his philosophy did not derive from any narrow sense of class-solidarity. It is true that he regarded government as the prerogative of the educated classes (so, in a certain degree, did Wolfe Tone), and education was in those days the prerogative of the privileged. Yet the upper classes had no more caustic critic than Charlemont. He believed that they had in their own interests kept Ireland ignorant, and hence helpless.

Reflecting upon 'the emancipation of Ireland from the fetters of English tyranny' (that is how he described the short-lived triumph of Grattan's Parliament), he wrote:

The unhappy divisions among our people had been the principal source of our long servitude. Ireland was naturally strong; her inhabitants were brave, hardy and numerous, amounting to more than three millions. But of these a small minority by artificial force despotically governed an immense majority of unwilling subjects, whom they treated as an inferior race … Thus did we possess many inhabitants but few citizens.

And of these 'inhabitants' he wrote: 'The only way to induce them to love and serve their country is to make that country really theirs by giving them a real and substantial share in it.'

You see that 'the love of country' was in those days a virtue that an enlightened Protestant felt it to be his duty to inculcate into his countrymen. The Anglo-Irish terror of Irish patriotism was a late post-Union growth, not unnatural in an enslaved and corrupted aristocracy who were more scared of their tenants than of their English masters, and who once more found 'inhabitants' more manageable than 'citizens'.

I do not know if Charlemont's philosophy has any practical bearing today, when no class has a monopoly of education or a prior claim to govern, but it is part of the Irish cultural inheritance. Like Grattan's Parliament, which it largely shaped, it is one of those shared experiences that will always bind Ulster to the rest of Ireland.

On the whole, Ulster has to forget as much history in the cause of Partition as the Republic has to forget in the interest of the Gaelic state. One must suspect that Charlemont is no longer honoured in Ulster, as so little effort was made to save his Ulster home from senseless demolition some years ago. It is a better augury that, in Dublin, Charlemont House survives and houses a national collection. There could not be a more fitting memorial to its former owner, who was a great patron of the arts as well as commander-in-chief of the Irish Volunteers.

Can Ulster Protestants turn their backs permanently on the many other traditions that bind them to the south? Yeats was considering the Ulstermen, too, when he made his fighting speech in the Senate. His peroration would have been impossibly arrogant from an imperialist; but from a nationalist, as Yeats was, defending the rights of a minority, it was one of those plain statements of fact by which democracy is honoured.

We against whom you have done this thing are no petty people. We are one of the great stocks of Europe. We are the people of Burke; we are the people of Grattan; we are the people of Swift, the people of Emmet, the people of Parnell. We have created the most of the modern literature of this country. We have created the best of its political intelligence. Yet I do not altogether regret what has happened. I shall be able to find out, if not I, my children will be able to find out, whether we have lost our stamina or not. You have defined our position and have given us a popular following. If we have not lost our stamina, then your victory will be brief and your defeat final and, when it comes, this nation may be transformed.

VI. FIGHTING THE SPRINGTIME

Sometimes what is a platitude to one person appears as a start-
ling heresy to somebody else. It seemed to me so obvious that
Protestantism has no fundamental tie with either imperialism or
monarchy that I hesitated to labour so dull and incontestable a
point. The result is that here is Mr Greenaway (24 May) saying
that I want to 'exclude from Irish Protestant life today all royalist
and imperial loyalties'. Of course I don't, as anyone who troubles
to read again what I said can verify.

I tried to emphasize that it is not the Church of Ireland only,
with its royalist associations, but the entire Reformation which is
at stake in Ireland today, and that, if we are to look inside ourselves for a focus for the beliefs that derive from the Reformation,
we are no more likely to find it in the Empire than in the USA – a
republic that, like ours, revolted from the British Crown. Moreover, in Europe almost all the Protestants who live as we do in
predominantly Catholic countries are republican. If the empire
was able to offer any special safeguard to Irish Protestantism, Mr
Hollis and the scholarly Catholics of *The Tablet* would scarcely be
so eager to lure us back into it.

Mr Greenaway's advice to us seems to me defeatist and un-
adult. It reminds me of the moral that Mr Belloc drew from the
small boy who was eaten by the lion in the Zoo.

> Always keep a-hold of Nurse
> For fear of finding something worse.

We southern heretics must trot behind our little Ulster brother,
our eyes round with admiration, while he firmly clasps Nanny
Westminster's hand. But that advice is 150 years out of date.
Grattan and Charlemont, from whom I quoted, were rightly critical of these nursery ways. We are grown up now, and Nanny
Westminster is preoccupied with her own affairs. Like Mr Hanna,
she sees nothing against Final Arbiters, provided they don't arbi-
trate at her. Irish Protestants must fight their own battles as Irishmen. They'll get no help from outside. They'll get jobs for their
children outside, and that's all.

Let me give an instance of how Protestant Ireland is being weakened, not fortified, by its imperialist obsessions. Who would deny that the *Ne Temere* decree of 1908 did more to confuse and debilitate Irish Protestantism than any Dáil legislation? When it was first promulgated, our Primate, Dr Gregg, wrote of it:

This uncalled-for decree from Italy had thrown national concord back by a hundred years. It is a wanton attack upon Irish unity, and can only deepen the fissure that separates Irishmen into two camps ... Resistance in God's name and in the name of conscience and liberty, resistance is the duty of us all.

This eloquent prophecy has been fully justified by events. *Ne Temere* added great bitterness to the Home Rule struggle and made our clergy preach abstention from social intercourse with Catholics. It made us distrust each other and prevented that fusion of peoples out of which a truly united Ireland might arise. I have been told that the Irish Catholic bishops did not favour the application of this decree to Ireland, for they foresaw what bad social effects it would have. I have heard it suggested, too, that it was merely a move in a game of high diplomacy for securing a concordat between Rome and England, and that *Ne Temere* might have been withdrawn as part of the price of the concordat.

An Ulsterman looking at *Ne Temere* with wide-ranging imperialist eyes is bound to misconstrue it. For, while the decree has been disastrous to Irish Protestantism, it has been harmless, if not actively beneficial, to English Protestantism. In Ireland, in a mixed marriage, the Protestant invariably signs the pledges or leaves the country, whereas in England, as in the United States, there is an overwhelming Protestant or indifferentist majority, and it is usually the Catholic partner who gives in. On the whole, therefore, the imperialist Protestant is the gainer and it is by a decree through which the Irish Protestant loses every time.

So we have waited for a lead from England, and none has come. And that high-sounding 'resistance in God's name and in the name of conscience and of liberty' has been a total flop. Has there been collectively as much moral force behind it as would alter a county council by-law, or a membership rule of the Kildare Street Club? Looking for evidence of it not long ago, I found two or three short pamphlets and a couple of printed sermons by Dr Gregg, Dean Babington, Mr Hammond and Canon Fletcher. They are mostly out of date, if not out of print, and the entire corpus of resistance literature has about as much dignity and authority as a handful of department leaflets on the spraying of potatoes.

It is easier to read the consequences in the country than in the big cities, where religious communities are large enough to be self-sufficient. In the country you will find pinned up in the church porches stern warnings to the young against mixed marriages and the *Ne Temere* pledges. I do not believe they have, or deserve to have, much effect. For the community is trying to thrust onto the shoulders of some helpless Miss or Master O'Connor-Jones a burden of resistance that only the united strength of all the children of the Reformation in Ireland, north and south, would be strong enough to bear.

Not long ago I saw one of these warnings flapping valiantly in the porch of a midland's church. It seemed to be phrased with unusual vigour, so I turned the door handle to examine for myself the inner defences of this citadel of spiritual freedom. But the door was locked, and further investigations showed that the church had been closed for some months. The rector and his entire congregation had melted away.

I believe that if Irish Protestants looked at the *Ne Temere* decree with properly focused Irish eyes, they would have won over our Catholic countrymen long ago to make representations to the Vatican for the withdrawal of a decree that has no tradition behind it, and has the prospect of ill-will and prolonged Partition in front of it. Moreover, any giant gains that the Roman Church may make among lovesick Protestants through this decree must be offset by the heavy losses it causes them in the still predominantly Protestant empire.

And why put needless obstacles in the path of the young? There is an Italian proverb: '*Non fate Guerra al maggio!*' or 'Don't fight with the springtime!' Catholic and Protestant isolationists will always get defeated in such a battle, so why engage in it? There is nothing wrong with a mixed marriage provided those who have to face its problems are allowed to find the solution themselves. Before 1908 there was a fair and friendly tradition to guide them.

In the meantime the Ulster Protestant puts his faith in the Border. To take a simile from Milton, I would compare him to 'that gallant gentleman, who thought to impound the crows by shutting his park gates'. For the *Ne Temere* decree is indifferent to borders and far more undermining to Ulster Protestantism than is Irish republicanism, which derives from the Protestant Wolfe Tone.

In the south, we put our faith in Mr O'Connor-Jones's staunch Protestant convictions; but we do not make sufficient allowances for his dislike of 'unpleasantness'. One of the reasons why his elder daughter went to Australia was because she married a Catholic, without signing the pledge, and there would be less unpleasantness for the couple there. When his other daughter married a Dublin businessman and *did* sign, he was very sad, but in the end he looked at it this way:

'Bob is a very good chap. He was at Dunkirk. And one must hand it to the Catholics for the wonderful stand they are making against the Communists in China. And after all, we Protestants believe in allowing the young folks to decide for themselves. We're more open-minded than we used to be. What I say is, if a man is honourable and does his best, I won't ask what altar he worships at. And nowadays it seems to me ...'

I need not unwind any further that woolly ball of homespun sophistry with which we bind our wounds. It is the best we can do, and far better than will-shaking and family rows. And, as it happens, Bob and his wife are very happy indeed. Yet Protestants must believe that the post-dated cheque with which this happiness has been bought is a very large one indeed, and that, in the name of Private Judgment, Mr O'Connor-Jones's grandchildren have been deprived of the right to that very thing.

VII. RESISTANCE IN GOD'S NAME

The best of the resistance pamphlets that I have seen, apart from Archbishop Gregg's early sermon, is by Canon Dudley Fletcher. Even this is very archaic now. There is a frontispiece of himself and his wife in the ninetyish bicycling costume, and his arguments have the easy free-wheeling innocence of the pre-atomic age. He urges that the Irish government should appeal to the Pope 'to withdraw a decree, which causes so much bitter resentment among the Irish people and hostility to his Church'. 'Why', he asks, 'should a foreign State dare to proclaim and enforce its foreign laws in our country?'

Canon Fletcher wrote before the Tilson Case had proved that the Irish government, so far from appealing to the Pope to abolish the decree, would permit its courts to give to this 'foreign law' the force of an Irish law, to which all Irish citizens, whatever their faith, must bow. It was at this point that the English Protestants and indifferentists, if they were to be of any use to us, would have taken notice. But Nanny Westminster did not bat an eyelid. *Ne Temere* is not going to be made *English* law, and that is all *she* cares about. Besides, Bernard Shaw, in his preface to *John Bull's Other Island*, has described the Church of England as 'a reformed Anglican Catholic Anti-Protestant Church', and she likes to sit mid-way between Rome and Reformation, exchanging winks with both of them. But the Americans did take notice, and Mr Paul Blanshard, in some three months of investigation here, has provided a better source-book [*The Irish and Catholic Power* (1954)] for the study of *Ne Temere* and kindred problems than all our Irish Protestant scholars have produced in half a century.

It is unfortunate that this book, which is not political or bigotted, unless it is bigotted to defend your own beliefs with dialectical skill and copious documentation, has been used by members of the Northern Parliament as a work of propaganda for Partition, since that was plainly not Mr Blanshard's object in writing it.

I have never read that our synods have discussed what form this 'resistance in God's name' should take, but, not long ago, a distinguished Church of Ireland scholar wrote to *The Irish Times* that there is no sin in taking and breaking a pledge whose imposition was an act of dishonesty.

When grave seniors, clergymen and scholars advise young people to commit what is normally considered perjury, a problem has arisen serious enough to take precedence of most others. At our synods those discussions about hymns, school buses, clerical stipends and the morality of turkey-raffles at church bazaars should be suspended, till a plan of resistance has been formed. Why should our rulers be thanked for Protestant buses, if they cannot guarantee to the small passengers some protection in the future against a moral and social pressure so strong that perjury is the only antidote that our scholars can offer to the risk of apostasy, exile or heartbreak?

Information is a necessary preliminary to organized resistance, and in this, as I have shown, we are scandalously ill-equipped. We ought to know, for instance, how it was that the German Protestants presented so strong a front against *Ne Temere* that it was not imposed upon their country in 1908. And how did the Hungarians manage to secure exemption till the collapse of their country in 1918? We ought to know what are the emotional repercussions in smaller states of mixed faith like ours.

I once asked the Orthodox Bishop Arsenije of Montenegro how the Orthodox handled the *Ne Temere* pledge. 'Oh, it doesn't bother us much,' he said. 'You see, we impose a pledge too.' I deduced from his slight smile that in this conflict of pledges the Orthodox always won. These perjury matches can hardly form a good basis for the long-promised union of Serbs and Croats. Nor in Ireland will they help us to realize Wolfe Tone's dream and 'to unite the whole of Ireland and to substitute the common name of Irishman in place of the denominations of Protestant, Catholic and dissenter'.

I think most headway will be made if we treat the problem as practical and not spiritual; for what can be more squalidly material than the attempt to make young men and women renounce their beliefs on behalf of their offspring, simply because they are dreaming of love? If a synod were to recommend the imposition of a Protestant pledge at Confirmation, it should be treated merely as a lever by which the State might be forced, in concert with the Churches, to outlaw, equally, all such pledges. It is sometimes necessary to arm in order to force disarmament. Such an arrangement, bad as it would be, would at least bring us face to face with realities. Mrs Tilson and the Irish courts would have no grounds for being surprised at Mr Tilson's breach of his pledge to the Catholic Church, if he had already, on marriage, broken his pledge to the Protestant one.

Almost any positive act of corporate self-defence would help to counteract the O'Connor-Jones defeatism, and infuse into us some energy to act as Protestants and as Irishmen. We are not half as helpless as might be inferred from Mr Greenaway's letter. Numerically, we probably represent about the same percentage of population in the twenty-six counties as we did in the pre-Famine years, when the Protestant Ascendency seemed safe forever. But for five generations we have been exporting those who would have been our spiritual and intellectual leaders. As a result our 'effortless superiority' has disappeared, leaving behind

it a tradition of effortlessness to hamper us. Most southern Protestants would now shrink from the vulgar effort necessary to
guarantee even equality before the law for our posterity, as in the
matter of pre-matrimonial pledges. Imagine a southern Protestant demonstrating about anything!

But, on second thoughts, Protestant bank-clerks, bus conductors, teachers, are as aggressive as anyone in defence of their
material claims, and are ready to inflict any 'unpleasantness' on
the community to get a few shillings a week extra. So leave out
the derisive exclamation mark, and simply imagine. We are up
against it now. How, when, where can we make our compatriots
know that we, too, the Irish heirs of the Reformation, have strong
convictions, which cannot be overridden?

Irish Catholics have a long tradition of resistance and can teach
us much. The Catholic population of Great Britain is, per cent,
only slightly larger than the Protestant percentage in the Republic
(8 per cent against 5 per cent). It is less than a third of the Protestant percentage in all Ireland. In addition, the majority of these
British Catholics must now be of Irish immigrant stock, with
less right to dictate to England than Irish Protestants have to
dictate to the Republic. But dictate they do. When Marshal Tito's
visit to England was planned, there were widespread and well-
organized Catholic demonstrations and petitions against it. They
did not lead to 'unpleasantness' and in the spring of 1953 the
Archbishop of York retaliated with courtesy in support of the
government. He recalled that Tito's persecution of the Churches
had not surpassed in savagery the Catholic persecution of the
Orthodox in Croatia.

There is no reason to regret these Catholic demonstrations.
If Catholics found Tito's visit unwelcome, they had every right
to say so, and their protest precipitated Dr Garbett into making
a statement on behalf of the 240,000 persecuted non-Catholics
of Croatia that ought to have been made ten years earlier, and
without government prompting. As a result, a breath of realism
swept through the press, Catholic and Protestant, and a far more
accurate account of what happened in Yugoslavia was at last
made public.

Resentment too long unexpressed is dangerous and unhealthy,
and Ireland would have nothing to fear if Irish 'non-Catholics'

of the north and south demonstrated vigorously in defence of their rights. But it has to be recalled that the Catholic demonstrations in Ireland would have failed to impress had they been complicated by anti-imperialist or Irish nationalist propaganda. Analogously, any Protestant demonstrations in Ireland would be abortive if they were linked to pro-British or imperialist propaganda. They would rightly fail, for the liberties claimed at the Reformation have nothing whatever to do with race or royalism, though they appear to be very closely allied to the concepts of modern democracy.

[1955]

23

REFLECTIONS OF AN
UNJUSTIFIED STAY-AT-HOME

Most Irishmen who read Mr Hamilton's article in the August *Twentieth Century*, 'Confessions of a Justified Emigré', will have been grateful for the candour with which he has described a Scottish problem. Many of us in Ireland have had to face the same moral and cultural dilemma in a more acute form. We have had to ask ourselves whether romantic nationalism is, as Mr Hamilton says, part of the innocence of childhood, an innocence that it is 'not merely man's fate but also his duty to lose'. Some mood is engendered by a mist-covered mountain, an ancient legend or a provocative sneer, and, while they are enslaved to it, quiet and intelligent people, post-office officials, clergymen's sons, drapers, will blow up viaducts and raid military barracks. They see no other way of turning into reality some dream of a United Ireland, a Free Scotland, a Restored Zion. Alternatively, is it possible that, when we are young, a fundamental obligation presents itself to us in the nursery colours that as we grow older we have to translate into sober adult terms? Is it right perhaps to recognize an overriding loyalty to the small community in which we were born, and is it perhaps only when a natural impulse is perverted or arrested that we reach out for our Colt .45 revolver and twenty rounds of ammunition?

Mr Hamilton's 'The Justified Emigré' seems to argue that romantic nationalism is usually excluding and futile. And certainly, if he looked at Ireland, he would observe how dowdy our dreams have been in their realization and how little they have satisfied the dreamers, and he would confidently augur the same disillusionment for Scottish nationalists. In spite of that his reasoning seems to me to be utterly wrong; our troubles are not those he predicts for a Free Scotland, and so far from being eased by emigration and the 'broad views' that justify it, they immensely increase as our countrymen depart for a wider sphere. I would argue, indeed, that it is no coincidence that the recent outbreak of Irish republican violence in England and the Six Counties should occur at a time when Irish emigration to England is greater than it has ever been since the Famine of 1846. Our nationalist hallucinations are of the sort that prey on a devitalized and exhausted people. Emigration for generations has acted on us selectively, draining away intelligence, enterprise and common sense. Is it strange that we should be at the mercy of the prigs and the fanatics?

I should have hesitated to suggest any analogy between our problems and Scotland's if the arguments that Mr Hamilton opposes to the romantic nationalists had not been nostalgically familiar to us here. My great-grandparents used them against Wolf Tone and Emmet, my grandparents against Parnell and Gladstone, my parents against Griffith and Pearse, but 'the rainbow-chasers' – that is what 'the realists' called them – won in the end and their opponents, once immensely powerful and numerous, have dwindled to insignificance and their protests to an inaudible grumble. And in a sense the chase has been justified, for, in pursuit of the elusive rainbow, the underprivileged have found their pots of gold and for over a generation we have enjoyed a profound peace almost unique in our history.

My forbears apprehending 'bloody confusion', as Mr Hamilton does now, were totally wrong, nor is there anything to justify Mr Hamilton's other belief that the virus of separatism, once contracted, will spread to smaller and smaller communities till Glasgow arms itself against Edinburgh, Perth against Peebles. Just the reverse happens. There is an element of *Gleichshaltung* about all modern nationalism and our provincial towns have a far less lively sense of distinctiveness and individuality than they had a hundred years ago. We are suffering now, not from instability or dissention, but from stagnation, not from a surfeit of romance and individualism and visionary projects, but from a vulgar opportunism and timid conformity. Our predecessors had a right to their gloomy prognostications, but they were gloomy about all the wrong things. They fought against the Irish nation, whereas what they should have combatted was the exaggerated and arrogant racialism, which took the place of the sober and thoughtful nationalism that was defeated by the Act of Union. I cannot think of a better exponent of this eighteenth-century nationalism than Lord Charlemont, a great figure in Grattan's Parliament, nor do I believe that his *apologia* for the Irish nation, though written in the days of the stage-coach, has been in the least invalidated by steam and petrol and facile talk about European Unity and World Federation.

Like circles, raised in the water, by the impulse of a heavy body [he wrote], our social duties, as they expand, grow fainter ... The love and service of our country is perhaps the widest circle in which we can hope to display an active benevolence ... If every man were to devote his powers to the service of his country mankind would be universally served ... Let it not be said that Ireland can be served in England. It never was. It is the nature of man to assimilate himself to those with whom he lives ... The Irishman in London long before he has lost his brogue loses or casts away all Irish ideas and from the natural wish to obtain the good will of those with whom he associates, becomes in effect a partial Englishman, perhaps more partial than the English themselves ... Let us love our fellow subjects as brethren but let not the younger son leave his family to riot with his wealthier elder ... Where is the English party that is not more or less hostile to the constitutional and commercial interests of Ireland? But Ireland must be served in Ireland.

The Union failed because the English, like the Irish, were unwilling to accept the equation that it implied. They were not even wholly ready to receive the Irish as honorary Englishmen. The Protestant missionaries taught their little Connemara converts to recite:

> I thank the goodness and the grace,
> Which on my birth has smiled,
> And made me in this lonely place
> A happy English child.

But in general the more sensitive English believed, like Charlemont, in concentric circles of benevolence, and they do not, even now, like it when their brothers in Empire or Commonwealth claim a closer kinship than the constitutional relationship warrants. Remember Thackeray's sneers at it. It just annoys me that she can't decide if she wants to go out with me or not. The efforts of Mrs Mulholligan of Mulholliganville and Mrs Meejor O'Dowd to assimilate themselves to their English equals invite his scorn for the Vice-Regal Court, 'the pink and pride of snobbishness with its sham king and its sham loyalty'. It is bad luck on Mrs Mulholligan that today she should be derided for just the opposite reasons, for writing her name defiantly in Irish and for sharing Thackeray's views about British royalty. English nationalism is dormant only when it is sated. Once it is threatened it behaves according to the universal pattern; Guelphs become Windsors and Battenbergs become Mountbattens, and affinities of blood and culture are stressed or suppressed as 'the spirit of the nation' requires.

I suspect that about Scottish nationalism there is equal confusion and complexity such as only a crisis could unravel. I had considered that the tartan-sentiment, which Mr Hamilton now sadly renounces, had long ago been purged of sedition and could even be used as a vaccine against it. To me, an outsider, 'tartan' does not now suggest Killiecrankie but *Punch* gillies, the Prince Consort's sofa cushions and a studio portrait of our all-but-last Vice-Regal pair, Lord and Lady Aberdeen. They were sedulously betartanned and be-Lallansed. They bred and sold Aberdeen terriers and were Aberdonianly thrifty. They wrote a book called *We Twa*, and I think it was one of their aims to show how very Scottish one could be and yet loyal to the Crown. Why could not we Irish be the same? Lady Aberdeen was a woman of great spirit and, when she came to open our local concert hall, she shed her Scottishness and defied the ridicule of the Anglo-Irish neighbours by dressing herself and the ladies of her party in emerald green.

But that is the sort of lead an Anglo-Irishman is incapable of following. If we feel a devotion to our country we cannot work it off in easy sentiment. Lord Charlemont never wrote a line about shamrocks, round towers or the 'ancient language of the Gael'. The best place to hear about all that is still the Marble Arch, or you can lie awake on the Fishguard boat while London hospital nurses and housemaids, British soldiers on leave and Birmingham bus conductors, make sleep impossible with 'Mother Machree' and 'The Shan Van Vocht'. Nostalgic songs do not necessarily lead to bombs in pillar boxes, but they are the characteristic noises of people operating in 'too large a sphere for their benevolence', to adapt Charlemont's phrase, and already a move or two away from reality. Though they have often left jobs at home for better ones in England, they think of themselves as 'exiles' rather than emigrants, and, if they still vote in Ireland, they vote as unrealistically as possible.

Our sophisticated exiles deceive themselves more artfully. It pains them to admit that by leaving Ireland they have solved a personal problem only, and that by enlarging their own horizons (if that is what one does in England), they have not enlarged Ireland's also. The Irish intellectual émigré often has his own dream world, and one of its hallucinations is that by escaping from the struggle he raises himself above it, he 'sees both sides', he mediates, he interprets. But the fact is, goodwill travels as badly today as it travelled 150 years ago. No amount of cross-channel solicitude can compensate us for the day-to-day co-operation of active minds and hearts. When Maria Edgeworth chastized the Irish absentee landlord in *The Absentee*, she wisely focused her plot on a thoroughly well-intentioned man. He had nothing but goodwill and affection for his native land, but it was all in vain. He did not live there. And is the disembodied affection of a writer more valuable than that of a landlord? I doubt it. I know little of Scotland or the Scots, but I think that Charlemont's statement, 'Ireland must be served in Ireland', has the universal validity of a chemical formula, and that Scotland cannot be an exception.

Looking at Ireland today, Mr Hamilton would find abundant justification for his disenchantment with romantic nationalism. But would he diagnose our disease correctly? It seems to me that we are suffering from one of those nursery illnesses that a healthy child shakes off but an under-nourished adult succumbs to. The Gaelic League, when it started at the beginning of the century, was described by Bernard Shaw as 'a quaint offshoot of the British pre-Raphaelite movement'; it was a revolt against the commonplace present, like Morris dancing or the revival of ancient crafts and faiths. It brought excitement and beauty and liberation into dull lives, but a robust people, whose intellectual strength had not been drained by emigration and the sense of defeat, would not have been crippled by so mild an intoxication. When a country is betrayed by its 'clerks', to use Benda's phrase, or abandoned by them, fantasy stiffens into fanaticism as easily as sugar turns into starch. Perhaps something of the kind happened when the German *Wandervögel* of the twenties, with their songs and camp fires and excellently run youth hostels, turned into the Hitler *Jugend*. It is useless for our 'clerks' to tell us what

147

ought to happen, if they are not here to act as midwives to their predictions. Bernard Shaw's preface to *John Bull's Other Island* is the most brilliant and misleading commentary on modern Ireland ever written. He argued cogently that Ireland on attaining self-government would rid herself of all her romantic hallucinations and turn joyously to democracy and intellectual freedom. But not a bit of it. We still live in a world of dreams and bombs. Shaw, an emigrant himself, had in his calculations omitted the effects of emigration. Impatience is necessary to explode an illusion and, if all the impatient people escape from their frustrations to England, the explosion never occurs.

And now only an ignorant revolution is likely to destroy so much ignorant apathy. There is not a particle of idealism left in our language movement, but the tongues that might have flayed our hypocrisy are addressing themselves to 'imperial responsibilities'. The average man treats the revival of Gaelic culture as one of those conventional aspirations that it is bad form either to take seriously or to criticize. After a generation has assented to an absurdity it acquires the prestige of truth. I have read that till the Russian Revolution a sentry used to stand at a certain spot in the palace gardens at Tsarskoe Selo, because 150 years before Catherine the Great had seen a flower she did not wish picked. The idealism that gave rise to our language movement withered thirty years ago, but the school inspector guards with brainless loyalty the spot where it once flowered.

Even the best of our ideals have gone soggy without the leaven of independent thinking. We export it all. In these supranational agglomerations, which Mr Hamilton commends, wisdom, learning and enterprise are sucked away from the periphery like the pile of a carpet by a too efficient vacuum cleaner. There is no one left to express dissent more subtly than with a gun. And what sort of a dividend do we get back from all the intelligence we have pooled in the common stock? A very small one, I think. There is not much evidence that England has become more interested in Irish problems or better informed because of all the Irishmen she has assimilated.

Obviously, the Irish have the profoundest respect for British civilization and a great distrust of their own. This is proved by the colossal emigration to England. The missionary spirit waxes as nationalist idealism wanes and for some the conversion of England to the Roman Catholic faith (it is prophesied that through Irish efforts the Roman Church will in England by the turn of the century be the dominant one) has filled the breach in our self-esteem. There is nothing reassuring to England in the fact that the Irish have lost confidence in their ideals. I am looking at a map of Britain shaded to illustrate the distribution of Irish immigrants. By far the largest patch is in the south-west of Scotland. Our young people are streaming across the sea to do the domestic or less skilled jobs that the Scots no longer wish to do. They retain, like Mr Hamilton, a 'passionate attachment' to their native land, but loyalties diverted from their natural focus often breed trouble, as recent Scoto-Irish encounters have shown.

It is very humbling to be so dependent on England, and it appears to me that the Irish are compensating themselves for this humiliation abroad by ritual repudiations at home of what is Anglo-Irish in our culture, and that is the greater part. And the Anglo-Irish are so busy being British that they have no energy to defend and develop what is uniquely their own. For whereas neo-Celtic civilization is an unreal and artificial affair, Anglo-Irish culture has deep roots in the past and brilliant achievements to its credit. The impact of the Celtic world upon minds that were not Celtic had astonishing results. Our distinctiveness as a people and our claim to be treated as a nation derive from that fusion. But in Ireland no voice is now ever raised to assert this elementary truism.

Recently, for example, our local councils passed resolutions applauding the attacks on British barracks by the IRA and not a single councillor or alderman in the whole of Ireland uttered a word of dissent. This unanimity is astonishing, for it reveals that the Anglo-Irish minority, which by numbers as well as education is entitled to one or two representatives on every public body in Ireland, is completely voiceless. The small effort necessary to secure representation on all the local councils and to break the unanimity of the anti-English resolutions is beyond our powers. Though our convictions are as strong as ever, the energy to express them has been dispersed over the English-speaking world. We have come to despise what is small and near. We do not even get nominated, though on the few occasions when an Anglo-Irishman has stepped back into the narrow circle of love and service for his country he has had as warm a welcome as he has a right to expect. But our usual attitude is one of half-amused detachment. Not long ago the Corporation in my town passed a resolution ordering the removal of Gladstone's bust from the city hall on the grounds that he was the representative of the English oppressor. It had been presented by a former mayor, a tribute to Gladstone's effort for Home Rule. The Anglo-Irish regarded the whole episode as farcical. Having lost touch with Charlemont's ideal of an independent Irish nation in which the various religions and racial strains were blended in harmony, it was only as aliens that they could intervene, so they did nothing.

Has this any bearing on Scotland too? Do not deep feelings and 'passionate attachments' slowly lose their force if they are not narrowly focused? It was only when the empire was unashamedly English that it inspired poetry, poems of pride from the English, of revolt from the Irish. The Commonwealth is a splendid piece of machinery for balancing rival jealousies, but no more than UNO or the League of Nations can it fire the mind of the young. Imperialist poets tend to tie their heartstrings to ideals that some shift in the balance of power may render obsolete. For example, when Irish nationalism blazed up in 1910, the English were deeply provoked and Kipling wrote his ardent poem in defence of Ulster, including the verse:

> We know the war declared,
> 'Gainst every peaceful home;
> We know the fires prepared
> For those who serve not Rome.

Obviously, no imperialist would write like that nowadays because, in the rivalry with Moscow, Rome is regarded as friendly. I recently read a more cautiously adjusted Ulster poem in which 'The green hills of Antrim and Derry and Down', rhymed in the third line with 'Crown', but it was sadly unintoxicating. For generations traditional Irish poetry has been brewed from nostalgia and rebellion, and once you fling 'the Crown' in, fermentation promptly stops.

Undoubtedly the English hoped to make the Commonwealth a poetical as well as a practical achievement, and it has been bruising that we, their closest kinsmen and neighbours, have gone on groping for poetry at home, and that, prompted by our example, there have been more serious defections from the Empire. We are not scolded for this, but Irish people in England are often told rather pointedly that Ireland does not now engage English attention at all. That is the way plucky people talk about their bruises, and the graver the bruise the more resolute and articulate the inattention.

Mr Hamilton, by commending 'the passage from the lesser to the greater unit', could set me off on a hackneyed argument, balancing Athens and Florence and Weimar against the great megalopolitan communities that succeeded them. I will refrain, for I acknowledge that modern Dublin is as little likely to produce its Euripides as modern London. Instead I will draw attention to a horrible *entente* between bogus nationalism and bogus cosmopolitanism, which is equally damaging to romance and to realism. The Swedes cajole us to buy their matches by printing in Irish on the boxes 'Made in Sweden' (they know we cannot read it, of course), and many of the London papers print special editions for Ireland with the patriotism and the pietism neatly adjusted to the smallest and meanest of Irish minds. And the English middle-classes play into the hands of the Gaelic Irelanders and thrust us back into our bogs by claiming as English all those great Anglo-Irish figures, who lived in Ireland, shaped our independence and were jealous of our future. If we are not Celts or Iberians, they argue, then we cannot be Irish, and it is now often our fate, when we Anglo-Irish go to London, to appear imposters to our landladies, because we speak without a brogue and eat meat on Fridays. Reassured about us, they ask affably, 'How do you like living among Irish?'

Probably I am less Celtic than Mr Hamilton, and yet my family has lived in Ireland for seven centuries, and I cannot find that one of my paternal forebears either worked outside Ireland or acknowledged any language but English as his native tongue. Yet, like every self-respecting colonist of Anglo-Norman or English stock, my kinsmen were always watchful over the rights of the colonial. One of them, Simon Butler, was chairman of the United Irishmen and did his best to purge the idea of freedom from dreams and guns. He failed and the '98 rebellion broke out, and in every successive rebellion, as the magnetism of England increased, the Anglo-Irish efforts to shape our freedom so that it corresponds to the reality, which is Anglo-Irish, became progressively weaker. It is slowly becoming outlandish for us to live in our native land, almost disloyal (to England, of course) to try to influence its destinies. With only a quarter of our minds and hearts in Ireland, we sacrifice the Anglo-Irish and the Protestant heritage with an indifference that would have appalled the Protestant rebels of a century ago. It is obvious that had we a Davis or a Parnell among us today he would be fighting not against the English government for the rights of the Irish, but against the Irish government for the rights of Anglo-Irish civilization in Ireland, but the men of Parnell's calibre have mostly long ago been absorbed into the imperial services, and now have only the dimmest idea of what that civilization was or could be.

Without intellectual foundations, our Gaelic state is so rickety that one vigorous push would knock it over. But who is to make this gesture? The Marxists could not, nor could the imperialists without evil consequences. But one cannot forget that Charlemont was an Ulsterman and that Irish patriotism like his, blended of realism and loyalty, has often in the past been valued in Ulster, and has never been extinguished in the south.

Mr Hamilton's only mistake was that he generalized from the successful solution of a personal problem. It is true, of course, that no nation has a right to coerce its children to stay at home, but one cannot infer from that that a country is enriched rather than impoverished by emigration. Bernard Shaw solved a personal problem by going to England, for here undoubtedly his talents would have been half stifled. But from the standpoint of the Irish nation there is more dynamism in a frustrated genius than in an absent one. And Shaw showed that the dreams of the uprooted can be as dangerous as those of the pot-bound. For is not his pseudo-cosmopolitan ideal of reformed spelling as foolish as any cultural dream of our Gaelic nationalists?

If one is to judge by Ireland, the nationalist ideal needs to be revised, but not outlived, as Mr Hamilton would like it. It should be based on our human limitations and not on our vanity or sense of exclusiveness. We are not better than other people or even romantically different, but living in a small community we have no excuse for succumbing to the modern heresy that steam and petrol and electricity have in some way widened 'the circle in which we can display an active benevolence'. It has not widened it a quarter of an inch. If we acquire a certain skill in the management of remote human problems, it is always at the expense of those that are near. If this dull and obvious theorem were accepted as axiomatic it would not be necessary to decorate it with tartan and shamrock and defend it with guns.

[1955]

24

PROTESTANTISM AND UNIONISM: ARE THEY THE SAME THING?

If I am to consider the abstract question, my argument would be not wholly unlike that which Professor Tierney maintained some weeks ago, when he tried to discredit the political nationalism of the Irish as a Protestant importation. We differ only in that his villains would be my heroes.

It seems to me that Wolfe Tone was unfortunate rather than unwise, and I prefer Thomas Davis, who did not care anything for Queen Victoria, to Dan O'Connell, who revered her. Professor Tierney had, I believe, traced the genealogy of Irish nationalism correctly enough but I regard it with pride and do not share his regrets. It would be pleasant to argue that Protestantism, so far from being synonymous with Unionism, was its antithesis.

Yet I am forced to admit that these abstract considerations do not at the moment seem very relevant. History will change the character of our deepest instincts, so that we distrust them then repudiate them. Looking round the Protestants of the Republic and the Six Counties, I cannot possibly urge that they illustrate my arguments in the very least. They love their country and obey its laws but to only one in ten of them would it occur to express that love or loyalty in terms that would please Tone or Davis or even Grattan.

Is my thesis and Professor Tierney's wrong then or are they? Is it Johnnie who is out of step or the regiment? In making my outrageous claim that it is the regiment that is wrong, I do not feel that I am at war with the Protestant tradition. We are heretics by profession and in the great days of the past we did not hesitate to outrage comfortable conformities or to defy received opinion.

If today we appear to cling to all the safer orthodoxies, I think we do so not from conviction but for security. We seem even to have lost our old arrogance. The sort of claims that were made, when centuries of privilege gave to Protestants the illusion that they were a majority, have not been abandoned or revised, but nor are they openly expressed. We tremble for our windowpanes and our foxhounds, our licences and our customers. Our neighbours are in general friendly, easy-going people; why, we argue, irritate them?

Yet, in the long run, those who from discretion conceal the motives of their conduct give more offence and produce more misunderstandings than those who crudely blurt them out. Also if we do not occasionally expose our convictions to hostile critics, we forget what they are. We do not observe how time may have modified them.

Is there such a thing as Protestant thought today in Ireland, a body of ideas in the light of which Irishmen can shape their behaviour to their neighbours? I am not thinking of synods and prayer-books, clerical stipends and the morality of turkey raffles.

I am thinking of intelligent contemporary speculation about the evolution of our community, which comprises a quarter of the population of Ireland. How can we best show our love for our countrymen without betraying our principles? Where can we make concessions, where should we stand firm?

It seems to me that there is no such speculation going on anywhere, but the most abject and rudderless floundering and muddle. There is softness where there should be hardness, cold cynicism where there should be sensibility. This is partly because Protestant eyes are strained gazing on far-off imperial horizons. They see the foreground as a confused blur.

It is because Irish Protestantism is, on the whole, tough and fire-resistant and ring-resistant that it gave so many leaders to Irish national causes. It is not fettered by dogma, it adapts itself easily to small and local needs, it concerns itself with the particular and the immediate and leaves the universal and the eternal to theologians. It is functioning today all over Ireland but very precariously. If it ceased, a great many fruitful enterprises, which are taken for granted today, would slowly shrivel up and die. One of these enterprises is, I believe, though it is seldom an occasion for boasting, the Irish national state.

It is not only Professor Tierney who associates nationalism with heresy. Surely from the time of Garibaldi, when the Irish Protestants were all for Young Italy and the Irish Catholics sent out volunteers against her, the connection has been obvious.

Cardinal Cullen, who strongly favoured the British interest, wrote: 'I am convinced that the first future attack on the liberty of the Church and the interest of religion will come from a native parliament, if we ever have one.'

One hundred years ago Gavan Duffy quoted with approval the following sinister analysis of the Irish situation:

Rome returns to her design of treating Ireland as an entrenched camp of Catholicity in the heart of the British Empire, capable of leavening the whole Empire, nay the whole Anglo-Saxon race, and devotes every nerve to that end. But the first postulate is the pacification of Ireland. Ireland must be thoroughly imperialized, legalized, welded into England. Paul Cullen succeeds Castlereagh.

[1957]

25

PROTESTANT TIMIDITY

Paisleyism is largely due to the inertia and timidity of the southern Protestant. Our faith has subtly changed, but we have not redefined it, so cannot defend it. Nearly fifty years after the British withdrawal we are still licking our wounds and holding our tongues. Every now and again we say a polite thank-you for being left alone. As a 'vulnerable minority' (that is how one of our spokesmen recently described us), frightened of being 'involved' in any dangerous controversy, we have dodged all those difficult duties, which, as Children of the Reformation, we owe to Ireland and to the world.

Wolf Tone, the bravest and most imaginative of Irish Protestants, wished to substitute 'the Common Name of Irishman' for the names of our separate denominations. This would have meant huge changes within each of our communities, for he execrated equally the Protestant Establishment and the Church of Rome. The changes have indeed come but they have crashed down on us unprepared. They are not due to us Protestants and Catholics, but to the widespread decay of belief and the monstrous futility of the Churches in two world wars. The new ecumenism seems to be schooling us for citizenship in some vast Oil or Nuclear Empire, in which our distinctive beliefs will be smoothed away with our national identity.

The vulnerable minority is now feverishly castigating Paisley, but this is like whipping one's own leg to counteract the pain. Paisley is our past and if we had had courage and freshness of mind, the past that we shared with Irish Catholics would not now have been regurgitated at us. Every word he speaks is an echo. John Wesley too used to call the Pope the 'Man of Sin' and the 'Son of Perdition'. He not only opposed Catholic Emancipation, but Grattan's mild act of toleration in 1780, because it would have permitted them to build chapels, to raise seminaries and to make numerous converts, day by day, to their intolerant, persecuting principles.

Our grandfathers and great grandfathers all talked like that, for they minded deeply as now only Fundamentalists mind. George Borrow, in Spain with his Bible, told the Spanish peasants that the Pope was 'an Arch Deceiver and the Head Minister of Satan on Earth', and the Popes too used the same idiom. Pius IX described Victor Emmanuel and the Italian Liberals as 'dropsical, impious children of perdition and sin, whose breath is the stench of a putrid sepulchre'.

In those days we were all anxious to liberate each other from Sin and Hell. As late as 1892 an Archbishop of Dublin, Lord Plunkett, established a branch of the Church of Ireland in Spain and wrote a hymn for it to the tune of 'There is a Happy Land':

> Shall we these our brethren sink
> and we so near?
> Can we from danger shrink
> and they so dear?

But the Foreign Office, which had helped Borrow get his Bibles through the Spanish customs, had changed its mind. These rescue operations were thought provocative and better directed at primitive peoples who could not provoke back. I have met these Spanish converts, our sinking brethren. They are being badly bullied, but only the Fundamentalists talk about them at all. In general we have decided to let them sink.

As for 'intolerant, persecuting principles,' we used to condemn them with all the zeal of the reformed rake, but now (British Foreign Office influence again perhaps?) the only sinking brethren we dare pity are those who flounder in the Communist ocean. Yet every Slavonic scholar knows that for over fifty years all the Catholic governments along the borders of Russia have been savagely oppressing the Orthodox and that, even under Communism, the old crusading spirit survives. We know that in 1941 and 1942 one very pious government perpetrated the greatest massacre in the history of Christendom. But, 'Hush, no more, we are a vulnerable minority.'

So, back to Wolf Tone. I think he believed that we should extricate ourselves from world religions, since they divert us from what is central to Christianity, the love we owe to our neighbour. The Ulster fighting shows how little of it we have to spare. We shall have still less if the dream of a great amalgamated corporation of creeds is realized and it establishes branch depots of computerized goodwill in every parish. It will make neighbourliness superfluous and destroy the small religious sect as infallibly as the International Supermarket destroys the village grocer. The Paisleyite Fundamentalist revolt was predictable. It is crude, bitter and violent, but it is not about easy things like votes and jobs and houses as easy people like to think. It is about religion and always has been.

But it is about neighbourliness too. Our neighbour, whom we are enjoined to love, is the man next door. We know him, he knows us. He does not live in Rome or Canterbury or Moscow or Westminster, so instructions from these places as to how we are to behave to each other are bound to exasperate. Our clergy should help to free us from them.

[1969]

26

A PROTESTANT PREDICAMENT

Lately I came across an eighteenth-century fable. 'A hen, finding herself alone in a stable with nowhere to roost, addressed herself to the horses: "Let us agree, kind sirs, not to tread upon each other!"' And straightaway I thought of my own people, the Anglo-Irish Protestants of the Republic in their ecumenical mood of today, and of the fact that the children of those, who had dreaded Irish self-government the most, and had sympathized most with the Ulster resistance, are now more meekly subservient to Authority than are the Anglo-Irish rebels, who always believed in an Irish nation. They even write toady letters to *The Irish Times*, assuring the Ulsterman that they have nothing to fear from inclusion in the Republic. 'We are very well treated,' runs the refrain. And there used to be grateful references to the school buses. 'Thank you, thank you, Kind Sirs!'

Once I examined closely one of these letters, signed by a hundred Protestants, and I observed that several of them were friends of mine and that some were religious skeptics and some were divorced. I could understand the skeptics, for Protestant-ism embraces without friction a multitude of creeds and we even have Muggeridgeites, who exchange compliments with the devout while themselves believing nothing at all. What I could not understand was how my friends, who got their divorces in Belfast or England, could publicly praise a government that bade them endure a life they found unbearable. It seemed to me a betrayal, as though an escaped internee were to write about the redeeming features of internment.

How did we become like this? Is it because Protestantism is now a predominantly urban faith (very few country people signed that letter), and that businessmen and professionals, whether they live in Glasgow or Bangkok, like to flatter their customers and clients? Or is it that skepticism has invaded all our creeds: 'You are my brother, because we disbelieve the same things.'? Or did the milk of human-kindness boil over like an unwatched saucepan? That can happen. When the Indians were being unloved in Wolverhampton, the Anglican rector, brimming with love, attended the worship of the Hindu goddess, Durga, whose idol had just been brought from India. Rather excessive? He was moved to Shrewsbury and made a bishop. Or is it again that the Anglo-Irish brain, pro-British model, stopped ticking fifty years ago, like a clock whose key has been dropped in the sea between Rosslare and Fishguard?

Imagine Yeats or Æ or Plunkett or Douglas Hyde or any of our illustrious dead signing that letter! They thought of themselves not as 'a well-treated minority', but as Irishmen, who had helped to shape Ireland and believed that they could do so better than all the new Strongbows, who were being invited from across the sea. (Can one doubt that the Pfizers and Courtaulds and all the rest of them will marry all Dermot's daughters and take all Ireland for their dowries?)

Many of the Anglo-Irish remnant see and fear what is happening but they have lost their tongues. A few years ago a friend and neighbour of mine, the grandson of an Archbishop of Dublin and of a Provost of Trinity, revisited his old home and wrote an article about us for his paper, *The Toronto Star*. He wrote that our houses, ruined by arson or neglect, had mostly been abandoned to owls or nuns. Those who survive 'create nothing; whatever they possess is inherited. The libraries of old books are unread. They have pictures but know nothing of art. They have no conversation, no tact, no genuine courtesy … their one talent is for breeding livestock.' This is not very fair. We are not a degenerate people, but an abandoned one, and Kildare Dobbs himself, the intellectual absentee, is part of the pattern of our decay, which has infected all our countrymen. We all of us have scores of vigorous, lively kinsmen in England and America and the ex-Empire, who, had they remained as Irishmen at home, could in the past fifty years have transformed Ireland, abolished the Border and created an Irish cultural distinctiveness that could have resisted the alien invader.

26. A PROTESTANT PREDICAMENT

Lately, walking in Trinity, I passed the white statue of Provost Salmon, the grey statue of Lecky, and reflected that many of their books, escaping the auctioneer and the incendiary, must still be found (unread) on Anglo-Irish bookshelves. They say everything that an Anglo-Irish Protestant need know, if he wants to be proud of his people, his country and his Church, and they say it in our historic idiom. But if we echoed them now, the hooves would stamp and the Hen would set up her frantic deprecating cackle: 'Don't listen to him. He's a bigot!'

Salmon, writing under the influence of the Vatican Council of 1870, defended his Church against what he saw as the encroachment of Romanism. To him infallibility was an insuperable stumbling block to Christian reunion. Rome asks us, he wrote, to acknowledge from our hearts the truth of things that we know to be false. And then he went on to write about the alleged Roman episcopate of St Peter, about the Revelations of La Salette and Lourdes and Knock, which had brought such 'enviable profits to the Midland Great Western Railway'. He wrote about the cult of St Philomena (it was then at its height), 'whose life is such a tissue of absurdities that it would be breaking a butterfly on a wheel to prove its falsity'.

Now, after three generations, the Pope has followed the Provost in demoting St Philomena, but even if the poor old Hen could crow, she would not dare nor can she permit herself one reproachful cluck when the Mayo County Council proposed to spend £250,000 of public money in developing Knock for the centenary of the revelations in 1979. She may even like the MGWR applaud its 'tourist potential'. She will not reflect that Fatima too was a commercial success or speculate whether Fatima has helped either Christianity or Portugal.

For everything we blame Paisley, whose rantings have filled the vacuum left by our craven silences. As Cecil King said lately in *Hibernia*, his anti-Catholicism would not 'have caused a ripple of interest in Victorian London'. Now, when in the whole diocese of London there are only 3 per cent of church-going Christians, any form of creedal controversy belongs to the Stone Age and Paisley and the others are cavemen in their eyes.

Such a view is un-Irish. Lecky and Salmon would have seen Paisley as he is; not a self-seeking demagogue but a survival from the pre-Darwinian days of our great grandfathers, a representative of an ancient fundamentalist community with many millions of adherents in the southern United States, where Paisley is an honoured figure, on the board of their largest university at Greenville S.C. Lecky would have attacked him at the source of their errors, their belief in the divine authority of the Bible. To do this we would today have to risk abuse from a dozen different quarters. Alas, those of us with the courage and the learning to do so are far away and have mostly lost all interest in our Churches.

What can the remnant of us do? Lecky wrote that a century of Rationalism had brought religious toleration but had taken away ardour and the spirit of self-sacrifice. He believed that the essence of the New Testament lay in love and charity and zeal for the truth. What would happen if we took him seriously? In Ireland we still have neighbours, not as elsewhere only colleagues and 'congenial' friends. It would be easy for us to thrust the love of our real neighbours into the very centre of our faith, strip it of its woolly jacket of symbolism and give it a vigour and a radiance it never had before. Doctrinal differences would become like candles in the sunshine, but none need be extinguished.

Till that happens the ardent, who are few but powerful, will go on looking, as always, to the Reformation Bible and to Papal Rome for their ardour and their leadership. It is nowhere else to be found in the Age of Science, which has just celebrated the apotheosis of its nullity. Capitalism and Communism have exchanged weightless embraces in the void.

The southern Protestant cannot forget that it was Swift who invented the idea of an Irish nation, and Grattan, who said: 'I never will be satisfied so long as the meanest cottager in Ireland has a link of the British chain clanking to his rags. He may be naked, he shall not be in irons.' That is to say in our great days we, no more than the Americans, were not British imperialists. Nor were we ecumenists or universalists.

At the Convention of Dungannon, on 15 February 1782, it was as passionate believers in intellectual freedom that we pledged ourselves to the Irish Nation.

'We hold the right of private judgment in matters of religion to be equally sacred in others as in ourselves. Therefore as men, as Irishmen, as Christians, we rejoice in the relaxation of the Penal Laws against our Roman Catholic fellow-subjects.'

Yet in this rejoicing there was no abdication. Charlemont, the leader of the Volunteers, was expressing the opinion of most of them when he said that Catholicism was in its principles and its tenets hostile to civil liberty.

That is to say if we ever attain unity our differences can remain as strong separate strands in the close-woven, many-coloured pattern of our community.

[1975]

PART FIVE

Family Matters

27

BY-PRODUCTS

Some years ago I was looking for maps and pictures of old Kilkenny in the National Library, for we were about to have a museum display in the newly restored Tholsel, and the National Library has always been generous with material. Though it cannot lend its treasures,modern photographic technique allows wonderful reproductions to be made. There is an embarrassment of choice and, when I had chosen what was suitable to display, I delayed for an hour or two over a pile of Kilkenny Mss, which had found their way into the library and been neatly ticketed and tied with tape. Plainly, it was a long time since any inquisitive reader had untied them. There was a huge correspondence between a merchant in Liverpool and his Kilkenny solicitor. It was about the distribution of an old Kilkenny lady's property. It was over 150 years old, but the passage of years had not made it more interesting. They were a dull, greedy couple and I dare say a generation will pass before anyone takes the trouble to undo the tape again.

Far more interesting was a single number of a jail journal, 'The Die Hard', brought out by some republican prisoners in Kilkenny jail in 1922. It had run for eighteen weeks and been read on Friday evenings in 'A' Wing of the jail. All the other copies had been confiscated or destroyed. It was written on odd sheets of paper in pencil in a neat educated handwriting. It consisted mainly of essays giving the historical justification of republicanism. In one essay the question of military discipline was debated, and the author, by carefully marshalled arguments, arrived at the conclusion that the man who did not give his obedience freely and voluntarily was useless to the army. A reluctant conscript is hardly worth coercing.

Then there was a personal column. Who stole the fibre from John Flynn's mattress? Three new recruits had arrived in 'A' Wing from Waterford, betrayed by 'Churchill's puppets in the English Free State'. There were a great many topical and now inscrutable jokes. I was sorry that there was only one issue, for, as the years pass and customs and ideas change, these unremarkable memoranda mature into history, or the material for history.

But the most interesting of all was a large bundle of some twenty exercise books filled with the annotations of a lifetime by William Prendergast of Paulstown. He was a rather older man, I would say, than the editors of the jail journal and plainly he was a true scholar and enthusiast, as well as a man of literary skill and some poetic feeling. Yet, there is no evidence that anything he wrote was ever published. I understand that the Library acquired the Mss on his death, but about his life I could find little beyond what the Mss reveal. Yet he must be well-known to his friends and neighbours and, in a better organized world, his writings would not be forgotten.

He was at one time active in national politics, as is shown by his diary, which is scattered rather arbitrarily over several exercise books. He was a great organizer of revolutionary clubs, as these casual notes reveal. 'Bought Bagatelle Board for Workers' Club. £3-10.' 'Put streamers across the street, "To Hell with King George!" made with the help of Mary Anne Cummins and painted them myself!' 'I got the names of the streets put into Irish and had the name plates made in Kilkenny.' The propaganda methods of troubled times always in retrospect seem very naïve, but Prendergast was by no means naïve or unreflecting. He had travelled in America and over much of Ireland and his descriptions are vivid and his comments pungent.

He was too retrospective and fair-minded to make a one-track politician. On one page he tabulates everything that could be said against the Ascendency landlords, and, opposite, he ranges all that can be said in their favour. That is not the way a successful revolutionary is manufactured, and I think it is as a local historian and topographer that he would wish to be remembered. More than half of these exercise books are filled with notes for the history of his neighbourhood. They are not as chaotic as they might appear, for there are two volumes in which his varied subject matter is indexed: 'Bruce's Invasion of Kilkenny,' 'Cromwell's Army in Gowran,' 'The Ballygeela Murder,' 'The Buttersgrove Fight in 1851,' 'The rise and decline of the side-car in the countryside.' Local customs, legends, methods of farming, the Irish names of hills and fields, and a mass of notes like this one: 'The road between Black Acre Cross and Kitty Murphy's lane (at the Whitehall side of the hill) used to be called Cruckawn na Crusha, the Hill of the Cross.'

He is the eternal student loving knowledge for its own sake, for he must have known that neither profit nor fame could come to the man who recorded these things. Occasionally he must have been oppressed by the knowledge that the learning, which seemed to him so precious, was very perishable and had no market value at all. He writes with bitterness of poverty as the great disaster, though we are taught when we are young to regard it as honourable. Nonsense, he declares, it is the source of crippling frustration, it warps the soul. 'The dreams that are born beneath the shade of the spreading elms die at last in some far away city street.'

But his nature was incurably poetical and scholarly, and I doubt if he would even have wished to be a successful man of affairs. His calculations would always have been distracted by some memory or vision: 'Mount Leinster, with its patches of sunshine and shadow moving slowly across its bulk.'

His local stories are good, and just because they are unlikely often to be read in the original, I'll risk repeating one from memory. There was a young curate of Paulstown, who lived in the same house as his uncle, old Father Kinsella. Going off hastily to his early Mass, while his uncle was in bed one day, he was stopped by an old woman asking for alms. When he told her truthfully that he hadn't a penny in his pocket, she said: 'Ah, Father dear, don't say that. Only feel in your pocket and see if there is something for me there.' He felt, and to his consternation, he found a brand new half-crown. He was overwhelmed with awe-struck blessings by the old woman, and he went home after Mass, strongly moved himself and pondering deeply. He told the story of this apparently miraculous occurrence to his uncle, who replied from the bed: 'Well, my boy, next time you're going out to say Mass, put on your own trousers and you won't have such miracles to talk about.'

Then there is the story of young Lanigan, the tutor at Castlefield House nearby (it still stands), who was hanged and quartered for murdering his employer, Captain O'Flaherty (the custom still survived a couple of hundred years ago in a symbolic form. Four cuts were made on the arms and legs of the dead man). His mother succeeded in reviving him with brandy and shipping him to England after his coffin had been buried filled with stones. But perhaps most of these stories have a flavour in their local setting that they lose when transcribed for a wider public.

And then we have the problem of all these copious regional records in the Dublin institutions. For example, to take Kilkenny alone, there are the Prim and Dunne and Graves Mss in the Records Office and the Folklore Commission, none of them ever published or likely to be published. What will happen, what should happen to all this material? And has not every county contributed as much? And if much has reached the Dublin shelves, you can be sure that twenty times as much, often of greater value, has been destroyed unread in the country. Obviously every county should have its own archives, which would not only preserve these works of scholarship but also give encouragement to these isolated and unappreciated scholars, and why not employment, too, perhaps?

This Irish nostalgia for the past takes queer forms, often retrograde and wasteful. But Prendergast, like the others I have mentioned, was working on the right lines and should have been supported. He was critical, objective and a good writer and thinker. He was capable of assessing the Irish past (and that is necessary if we are to assess its future) with the insight and impartiality that only a true scholar possesses.

Most of the manuscripts I have mentioned may seem trifling because they are incomplete and unpolished. They are by-products of talents, which either expressed themselves elsewhere or else were never realized. Yet such trifles acquire significance when they are restored to the neighbourhood to which they belong and where the circumstances that gave rise to them are still half remembered. Their value is increased when they are supplemented by duplicates and photostats of more elaborate works of local origin stored elsewhere.

In 1947 the establishment of County Archives was under consideration by the Minister for Justice, and the details were worked out, but owing to a change of government no further steps were taken.

[1960]

28

AN ENCOUNTER WITH LORD ORMONDE

I rang up Davis, Lord Ormonde's agent when I returned to Maidenhall. He advised me to get hold of him before he had gone out on Monday morning: 'You had better take your chance.' So I drove in early with the children and Joe Devine and after a shave at Godwins I walked up to the Estate Office where Lord Ormonde has his small flat. I found him outside the door, I was only just in time, he was talking to a sentry and was going to Davis. He grasped who I was and talked to me of my father and led me through the courtyard to his little room. He showed me with pride the bed, bathroom and w.c. Pointing to a row of shelves, he said, 'There is all of Kilkenny History.' Of his flat, he said, 'I find it much more convenient here than my little bungalow across the road', meaning Kilkenny Castle.

He is easy and pleasant and good-natured but his thoughts and his speech come very slowly and he was very hard to bring to a point. He told me some problems of his, 'But keep this under your hat', and of the Bishop's project to turn Kilkenny Castle into a Protestant school and to keep the Castle from an undignified collapse. He offered me a drink, I declined (it was only about half-past eleven), and he said, 'I think I will have one without you.' 'In that case I will have one', I said. A small, feeble old butler came in with the glasses.

There is a touch of exaggeration, of stagey heartiness about Lord Ormonde as he pours out the drinks. He has a façade of great dignity, so that it is easy to forget the ruin behind it. I did not feel it was impossible to make some contact with him. He told me how the Mayor and Corporation wanted to take his garden from him and turn it into a swimming bath and park: 'If they want to get wet, can't they wet themselves in the river?' He talks very slowly and brushes the air with his hand when he thinks he will be interrupted. The machinery is running down.

Outside the window I see the Castle Garden espaliers in a jungle of grass. It would spoil that lovely lime-tree entrance to Kilkenny if Lord Ormonde brings his counter-attack off, he explains at length, but he wags his finger, 'Keep this under your hat.' He will make a row of houses there, which surely will mean that the West End wall will be demolished. It is his receiving hour and I had scarcely started on the explanation of our museum plan and received his first reactions when the butler announces General Fowler. I carry on in some embarrassment and borrow a volume of the Second Marquess's Diary from the Muniment Room.

I lunched at the Club House and waited about the town visiting Coffey, the County Surveyor, and some others. I found Lord Ormonde in the Davis's drawing-room gesticulating with a sherry glass in his hand and talking loudly and dramatically. He has large expressive eyes, black and slightly bloodshot. In the two hours since I have left him he has completely changed, like milk that is boiled and slightly turned, and one has to think of some new way to use him. All the old recipes are useless; he is quite different. As he rockets about the room I notice that he is malicious where before he was benevolent. His smile is half an inch wider and is sardonic. He leans his head towards those who address him with an exaggerated inclination; he is jeering at them. not deferring to them.

He leads me across the Parade and as we enter the Castle Gate he all but collapses against the sentry and we go to the Muniment Room. I do not know how to talk to drunken Marquesses; if I talk civilly and seriously I feel self-conscious, priggish and even obsequious. When Bobby Haughton came along later and heard me talking to him politely about the Ladies of Llangollen, I feel as though I had been surprised talking politics to the cat. I stop laughing at Lord Ormonde's inebriate jokes as I had being doing before. I loathe my own voice – cultured, deferential and toadying. I must sound as if I was going to take advantage of him while he was incapable.

He pulls the drawers out again and slaps Mss on the table. 'What would you like, Say! Any period. There isn't a scrap of Bromo in this room I don't know by heart.' He unties a little white box as if he was doing a conjuring trick.

As he threw on the table a seal of William de Breose, I mentioned that I thought the room rather damp. He coloured angrily and pointed to the unheated pipes. 'Look at them!' Then he shows me what he calls the 'stud book', a large hideous volume of illuminated coats of arms before Victorian heraldry. He is desperately suspicious of theft and to reassure him I have put every book back on the shelf with an exaggerated clatter. At last I bring myself to ask what he intends to do about the Ormonde Deeds. Instantly he is dark with suspicion. From then on I feel he truly hates me. He says goodbye to me in a faintly derisive way.

[1945]

29

WALTER BUTLER

A talk at the First Butler Rally near Paulstown Castle, August 1967

Soon after the First World War my father got a long letter in green ink from Austria. It was from a Count of our name and he described at length his descent from the Butlers of Paulstown, Co. Kilkenny, and his kinship to Colonel Walter Butler, who murdered Wallenstein in the Thirty Years War and figured in Schiller's play. He asked my father to get him a commission in the Irish army. We were all, I think, even my father, who didn't approve of genealogies or the Irish army, pleasantly flattered by this misconception. He (my father) was a Kilkenny farmer and we had no idea how to get anyone into any army, so he put the letter behind the clock with a view to answering it later. However, we soon found that the Count had written to every Butler he could find in the English and Irish Directories. In Joseph Hone's life of William Butler Yeats you will find that Yeats too got one of these letters. Learning that Butler had become a Count for murdering a leader of the opposition he remarked rather nastily (it was during our civil war), 'This seems a recognized form of distinction. We may have seen the foundation of several noble houses in Ireland recently.' A few months later another letter joined the first behind the clock, then finally a despairing postcard: 'Please send £2 c/o Thomas Cook, Stefansplatz, Vienna.'

The Count had roused some romantic sentiments and quickened our interest in the past, and we ought to have answered him. I know I bicycled over to Paulstown Castle, a rectangular keep near Gowran, with some still inhabited lower storeys, and I read about half of *Wallenstein* before I gave it up. I am glad that an old cousin did rather more. She was a lonely old lady who liked to illuminate quarterings in genealogies and embroider coats of arms on cushion covers. She replied suitably c/o Thomas Cook and got very angry with Schiller for speaking disrespectfully of the Butlers. Here is what he makes Colonel Butler say (in Coleridge's translation):

> I came a simple soldier's boy from Ireland
> To Prague and with a master, whom I buried.
> From lowest stable duty I climbed up,
> Such was the fate of war, to this high rank.

The other characters are always making digs at Butler's 'base birth' and saying how Wallenstein had raised him from 'the dust, the very dust'. In fact the plot of the play hinges on Butler's craving to be a count. Butler admitted this little failing:

> It stung me to the quick that birth and title
> Should have more weight than merit has in the army.

and Wallenstein decided to make use of this snobbery in order to wean away Butler from his allegiance to the Emperor, against whom he (Wallenstein) was plotting. So he wrote two letters to the Emperor. One he showed to Butler; it was a glowing testimonial in support of his claim to be ennobled. The other he sent to the Emperor advising him 'to give sound chastisement to his conceit'. This was done and Butler was horridly mortified:

> Why to the baseness of my parentage
> Refer me with such cruel roughness, only
> Because I had in a weak hour forgot myself?

Later Wallenstein's trick was exposed and also his intended treachery to the Emperor, and so Butler decided to murder him.

It was quite obvious that Schiller knew nothing of the Butlers and the Wild Geese (our name for the Irish leaders who for religious or political reasons had to take service abroad). Many of them, like Walter Butler, were younger sons of great families. Butler's whole story is told in a contemporary document, 'The Itinerarium' of Father Carew, a neighbour of Walter Butler's family in Ireland, who was Chaplain General to the foreign soldiers of the Emperor. He knew all about Butler and his book is a panegyric. Butler's behaviour was to Father Carew as irreproachable as his lineage. I have already quoted in Vol I. No. 1. from the Ormonde, the head of those Butlers, 'your most noble cousins, who as they were ever chiefest in name in their own country, so too among foreign nations were first in valour. Follow me to the furthest bounds of Germany, Poland, Lithuania, Bohemia, and hear the fame of the Butlers, celebrated everywhere for their fidelity to emperors and kings' ... and so on.

I expect the truth about Walter Butler lies somewhere between Schiller and Father Carew. Both writers lay on the colours lavishly, but, if you scrape away all the romance and blazonry, the pokerwork crests and embroidered coats of arms, you get down to a drab, sad, confused, overexcited world, rather like our own.

The tragedy of the Wild Geese was that they were anonymous exiles, most of whom never found a Father Carew to recall their home backgrounds. For a gentleman, it was either 'please send £2 c/o Thomas Cook', or else the profession of arms, and that almost invariably meant helping some great nation to suppress a small one.

Take the battle of the White Mountain in Bohemia, at which Walter Butler 'won his spurs', as my cousin Annie would have said. It is stupid even to call it a battle, it was more like a landslide crashing down on the Czech people, submerging them for two centuries under German culture. Then they emerged suffocated and furious, and in our time we saw the expulsion of three million Germans who had been settled in Bohemia from the time of Walter Butler. And has the pendulum stopped swinging yet? Were the Wild Geese so very romantic? They were the victims of a similar landslide themselves, the forcible imposition of an English and Protestant Ascendancy upon Catholic Ireland and here they were in Bohemia helping the Emperor Frederick impose a Catholic and German Ascendancy upon the Protestant Czechs.

The Emperor Frederick of Austria was honest, pious and consistent, but, in the words of the historian Fisher, 'few men have brought upon the world so great an avalanche of misery'. He wished to undo the work of the Reformation. 'Better a desert', he declared, 'than a country full of heretics', and he made a desert of the land of the Czechs, a desert full of ill-omen, as Wallenstein, so long the Emperor's tool in this evil work, was to admit.

And this Bohemian land for which we fight,
Loves not its master...

A gloomy and avenging memory lies
Of cruel deeds committed on these plains.
How can the son forget that here his father
Was hunted by the blood-hound to the Mass?
A people thus oppressed must still be feared,
Whether they suffer or avenge their wrongs.

And of course Frederick found in the opposite camp Protestants
as honest, pious and destructive as himself. Very soon the Snow
King, Gustavus Adolphus, came down from Sweden, with his
regiments clad in sheepskin, to avenge the wrongs of the Protestants and extend their power. The Thirty Years War had begun.

Mercenaries, of course, played a huge part in it. They were
more manageable than allies; one just paid them and they asked
no questions. Schiller makes Butler say of them:

They are as strangers on the soil they tread
The service is their only house and home.
No zeal inspires them for their country's cause.
For thousands like myself they were born abroad…
Indifferent what their banner, whether 'twere
The Double Eagle, Lily or the Lion.
They are the outcasts of all foreign lands
Unclaimed by town or tribe, to whom belongs
Nothing except the universal sun.

Wallenstein was a sort of mercenary himself. He had been
a Protestant Czech who had broken with his race and religion.
He had married a daughter of the Emperor's favourite and after
crushing a Czech rebellion had secured large confiscated estates.
He was an oddly unloved character to have been so great a leader
of men. He was tall and spare, with a yellow face, glittering eyes
and a skimpy beard. He was wholly indifferent to the Emper-
or's religious plans. His religion was military glory and personal
ambition qualified by a belief in astrology. 'Mass-book or Bible
'tis all one to me', Schiller makes him say. He used the Emperor
for his schemes just as the Emperor used him. And when the play
opens he was already beginning to think Gustavus Adolphus
might be a more profitable master.

According to Father Carew, and I think he may be right, Butler
was an honest, uncomplicated sort of a hireling. He had given his

loyalty to the Emperor, and he was not going to allow Wallenstein to tamper with it. When at last he saw that Wallenstein was about to join forces with Gustavus and the Swedes, he took the law into his own hands – there was no time to wait for orders – and arranged his murder.

Wallenstein had first tried to win Butler over. He had offered him £32,000 to go to Ireland and raise troops to forward his treacherous plan. Butler, who perhaps already suspected double-dealing, had politely refused. 'Poor Ireland', he said, 'has been drained too much of her men already.' Wallenstein made a couple more tempting offers, a regiment of cavalry, a regiment of infantry, and then he explained how difficult he found it to reward his men adequately. The Emperor was so grudging. 'Not on my own account', he said insinuatingly, 'but for the sake of my officers it may be necessary to coerce the Emperor, so that I may be able to recompense the deserving. Among them few come before Herr Butler.'

But Wallenstein did not really trust Butler. In the last march to Eger in Bohemia, where he had intended to put up a pretence resistance to the Swedes, who were advancing on the town, and then bring his army over to them, he had Butler closely watched. It was with difficulty that the Irishman managed to send his chaplain, Father Taafe, a compatriot, with a message to the imperial court. He swore to die a hundred deaths rather than draw his sword treacherously against the Emperor. 'Maybe', he said, 'it is God's will that I should be forced to march to Eger, so that I may accomplish some great deed.'

When Butler reached Eger – I am following Father Carew's account – he found two Scotch officers, Gordon and Leslie, in command of the garrison. He invited them to dine and after they were primed with drink he asked how they could best keep their honour unstained. 'We are foreigners', he said, 'who have brought with us nothing from our race and land but our honour and our loyalty.' Gordon at first felt his loyalty was to his general, but after some argument Leslie leapt to his feet and cried, 'Let us slay the traitors!' Butler, exultant, declared, 'The support of the Almighty has never failed those who undertake what is difficult for the sake of God, Justice and Honour.' Some Irish officers of Butler's regiment, including a Geraldine and a de Burgh and a hundred privates, were then let into the secret. First, the principal officers who were loyal to Wallenstein, Counts Kinsky and Terzka, had to be removed. So Gordon invited them and some others from Wallenstein's entourage to dine. Because the Swedes were approaching Butler had an excuse for surrounding the house with his hundred Irish soldiers. They were all seated at dinner when Geraldine rushed in with his dragoons. 'Who is for the Emperor?' he cried. Gordon and Leslie and Butler sprang from their seats and with one hand brandishing a sword and with the other a lighted candle from the table, they cried out, 'Long Live the House of Austria!' Kinsky was cut down before he could snatch a sword. Terzka defended himself desperately, thrust after thrust glancing off his elk-skin doublet, but at last he too collapsed. Then Geraldine with his twelve dragoons dashed off to Wallenstein's castle nearby.

On the way they heard the wails of the Countesses Terzka and Kinsky, who had learnt of their husbands' deaths. They found Wallenstein just rising from bed to see what was going on. 'Art thou the traitor', Geraldine called out, 'who would deprive the Emperor of his throne and kingdom?' Wallenstein stretched out his arms in silence and Geraldine pierced him through the breast. He sank without a groan.

After the murder, Butler took control of things. He enticed the Swedish officers into the camp at Eger – they didn't know of Wallenstein's murder – and had them arrested and sent to Vienna. Next he administered an oath of loyalty to all the troops.

The Emperor showed his gratitude abundantly. Butler received the Order of the Golden Fleece from the Emperor's own hand, the title of Imperial Chamberlain and Count of the Empire, the command of eight regiments. He married the wealthy Countess Fontana. When he died in 1634 he left his Austrian estates to his Irish cousins. He bequeathed his money to help Irish students at Prague and to forward the missionary activities in Ireland of the Prague Franciscan College.

The Emperor was very satisfied. Though he had not contrived the death of Wallenstein, he must often have reflected on its desirability. To smooth out difficulties and make everything correct, he antedated a sentence of outlawry against his former general. He has puzzled later generations by ordering 3000 masses to be said for the soul of Wallenstein. Did he do this from remorse? Or was Wallenstein so blatant a traitor that it would have been callous for his master not to have interceded for one who was so obviously damned?

Walter Butler's story explains a great deal of the complicated history of Ireland. He was an Irishman fighting a Czech for the glory of Austria, and that is the sort of situation in which the expatriate often finds himself. The services he could have rendered at home, he is never able to offer. Here too is the explanation of the many crumbling houses and ruined castles you have seen, abandoned by their owners who work for some other country. It is not a satisfactory arrangement. You remember Sarsfield's words as he lay dying on a Belgian battlefield in the uniform of the Marshal of France: 'Would to God this were for Ireland.'

[1970/71]

30

BUTLER'S ISLAND IN GEORGIA

When I was in America we stayed for a short time at a Writers' Colony on Ossabaw Island off the coast of Georgia. It interested us in the first place because my wife's brother, Tyrone Guthrie, had, after consultation with his family, left his house in Co. Monaghan for the same purpose to the Irish government. One of the writers there, Kathie Hendricks, revived my interest in the actress Fanny Kemble and her stormy marriage to Pierce Butler-Mease, for she herself was writing about Fanny, and to supplement this very short sketch I have asked her to provide me with a bibliography. Both Fanny and her daughter had written fascinating books about Butler's Island, which lies to the south of Ossabaw on the Florida frontier.

Butler's Island, before the Butlers settled there, must have been how Ossabaw is today, for Ossabaw, when the slaves were liberated, had reverted to primitive wilderness. It is vast and traversed by a hundred miles of rough road, across which the wild boars stray, as well as deer, raccoons, wild cattle, ponies and donkeys. In the summer you may meet, as you stroll through the live oak forests, three different kinds of poisonous snake, rattle, coral and moccasin, but in the winter they and the thousand alligators mind their own business invisibly. But I am not writing about Ossabaw, so I will just say that the colony works admirably.

When Kathie and I decided to visit Butler's Island, I anticipated something as luxuriant and romantic as Ossabaw, but it lies close to the once fashionable town of Darien and is joined by two causeways across the river Altamaha, which surrounds it, to the mainland. It is a featureless, treeless, grassy swamp, traversed by a highway, and all that is left of Pierce Butler's plantation is a few stumps of brick buildings and a factory chimney clothed in American ivy three feet thick so that it looks like a vast and exotic cylindrical tree. Two metal shields have been erected there to commemorate both Fanny and her daughter Frances.

When a kind, good, honourable, conventional human marries a genius, a terrible risk has been taken. Pierce Butler, who was one of the Butlers of Ballintemple in Co. Carlow (his descendent is one of our Society's vice chairmen), joyously took this risk. He saw the fascinating Fanny on her tour around America and Canada and, following her from city to city, he begged her to be his bride. He was charming, rich, well bred and cultivated, and in the end she agreed. It never occurred to him that it was important to tell her that he was a slave owner and that much of his wealth came from the rice plantation on Butler's Island. When at last she leant this, it filled her with horror, for, as she said, 'I am prejudiced against slavery, for I am an Englishwoman in whom absence of prejudice would be disgraceful.'

Probably Pierce thought such a charming and versatile lady would adjust herself easily to his rich and fashionable Philadelphia friends. But it was not to be so. They thought he had made a *mésalliance* and the Quaker ladies deplored her connection with the stage. Fanny found them all dull and dowdy beyond belief; the daughter of Charles Kemble of Covent Garden, the niece of Mrs Siddons, she had associated with all the leading figures in London intellectual society. In all America she could only find a handful of kindred souls. One of these was Dr Channing, the celebrated Unitarian divine and abolitionist. (One of her biographers says that Pierce himself was a Unitarian but I have not been able to verify this.) These high-principled New England acquaintances filled her with shame, when she found that her husband's affluence was based upon slavery, 'that grievous sin against humanity'. She insisted on going with her husband to Butler's Island. He warned her of the long arduous journey and squalid accommodation she would find on the island, for they would have to share a home with the overseer. But Fanny was as courageous as she was passionate and she saw it as her duty to go. From the start she hated all she saw, even what strikes us now as unique and delightful in the Georgian landscape; the great grey beards of the Spanish moss intertwined with jessamine, which drape the rugged forests of live oak, she saw as 'mourning veils, the most funereal spectacle in all the vegetable kingdom'. Pierce hoped she would make friends with the ladies of Darien, then a prosperous little town with many rich and beautiful plantation houses around it. Those were the great days of the Southern belle and chivalrous Southern gentlemen of whom so many novelists have written, but Fanny considered them a barbarous aristocracy: 'I would rather die a thousand times than lead the lives of these planters' wives and their daughters. Their vapid existence would deaden my intelligence.'

The only people who interested her were the Negroes on Butler's Island. She became their great confidant and what they told her she wrote down in her journal, which later on, as she informed Pierce, she intended to publish. Pierce pleaded with her to do nothing of the kind. They loved each other and their two daughters and Fanny felt herself torn apart between her conscience and her affections. She postponed the publication of her journals, except in a much-modified form, but the tension between the husband and the wife became increasingly acute and ultimately Fanny deserted her husband and 'this dreadful America' and returned to Europe. Pierce was given custody of the two girls.

Back home again Fanny was fêted wherever she went, but she could not forget the human suffering she had seen on Butler's Island and slowly her book took shape. After its publication she was blamed for the fact that Britain, which had been friendly to the Southern States in the Civil War, abruptly turned against them. But though the book is extremely well written with deep and sincere feeling, the accusation is inaccurate; it was not published till the defeat of the Confederate Army was assured.

The Journal of a Residence in Georgia caused an immediate sensation in England and brought her a multitude of enemies in the USA. Some said she was a pathological liar, others that she had been listening to a pack of yarns which the slaves, imposing on her English innocence, had spun for her. One of her close friends wrote: 'How I weep that a heart so warm and true as hers should be warped by a brain so weak!'

In fact there was nothing wrong with Fanny's brain; her writing is witty and forcible, her arguments cogent, but she was making one generation shoulder the guilt of many centuries. I do not doubt that the conditions in the slave hospital were as appalling as she describes and she did a little to alleviate them. When Joe was sold to a plantation in Alabama and his young wife, Psyche, was beside herself with distress, she implored Mr – (that is how Pierce is described in the journal) 'for his soul's sake not to commit so great a cruelty'. She discovered later that Pierce, while refusing to acknowledge her right to interfere in a business matter, secretly cancelled the sale.

As slave-owners go, Pierce seems to have been a good man; Dr Holmes of Darien, whom Fanny respected, said he was 'humane and indulgent almost to a fault', and in a museum at Savannah there is an engraved silver mug that Pierce presented to his head slave in testimony to the courage he had shown during a hurricane, when the other slaves had lost their heads. Fanny was judging him by those high standards by which she judged herself and which brought her the friendship and esteem of men like Browning and Thackery, Emerson and Walter Scott. Mrs Harriet Beecher Stowe said she would make six clever women and there would be a remnant.

She must have been a magical person for, despite sharp disagreement about the issue of slavery with her daughter, Frances, they remained devoted to each other. After the Civil War had ended, Frances had gone down with her father to Butler's Island to save what could be saved of the rice and cotton plantations. Even before the Civil War, Pierce had suffered a disastrous blow. The cotton empire was failing and Pierce had to sell five hundred slaves in 1858. When he and Frances came back in 1866, they were faced with an almost impossible task of which she wrote a record in her book, *Ten years in Georgia*. Without Fanny's brilliance, she had courage, endurance, sincerity, and her book is still very readable.

Fanny had been disgusted by the way in which she and Pierce had been welcomed with cries and tears by the Negroes on their first arrival, 'as though they were descending divinities'. But maybe this head-turning experience was more damaging to the mostly commonplace planters than it was to the Negroes. They seem to have liked Pierce better than the other planters for many of them when liberated returned to the island. The Negroes had kept the Butlers' furniture safe during the war and they arrived with presents of eggs and chickens when Frances and her father returned after it was over. Frances had shaken hands with over four hundred Negroes after church service and 'We be yours as long as you live', they had told her. She hired a Negro teacher for them from Philadelphia and, encountering boundless difficulties, she showed the same heroism, the same independence of spirit that her less ordinary mother had shown fighting a different cause.

She found that the freed Negroes were 'affectionate, trustworthy, honest but lazy'. They were quite happy not to work, for they were content to live on corn, sweet potatoes, fish and game. The seven hundred Negroes of Butler's Island shrank to three hundred and then to fifty, and she even considered employing Chinese labour. The Civil War had demoralized everything and everybody. She slept with a loaded pistol beside her bed, the overseer was useless and none could be trusted. A drunken Yankee soldier had stolen a silver mug and presented it to a neighbour. Is that possibly how the head slave's mug comes to be in the Savannah museum?

In 1892 a tornado swept across the island, rooted up the rice crop and tore down the chimneys of the lime kiln. And that was the end of the Butlers. Or was it? Knowing how freed slaves sometimes took the names of their employers, I looked in the telephone book at Darien and found that there were a dozen Butlers there, all of them black. I remembered how Fanny had complained that the planters scorned and insulted the Negroes and yet took them as concubines. Possibly some of these black Butlers are our kinsmen.

In this very difficult period, the three Butlers acted as their consciences dictated. A conflict of conscience can be a source of immeasurable tragedy, and in their different ways they shouldered the guilt of generations. When she was old Fanny wrote: 'Forgive me, my dearest dear Pierce, that I have bitterly cursed your existence.'

[1973/74]

31

THE BUTLERS OF PRIESTOWN

Lately an old cousin, Geraldine Butler, died at Priestown, a small house in Co. Meath that was part of the Dunboyne estate when in 1320 Sir Thomas Le Botiller, Knt, third son of Theobald, fourth chief Butler of Ireland, married Synolda Le Petit, heiress to the barony of Dunboyne.

Geraldine's heir, Chris Pitman, a member of our Society, acquired a bundle of family papers dating back to 1704 and, with the help of Sir John Ainsworth and the Hon. James Jocelyn, who reduced them to order, summarized and Xeroxed them, he has made possible a consecutive history of a junior branch of the Dunboyne Butlers.

Ours is a very unusual family, producing in several centuries three or four members who were above the average in talent or merit, three or four who were below; but time, aided by family piety and a dry, mouse-proof box-room, can make even the dullest of us interesting. Time lends enchantment to lawsuits, to carpenter's bills ('I promise to make James Butler Esqre a bottle-rack as compleat as Mr Steele's bottle-rack, as witness my hand. Richard Branan. Novem. 1757') and to Theobald Butler's undertaking, 1735, to pay his workman, Mikile Pettit, (a relation?) £3 a year, to squabbles about wills, property and marriage settlements. Where there is no literary talent, personal letters are torn up and nothing is left to show that our forebears were not as greedy, snobby and litigious as the surviving remnants suggest. Yet it is on such meagre records that we mostly build our identities and we must cherish them, for men, like plants, draw strength from their roots, no matter what the soil in which they grow.

Theobald Butler, the first to live at Priestown, followed the trend of the times. On 11 June 1704, the rector and two church-wardens of Shandon Church, Cork, testified that he 'had received the Sacraments of the Lord's Supper, according to the usage of the Established Church'. An Ensign in the Earl of Inchiquin's reg-iment, he collected other certificates from Lord Inchiquin him-self, from the second Duke of Ormonde, the Bishop of Ossory and many more. They all concurred in saying the he was the great-grandson of the second Baron Dunboyne and Lady Mar-garet O'Brien, his wife, that he was the only Protestant heir of a considerable inheritance forfeited in 1641 and that his family had suffered greatly 'in the late unnatural Rebellion'. The certificates were sent off to Queen Anne.

There is no evidence that Theobald or his father used their Protestantism against the Dunboynes.* He only wished to secure some annuity such as his father, the rector of Glenbeigh, Co. Kerry, had received, or, in view of his eight years of military service, a commission in Portugal. It is not clear if he got his set-tlement, but, after the death of his wife, Maria O'Hara, he married the daughter of a rich Dublin publican, Sir Nathaniel Whitwell, Lord Mayor of Dublin, and bought the property of Waterville, Co. Kerry, with its famous Butler salmon pool, which only lately passed to Mr Mulcahy of Quigley Magnesite.

Our forebears had the usual three obsessions, family, property, religion, in that order, and the usual skill in twisting the third into the service of the first and second. They were candid about it and used to quote that famous old Mrs Butler, who refused to restore certain lands to the Church, saying: 'Twere better that one old woman should burn for eternity than that the Butlers should lose their property.' But few men can have used religion so grandly in the service of their family, as the 12th/22nd Baron Dunboyne, that celebrated Bishop of Cork**, who to the horror of the Pope became a Protestant in order to marry his cousin, Maria Butler of Wilford, and thus to secure the continuity of an ancient Catholic line and prevent it falling into the hands of his distant Protestant cousins.

---

* The Dunboynes had remained Catholic, though the Duke of Ormonde, when he recovered their estates for them, had proposed to bring up the thirteen-year-old heir a Protestant and to arrange a suitable marriage for him with a Protestant Miss Legge.
** The Bishop was 12th Baron by patent and 22nd by summons.

He was resolved that his son would be brought up a Catholic, but there was no son, so deeply penitent, he recanted a second time. Against the advice of Archbishop Troy, he left Dunboyne Castle and the estate to the Church, so that of all the Meath property that the Dunboynes had held for nearly six centuries, only Priestown remained in Butler hands.

Lord Dunboyne's failure to propagate caused a flutter among all the distant and despised Protestant cousins, who traced their descent, like Theobald of Priestown, to James, 2nd/12th baron. Till I read the Priestown papers I did not know that our great-grandfather, Dr Butler, in a casual way, and his eldest son, James, with intense concentration, had for some forty years tried to dislodge the 13th/23rd baron, the ancestor of our genealogical advisor. James was urged on by his wife Isabella (Rothwell) who was more intelligent and ambitious than he and who had good social connections. The Rothwells were a wealthy and influential Williamite family, whose great house Rockfield, near Kells, was only sold by them in 1967. She was James' first cousin for the Rothwells had intermarried four times with the much poorer Butlers of Priestown. She persuaded Lord Headfort, her neighbour in Meath, to champion her cause. He paid the solicitor's bills and visited them in Germany.

For James, a Church of Ireland clergyman, impoverished by the Tithe War, unable to make a living out of Priestown, handed it over to his son, Thomas, and became Anglican chaplain at Bad Homburg in Hesse. The brief Homburg season had two peaks, a party given by the Landgrave to the Kurort guests and a party the guests gave to the Landgrave. When the fashionable crowds had left and the pews had emptied, Isabella beguiled the winter evenings poring over family papers and gathering evidence for her alluring theory that a certain Miss Dobbyn of Waterford had never properly married Edward of Clare. If she could only prove this, Miss Dobbyn's children would be bastardized and James and she … She wrote many letters to Waterford, Dublin, and London, but Sir Bernard Burke was discouraging and when another claimant, William O'Brien Butler, failed expensively before the House of Lords in 1860, James and Isabella gave up.

They were in Homburg in the exciting days of the 1848 Revolution in Germany but Isabella's comments are class-bound and uninteresting. When seven armed republicans were shot after drumhead court-martial in Frankfurt, she rejoiced and wrote to Thomas: 'If the same system was adopted in Ireland, Ireland would soon be quiet.'

All the sparkle and sensibility in our family letters – and there is much of it that I have no space for here – come through the family friendship with the Edgeworths and the marriage of James' brother, Richard, to Maria's half-sister Harriet. Maria and her father, the inventor, philanthropist, educationist, had made Edgeworthstown House in Longford a place of pilgrimage for the visiting scholar, almost as Maria's friend-enemy Mme de Stael had made Coppet and Tolstoy made Yasnaya Polyana. When the Edgeworths or their multitudinous relations take up the pen, ideas, notions, vivid images and descriptions light up the page like fireworks but Richard and Harriet had no children and on their deaths the letters revert back to the normal ecclesiastical-cum-agricultural, intermittently snobbish patter.

Maria loved Richard, as witness her ecstatic letters about the engagement to Mme de Stael's son, Auguste, and to Etienne Dumont, in Switzerland. So did all the Edgeworths.

Here is a short extract from a long account of a visit to our great-grandfather at Burnchurch Glebe near Bennettsbridge in June 1819. It was written to Sophie Edgeworth by her aunt Pamela Beaufort, an Irish archaeologist, and I owe it to an Edgeworth descendant, Christina Colvin, of Oxford. Our great-grandfather was at that time Vicar of Trim, Co. Meath, as well as rector of Burnchurch, Co. Kilkenny, but resolved on handing over Trim to his son Richard. James had already married Isabella but Richard had not yet married Harriet.

'… We soon sat down to cakes and tea. Then Mr Js Butler brought down his wife under his arm (Miss I. Rothwell, you know), … she is a pleasing amiable woman with a pretty person, a Rothwell face and red hair, her husband is a mixture of a crow and a Rothwell' (our great-grandmother was Martha Rothwell), *'and surprisingly ugly, but that is no mat as they are as fond as Turtles and coo shockingly and why an accomplished woman like she should like such an animal as he, heaven and herself can only guess, not I. Had she liked the second Richard she would have done very well. He is a dark plain man with a very agreeable countenance and charming eyes, which are very expressive and speak what is passing in his mind. He has a great deal of conversation and is very unaffected and modest. Thomas is very lively, his black eyes always dancing. He was in Canada and America wars. He is very good-natured and half-mad learning to fish. Whitwell is a handsome young man, good-natured and lively, very fond of*

his sister, and when he is not playing with the dogs, is pleasant. He is a half-pay officer of the Guards and was at Waterloo and says that all that story of the Duke saying "Up Guards and at 'em!" is an invention.'

The rest of the long letter with its accounts of visits paid to houses that are now ruined and families that are now extinct or emigrated, and to service at our great-grandfather's now empty and crumbling church of Burnchurch, would only be of interest to Kilkenny people. But here is a letter from Harriet Butler at Edgeworthstown to her brother, Sneyd Edgeworth, which is historically informative, for Kilkenny was at the centre of the Tithe agitation that swept Ireland some twenty years after the Union. There was a famous battle at Carrickshock in south Kilkenny at which twelve policemen were killed and the process-server (name of Butler) put to flight. Our great-grandfather's proctor, Drohan, was murdered near Bennettsbridge and, as Harriet shows, he and his family were molested.*

Edgeworthstown, 3 Jan. 1831.

'... I dare say you will see in the papers that there have been anti-tythe mobs in Kilkenny. News was brought to Dr Butler last Thursday that a mob would come to Burnchurch next day and force him to reduce his tythes. On Friday the Doctor and three of his sons were all armed and had plenty of powder and balls prepared and all ready for a siege. About 12 o'clock horns were heard at a distance and, as they looked from the upper windows, the whole country seemed alive with people pouring towards them. Mrs and Miss Butler stood at an open window on the second storey to show that they were not intimidated. As the people rushed to the number of 2000 a great number were filling the whole avenue from the gate; they all yelled in the most savage manner waving green flags and heavy bludgeons, the only arms they had. Dr Butler spoke to them from a window saying that he could not alter the laws nor could they and that as long as it was lawful for him to receive tythes he should expect them to pay them but that, if there was anybody, who had been charged too high, let him stand forward and he would do him justice – no one spoke but one man, who was not in Dr Butler's parish, and among the whole number, nearly 2000, were but four men paying tythes to him! A man then lifted up his stick and shook it in defiance at Miss Butler as she stood in the window and she with the greatest presence of mind kissed her hand to him in return. This delighted him and his companions, who all kissed

* Daniel O'Connell wrote to the people of Kilkenny that their conduct could only injure the cause of Repeal and in his campaign for the abolition of tithes, he asked them to vote for his candidate – Col. Butler!

*their hands too and they departed perfectly quietly without having done them
the least harm – satisfied with having threated and convinced that they wouldn't
succeed with Dr Butler.'*

And yet the Tithe War made life very difficult for the Protestant
clergy. Our great-grandfather had to leave Ireland for three years,
two of his three clergy sons left forever. In a letter to the Chief
Secretary, E.G. Stanley, later Lord Derby, on behalf of himself and
his fellow clergy, he wrote how he had to sell his horses and carriage and dismiss all his servants and labourers, how there was
no money to pay the proxies of his four curates or the school-
teacher, and how other clergy were in like case. The tithe system
was of course indefensible, though it had and still has its parallels
in many countries and faiths, but he was notably lax in collecting
from those who could not afford them. As a young man he had
paid a curate to replace him and had gone to Edinburgh to take
a degree in medicine so that he could give his medical services
free to his neighbours. He was a patron of the very enlightened
Merino Cloth Factory nearby, which was run largely on Robert
Owen principles and wove the coronation robes for George IV.
It may have been because of this that in 1820 he was given the
Freedom of Kilkenny.

Our great-grandfather's brother, General James Butler, was
Governor of Sandhurst and on the death of his son, General James
Arthur Butler, in 1881, the declining fortunes of Priestown were
revived by a large legacy to James and Isabella's son Thomas. My
grandfather, John Butler, was left the silver urn that William IV
and Mrs Jordan had given to the Governor for his care of their
two sons, cadets at Sandhurst. It is inscribed with the Royal arms
and the arms of Dunboyne. Our great-uncle Richard is the only
one of our family who seems to speak to our generation as well
as to his own. He had left Oxford at his father's urgent request
to take over the parish of Trim and remained there till his death
forty-three years later. He was the pattern of the country scholar
and the faithful pastor. His Balliol friends urged him to accept
a prosperous parish in Sussex and later Lord Carlisle, the Lord
Lieutenant, asked him to be his chaplain. The first was a great
temptation for, except at Edgeworthstown, he had few congenial
companions. Yet he wrote: 'Trim is my home and Trim church-
yard will be my burial ground.'

He succeeded in getting through his tithe problem better than his father had done. Under the Goulburn Act he had in 1823 made a 'composition for his tithes'. Which meant that the burden of them progressively shifted from the shoulders of the tenant farmer to the landlord, who was usually a Protestant. In Trim parish only one of the landlords lived on his estate and the absentees bitterly resented an arrangement that saved the clergyman his income at their expense. In Co. Kilkenny the gentry held aloof when the campaign was mounted against the clergy, but in Trim there was peace.

Richard was not ecumenical in the modern sense but he surpassed most modern ecumenists in his neighbourliness, dining often with his friend, the parish priest, and talking freely on contentious matters with his Catholic neighbours; he even addressed to them two circular letters, explaining with affection his own unpopular views. At his own expense he made a free day-school where Protestant and Catholic could be educated together. He often taught there himself and paid a permanent teacher.

As a scholar he expresses himself most freely to his old Balliol friend, Cosmo Innes, a Scottish medievalist and Professor of History at Edinburgh. He tells him of his part in the founding of the Irish Archaeological Society, for which he edited in 1849 *The Chronicles of Clyn*, the first warden of a Franciscan monastery, which James, Earl of Ormonde, had founded in 1336. He also edited the *Annals of James Grace*, a Kilkenny monk of the sixteenth century. He was one of those rare scholars who see knowledge as valueless unless it is a gateway to wisdom. To him it was a social not an intellectual disaster that his neighbours knew nothing and cared nothing for the history of their past, Irish, Norman, Anglo-Irish. 'Just as there is no bridge between the different ranks of society, so there is no bridge between the present and the past. The ignorant present is all that we have.'

Because of this, he published some of his books first in Trim, and his *History of Trim* has not yet been superseded. In Trim also he printed his *Annals of Ireland*, a translation from the Latin of Charles O'Connor of Belanagare with additions from other sources. It was a 'seminal' book, for it is clear from his preface that he hoped it would soon be superseded by John O'Donovan, which in fact it was.

Time has not diminished the perceptiveness of his preface and letters. The Anglo-Norman annals were mostly what he calls 'the ashes of history'; dreary catalogues of names and facts. Yet he claims that each dry entry was for the monks resonant with echoes, passed orally from generation to generation around the close network of affiliated monasteries. The entries were mere 'landmarks and boundary stones', within which lay 'fields of flowers and, *hominumque bovumque labores'*, which the flood of oblivion had covered. He regretted the poverty of his own imagination and wished that Ireland had its Walter Scott to rekindle those dead ashes. When Scott came to Edgeworthstown in 1825, Richard was there before breakfast and spent the day with him driving to visit the Droppings of Lough Gownagh and talking about the de Lacys, who built Trim Castle and figure in *The Betrothed*, which Scott was writing at the time.

Richard, then Dean of Clonmacnois (this title carried with it no duties or stipends but was a recognition of his services to archaeology), took another long journey with Harriet and Maria in 1836 to visit the Moores of Moore Hall in Mayo and there had long discussions with George Moore, the Catholic historian. To quote Joseph Hone's *The Moores of Moore Hall*:

The Dean had always sought the society of open-minded Catholics and these conversations recalled to him the theory he had held in his youth that a reformation, not from nor in but of the Roman Catholic Church in Ireland, might be possible. The men of sense and enlightened understanding among them, like his host at Moore Hall, would be willing to slip away from Roman peculiarities and virtually to be Protestants, although still retaining the name of Roman Catholic. They deplored together the strange fashion that had grown up since their youth of baiting all parties into consistency by ever recurring to first principles and rejecting compromise and common sense.

In a letter to Cosmo Innes, Richard had noted both the good and the evil consequences of what he called 'the Roman Reformation' of the eleventh century that Saint Malachy had brought about in Ireland. It had bound the easy-going Church to the disciplinary rigours that the Normans had applied in their own interests. It was from them that the tithe system stemmed and had been ruthlessly imposed on the recalcitrant. Though Richard was anti-tithe, he refuted the claim of a Dublin scholar that tithes under the Catholic Church had been voluntary. On the contrary he showed that after forty days the defaulter was excommunicated by the Civil Courts and lodged in gaol. And indeed the Anglo-Norman hierarchy discriminated as fiercely against the

Irish as the Protestants were later to do. The monastic annals, which he edited, stress above all the campaigns, floreats and obits of Butlers, de Burghs, de Lacys, Fitzgeralds.

He was no great partisan of the Butlers, believing that, if the Desmonds with their numerous and devoted Irish following had succeeded in their war against the English, Normans and Irish would have fused into one people. Possibly he would have seen the Butler victory over the Fitzgeralds at Affane as a set-back to Irish unity.

He was fascinated by the pre-Norman Irish traditions, which were slighted in all the Anglo-Norman chronicles. In his preface to *Clyn*, he refuses to believe as Clyn did that 'the strange and portentous legends' of the early Irish had no factual foundation. He thought they were the sober historical narratives of one people, interpreted by their successors, whose language and habits were different. We must look at them as 'the hieroglyphic records of forgotten but substantial history'.

An idea like this, obvious as it may seem, germinates best in the free air outside the academic forcing-house. Yet to formulate it in 1849 without access to metropolitan libraries was difficult. He carried it no further. Independently I have argued it in *Ten Thousand Saints* (1972), which I have printed in Kilkenny as he did in Trim. [The 2nd edition (Lilliput, 2011) was dedicated to Richard.]

Except for readers of Clyn and Grace and Dowling, or his biography by Harriet, the traces of his subtle mind have been mostly effaced by the heavier footprints of those who followed him. Yet till quite recently, when nature's timetable was disturbed by science, he was remembered annually in *The Irish Times* by some bird-watcher or botanist. He was the Gilbert White of the Boyne valley. He chronicled the lifespan of everything that flew or swam or grazed or flowered in his garden or the surrounding fields. He made a 32-year calendar from which you can observe in which year the corncrake arrived earliest, in which year latest, what happened to the herons when the heronry at Edgeworthstown was blown down after the great storm of 1839, or to the workmen who ate oatmeal at Moymet and Kildalkey in 1853.

The reformation within the Church of Rome, which Richard hoped for, is happening but there are few Irish Protestants now left, who are capable of contributing to a new Irish Christianity by advancing 'compromise and common sense' against 'first principles'. They have mostly gone with the corncrakes and the herons. Despite all the burnt houses of the twenties, I would not attribute their final migration to Irish Catholic or nationalist hostility but to those 'dividend loyalties', to which Shelia Leahy has earlier referred ['The Duke and The Poets', *Journal of the Butler Society*, Vol. I, No. 5]. The pull of England and the empire was so powerful that only the enterprising or those with strong deep roots could resist it. When Richard first came to Trim he had six hundred parishioners, but within a dozen years thirty had emigrated to Canada. Now there are eighty-five, and the churches where he had friendly colleagues have mostly closed or been amalgamated. The huge and hospitable episcopal palace of Ardbraccan has long ago been sold and there is a rumour that the whole diocese of Meath will lose its bishop and be joined to others. The Anglo-Irish who survive have done little to preserve a splendid inheritance. What is left of Edgeworthstown House and Trim rectory and its well-loved garden is almost unrecognizable. 'The ignorant present is all that we have.'

Richard saw the shape of the future clearly. Writing to Innes about an Edgeworth nephew in India, he said: 'India has been brought too near to us. The world has shrunk in our time and has lost its dignity. National distinctions are fading away and sectarian distinctions are growing stronger: the world will be divided not into peoples but into parties, a much worse division.'

I have probably falsified this family record by concentrating too much on Richard of Trim. He was unusual but probably had his too-usual moments, ignored by his devoted widow-biographer. To adjust the balance here are two awful family letters and an awful story. All three illustrate the tension of divided loyalties.

Our great-grandfather, to his son, Whitwell: Burnchurch Glebe, Bennetts-bridge, 4 March 1819:

You stupid fellow, the only thing you had to be proud of you seem to glory in having deprived yourself of. You are no longer an officer in the Guards. What are you? An idler so ignorant that you are not fit for any profession ... if you had the spirit of a gentleman, you would have lived on potatoes and salt sooner than sell your commission. You should have been a shopkeeper... I do not feel pleasure in the prospect of your visit.*

---

* I owe this to Whitwell's granddaughter, Synolda French, who preserved a large collection of family papers that I have been able to use.

Isabella, perhaps as a way of saying 'Don't mind him!', scrawled in the margin an affectionate message about handkerchiefs for James and the resetting of her engagement ring. A few years later we find Whitwell the owner of a 130-acre farm at Cooltrand near his father at Bennettsbridge. He came back to Ireland and never left.

And here is a letter of 1830 from the Rev. Edward at Cheltenham to his brother the Rev. James (the two who left Ireland because of the Tithe War):

It is very probable that I shall form a connection with an old and highly respectable English family... The Lady is by birth a perfect gentlewoman. Her eldest brother has two country seats, a house in town and £20,000 a year. Such a connexion can be no disadvantage to any of my family... Miss Skrine is not handsome and has no fortune but she is particularly gentlewomanly.'

And here is a story my father told me about his uncle Tom of the dancing black eyes. Our great-grandmother (Martha Rothwell) was standing on the porch at Burnchurch Glebe, when she saw a young woman in a shawl coming up the avenue carrying a baby.

'I've nothing for you, my good woman,' she said, when the girl was in hearing.

'That's as may be ma'am,' said the girl, 'but I've something for you.' She put the baby on the doorstep and saying: 'That's your son Tom's,' she retreated down the avenue.

The lessons of history, national and domestic, are not often easy to read, but one is self-evident. If you give only half your mind to the country of your birth, you will not necessarily be thrown out of it, but you will find less and less reason for staying there. Tom died in 1848, captain in the 79th Highlanders, *'sine prole'* is the glib, necessary lie of the family genealogist.

Maybe some generations hence the extended family, people loosely linked by ties of blood or friendship, will take the place of the small self-contained family unit, in which suffocating loves and jealousies so easily flourish. The new family would not be concentrated in one place or committed to one set of loyalties and prejudices. There would be room in it for Tom's baby and much else.

[1973/74]

32

FOREWORDS

I

It was Lord Dunboyne and George Butler of Templeogue, and myself, who started the Butler Society fourteen years ago. We were three very different people. Lord Dunboyne is a prince of genealogists and George Butler had an unparalleled knowledge of Butler history. As for myself, since I was born and lived most of my life in Kilkenny, it is natural for me to see this ancient city as the centre of our Society. George Butler is now dead and I am hoping that someone more vigorous than myself may be found to take over the Society and its *Journal*. One or two possibilities have presented themselves. At all costs we must keep things going. The Society has given pleasure and interest to many and, thanks to Bob Harrison and others, our membership is rapidly increasing. Everything promises well for our Rally at Cambridge and Kilkenny.

The Butlers are primarily an Anglo-Irish family and the Anglo-Irish, as such, are now in full retreat. Lately, Dr Lyons, the Provost of Trinity, said that today in Ireland four cultures are in conflict; the Anglo-American, the Gaelic culture in its modern form, the almost extinct Anglo-Irish culture of the old Ascendancy and the Ulster Protestant culture. The first culture is the most recent and, in Dr Lyons' eyes, the most dangerous of the four, for 'it might extinguish what remains of our local and regional identity'.

All this is true, yet Ireland is a lovely place to live; we are more prosperous, better educated, fed and housed than we used to be. We are less class bound, creed bound and inhibited, and we are most of us personally unaffected by the murder and arson in the North of which we read every morning and see on TV every night. Yet almost every day in the Republic a bank or a post office is robbed and in 1978 over two million pounds were stolen. We presume it is stolen by 'idealists' and spent on bombs for forcing the Ulster Protestants to join the Republic. And often we ask ourselves how so intelligent and warm-hearted a people can choose such primitive and stupid ideals?

History explains a little. For eight centuries Ireland was held by England as firmly as the Czechs, Croats, Poles, Letts and many others were held by their German, Russian and Austrian masters. Then gradually it became clear all over Europe that imperialism, even when the ruthless days of oppression were over, was failing to bring contentment. The magnetism of Berlin, St Petersburg, Vienna, London, had drawn away from the smaller peoples the intelligent and the enterprising, and richly rewarded them. The Czechs had manned the Austro-Hungarian bureaucracy, the Scots and Irish thrived in England more than at home, and those left behind for the most part got prosperity and improved government. But these small peoples were proud and undoubtedly there was 'impoverishment of spirit'. Loyalty to an empire or dynasty is a feeble substitute for the love and commitment we should feel for our native land. Disengagement had to come, but the disentangling of loyalties is as delicate an operation as a heart transplant. Through the centuries ruler and ruled had grown into each other and it was hard to tear them apart after years of ligaments. After forty-four years of European peace a world war, rising out of the tensions between Austro-Hungary and her Slav subjects, made violence appear to be the road to freedom and in every case the knots that bound the subject peoples were not unravelled but cut with a knife. A knife once grasped is seldom dropped.

Newly independent peoples are usually racists and not nationalists and see no way of living in equality with those who formerly ruled them. The Irish fared better than the Czechs, Poles, southern Slavs, who all now suffer a worse tyranny than that from which they were liberated. This may have been because the idea of an Irish nation with a distinctive culture of its own, woven from many different racial strands, was in the first place an Anglo-Irish one. In the late eighteenth century, inspired by the revolt in the American colonies, Grattan and Flood and Charlemont sowed the seed of cultural freedom and for eighteen years were allowed by England to tend it. Then came the '98 and the Union and after that the gradual weakening of the Anglo-Irish, tempted by imperial opportunities to England and harried by land leaguers and the like in Ireland.

Yet the idea of Irish cultural unity is hard to kill and, as before, it was among the Anglo-Irish that it revived. In the mid-century there was Thomas Davis and the Young Irelanders, at its end there were Standish O'Grady and Douglas Hyde. In reaction to imperialism these men favoured the cult of the regional, the Gaelic, the heroic. They wished to enrich what was Anglo-Irish, not to replace it. This led on the one hand to the Irish Literary Revival, on the other to the political and racist Sinn Féin and the 1916 rebellion. After that came civil war and terrorism and a further withdrawal of the Anglo-Irish, among whom nationalism was born and without whom it was bound to die. Sinn Féin Ireland, the second child of the Gaelic revival, is now as dead as the Anglo-Irish Ascendancy and there is nothing but Anglo-American culture to unite us.

Ireland today is a mutilated nation, which needs the good will of all its absent children. It is here that the Butler Society and other family societies can play their parts. We value the sense of continuity and belonging; family history and local history are the bricks from which the many-facetted Irish identity must be rebuilt. But what is the good of denying that since the twelfth century Irish history and culture has been shaped by successive waves of immigrants from England who imposed for 400 years, not always under duress, an English form of Catholicism, for 300 years an English form of Protestantism? The traces of these invaders are scattered over the whole land – abbeys, castles, streets and squares, country mansions and the work of generations of artists, architects and craftsmen. What else, in fact, have we but lovely and mysterious remnants of the Gaelic and megalithic centuries. But these are relatively scanty and they, too, have little relevance to Anglo-American Ireland, which is levelling everything that stands in the way of 'progress'.

In our last issue I mentioned the destruction for agricultural purposes of mottes and bailies, which date from the first coming of the Normans. In Co. Kilkenny we lost the fine motte of Knocktopher, which bore on its top traces of the castle of the second Earl of Ormonde and of Sir James Butler, father of the eighth Earl. I recently learnt that at the same time the large motte of Tybroughney, also in Co. Kilkenny, attributed to King John, 24 foot high by 22 yards wide at the top, was also destroyed. It was yielded, with the adjoining castle, to Cromwell by the Mountgarrets in 1653, but Cromwell, having no bulldozers, had spared them. When, to broaden the roads for our new EEC traffic roadside trees are torn up and eighteenth-century bridges are disfigured, the concern felt by the locals has little metropolitan backing. Yet when the historic pattern of our town and villages is destroyed, we become a country without a past or any claim to a distinctive culture of our own.

I am sorry that so few Anglo-Irish émigrés interest themselves now in what is happening in the land of their fathers. Recently I read the entertaining memoirs of Lord Drogheda, which may explain some of this indifference. His family, the Moores, have been in Ireland since Elizabethan times but he sold his family home, Moore Abbey, to a convent without regret and led a useful active life in England as journalist and Chairman of Covent Garden. 'However shameful', he writes 'the story of English rule, nothing can condone the atrocities committed by the IRA and the Provisionals, which the Irish government seems powerless to prevent. It would have been impossible for me to become in any way identified with the country.'

But can one really dissociate oneself from one's country? It is 150 years since Maria Edgeworth in *The Absentee* chastized the landlord who left his Irish estate to an agent and went to London. Absentee landlords are no longer a problem and the absentee intellectual is more like a fact of nature than a problem. It is useless scolding him for going where his talents are valued and not treated to jealous disparagement. So every year the Anglo-Irish (I am not talking about the Anglo-American) make less and less acknowledged impact on what is happening here. They were once the mediators between England and Ireland and might have remained so but opportunity after opportunity was squandered. Now it is clear that Tom Broadbent and Tim Haffigan would much prefer to bypass the hereditary mediators and to conduct their own negotiations. Will the results be as sad and foolish as Shaw anticipated? All this being so, one can still ask the old questions. Can one inherit an Irish title and an Irish home and have Irish forebears without inheriting also certain obligations? It is no doubt common sense to shed those that are no longer practicable, but in Lord Drogheda's case would not regret be more proper than self-congratulation?

A word about archives. We shall make little progress till some younger enthusiast, who sees our desperate need and is not merely looking for a job, throws all his weight against a half-open door. The Muniment Room in Kilkenny Castle was for centuries well-cared for and the second Marquess, a student himself, refused access to no serious scholar. Today, after nearly sixty years of self-government, we have nothing at all nor any consciousness of the need. Recently in another large Irish town the City Museum was closed to make way for a Reference Library and a collection of family and other papers that it contained, was scattered or withdrawn by their owners. A disused Protestant church, which had been given to the Corporation and might have taken the place of the museum, was used for a store.

A reference library is useful enough but no substitute for a repository of local history, which is the story of our forebears, our kinsmen, our neighbours, and, by no very long stretch, of ourselves. It has less to do with 'knowledge' or 'education', moveable and marketable commodities, than with a kind of regional dedication, which has become very rare. In praise of it James Graves chose a quotation from Camden as the motto of the famous old Kilkenny Archaeological Society that he founded in 1848.

If any there be, who are desirous to be strangers in their owne soile and forrainers in their owne citie, for such I have not written these lines nor taken these paines.

We lose members every year through death and it saddens me that the names of the many, whose help we have valued, must go unrecorded. We have lost our Spanish Vice-President, José Maria Butler Orbeta. We have lost Doreen Archer Houblon, at whose Kilmurry house the Butler Society has often been entertained. She inherited Kilmurry, once the home of Charles Kendall Bushe (1767-1843), from Butlers of the Mountgarret family. She herself was a granddaughter of the Earl of Carrick. Like José Maria, she was a remarkable person. A noted horsewoman, she was home-loving and dedicated to organic farming. She was self-effacing and few knew that she gave regular horse-riding lessons to Queen Elizabeth II.

I give on another page the dates and details of the Cambridge and Kilkenny Rallies and we hope that, at one or the other, we may most of us meet again.

[1978/79]

1988 was Rally Year again and it was largely due to my niece, Melo Lenox-Conyngham, that it was one of the happiest and most successful we have had.

My age keeps pace with the century and in two years we shall both be ninety so inevitably my thoughts often turn backward. Our first journal came out in December 1968 and it contains a very significant address by the sixth Marquess of Ormonde, which I have decided to reprint *in toto*, for it reminds us what we and Kilkenny City owe to the Ormondes.

I cannot here forget what we owe also to the Seventh Marquess; he is a year older than I am but he makes light of his years and crosses the Atlantic every rally year with his daughters, Cynthia and Ann, and sometimes his sons-in-law as well.

He has no male heir so there will be no Eighth Marquess, but Lord Dunboyne, our genealogist, thinks there might be an Earl of Ormonde, since the Elizabethan Tenth Earl, Black Tom Butler, had many descendants, some legitimate. He might be in Australia or Canada or the United States and might not think it worth the trouble of proving his case.

Address by the sixth Marquess of Ormonde [James Arthur Norman Butler (1983-1971)] at the handing over of Kilkenny Castle to the Kilkenny Castle Restoration Committee – 12 August 1967

I believe that from now on we can look forward to the Castle being a cultural centre of real value to the city and county. One need only look across the road to the old stable building, where the Design Centre is now, to realize that new life can be put into these old buildings. And I hope that will happen.

Let me tell you a little of its recent history. My uncle, the third Marquess was born in 1844 and lived at the Castle all his life until his death in 1919. During those years, King Edward VII and Queen Alexandra were entertained there. When he died, my father succeeded to the title. The Castle and the estate were inherited by my elder brother, George, who became Earl of Ossory and lived at the Castle with his son, Anthony, and his daughter, Moyra. It was during their time, in 1922, that the republican army seized the Castle and held it for two days before it was retaken by government troops of the Free State.

In 1936 with the increasing taxation and increasing costs, my brother decided to sell the whole contents of the Castle and that really put a seal on its ever being lived in as a private residence. A year later, my brother's son, Anthony, came of age and the estate was re-entailed about three years after that. Anthony himself died about 1940. In 1943 my father died at the age of ninety-three and my elder brother succeeded to the title. In 1949 my brother died after which I inherited the Castle.

The Castle had already stood empty for thirteen years when I succeeded to the title and as it was not lived in and as the damp climate was detrimental, deterioration was inevitable. So I set about thinking of every possible way in which I could get the Castle lived in again as the best means of preserving it. Various schemes were started. I thought perhaps it might be adapted as a college, a university or a school so I got in contact with Catholic and Protestant Churches in case they wanted it as headquarters for a training college. But all these schemes came to nothing.

The people of Kilkenny as well as myself and my family feel a great pride in the Castle and we have not liked to see this deterioration. We determined that it should not be allowed to fall into ruins. There were already too many ruins in Ireland. Recently a development committee was formed representative not only of the city of Kilkenny but also of the Irish government, and we were fortunate in having Mr Gibbons as chairman. Then negotiations started.

Knowing that any restoration committee would be faced with a large expense in doing the work of restoration, I was determined not to handicap them still further by putting a high price on the Castle. Yet had it been put up for auction many people in the world would have given tens of thousands of pounds for it. I always had Kilkenny at the back of my mind and I decided that whatever the future of the Castle should be, it should be for the betterment of the city itself.

I have no son myself. I have two daughters, so my next heir will be Charles Butler, who lives in America. He is married and also has two daughters. The eventual heir according to the re-entailment of 1937 will be the eldest son of my niece, Moyra, who came of age this year and is serving in a Rifle Brigade of the British army.

As well as the Castle I have been thinking of the parklands and their development. I think that two or three hundred yards in the vicinity of the building should remain unbuilt on and I know the restoration committee feels the same. Land is valuable around Kilkenny and I know development is envisaged. That is why I would like to ensure that there are two or three hundred yards clear of buildings so that the Castle can be seen in all its dignity and grandeur. That is my great wish but it is not an easy thing to do. Covenants cannot be made with committees. I do not think that Trustees can make covenants either. What I hope is that I can buy the land myself and offer it to the people of Kilkenny as an open space.

It should be added that shortly afterwards Lord Ormonde was able to realize his intentions. The parkland now belongs to the nation. Lord Ormonde had bought the land from the Trustees for £12,000.

I believe the Kilkenny Castle Restoration Committee, of which I and a neighbour Stanley Mosse were members, realized what a generous present Kilkenny and the Irish nation were being given. Stanley at the last meeting of the Committee before the nation took over expressed its gratitude and gave Lord Ormonde a silver bowl made in the Kilkenny Design Workshops.

But the nation persisted in thinking they had bought it for £50 and that someone had acted very astutely on their behalf. There were headlines in the Irish papers saying, 'Kilkenny Castle Goes For Fifty Pounds', and Lord Ormonde told me people kept writing to him asking if he had any other castles to sell. For years afterwards I had to write to *The Irish Times* explaining that it had been a gift not a sale.

[1988/89]

PART SIX

History and Literature under Review

33

JONATHAN SWIFT

I began these books* in a parochial frame of mind. Would they strengthen my conviction that something should be done to keep the roof on Swift's Heath and Jonathan's ancestors on its walls, or would they make me feel a sentimentalist concerned with irrelevancies? In the middle I went to Swift's Heath and found that a strategic retreat had been successfully carried out. The bad half of the roof was off and the ancestors had moved in a body to dry walls. The Vicar of Goodrich, the only one of his relations of whom Jonathan approved, remained where he had always been and dry. The Vicar's father, the Rev. William, and his grandfather, the Rev. Thomas, both of Canterbury, had obviously disliked the winter of 1962, but can now face the future fairly confidently under ruberoid instead of slates. I don't know what to say of Sir Edmund Swifte and his son, Barnham, Lord Carlingford – they are looking fairly well, but Mr Ehrenpreis says that Jonathan was wrong in thinking they were his relations. If so, what are they doing on the walls of Swift's Heath? This is one of those problems that cannot be solved at Bloomington, Indiana; he must come to Kilkenny and fairly soon.

Of course it is true that Jonathan disliked his Uncle Godwin, the first Swift to build here, and remembered Kilkenny principally for bloody noses and furtively consumed custards, and Swift's Heath is perhaps irrelevant. Yet it is by irrelevancies that we most of us build up the idea of genius. Like the shape of the

---

* Irvin Ehrenpreis, *Swift: The Man, His Works and the Age*. Vol. 1; Sybil Le Brocquy, *Cadenus.*

sun, it is usually best observed through bits of clouded glass. We are still perhaps a century away from understanding the mind of Swift and we cannot tell what stray oddments posterity will find illuminating. Let us preserve them all.

Both Mr Ehrenpreis and Mrs Le Brocquy have made excellent books out of miscellaneous junk. Mr Ehrenpreis's appendices bulge with wills and pedigrees, and he has found what fines Swift paid and what marks he got in his exams at Trinity College Dublin and a list of books that Sir William Temple bought for his library. Mrs Le Brocquy had used a financial petition from Vanessa's mother as a dust wrapper for her book and concludes it with a dozen pages of wills. One might guess that none of it meant anything to Jonathan and yet personally I see him clearer from having read the books.

In his zig-zag pursuit of genius, Mr Ehrenpreis stops for a chapter in Kilkenny and even follows the headmaster, Dr Jones, from a college to a bishopric at St Asaph's, where he was suspended for simony and for appointing a criminal to a canonry. Then we tack back twenty years to Trinity College, Cambridge, where Dr Jones had encountered Calvinism, whose austere intensity he may well, Mr Ehrenpreis surmises, have brought back with him to Kilkenny. Was it Dr Jones' austere intensity or his simoniacal propensities or his custards that most influenced Jonathan at Kilkenny College? We do not really know, but from such morsels Mr Ehrenpreis has stuck together a tolerable model of the 'Age of Swift'.

A genius bears the same relation to his age as a chicken to an egg. He has to smash his way out of it. Wherever this tremendous man leant against his age it began to crack. The English Ascendancy in Ireland rocked, he broke Marlborough and his clique and set the whole bench of Bishops of the Church of Ireland quaking. Seldom has the power of scorn been so effectively demonstrated.

Yet Swift was very vulnerable. It was obvious that his private life and his public life were in violent collision. Did their impact cause the spark that fired his genius? Or did it blast his ambition and finally disintegrate his mind? However you explain it, the collision mattered deeply. Mrs Le Brocquy believes that Swift was, in fact, the lover of Vanessa and had weekly meetings with her at the house of a book-binder, Thomas Kendall, in Dublin. The best books are often written round theories and Mrs Le Brocquy's convictions, vigorously argued, give to her writing a warm concentration of purpose that is lacking in more timid biographies. She believes that Kendall's wife, formerly Anne M'Loghlin, gave a name and a home to a small boy, Bryan M'Loghlin, and that he was Vanessa's child by Swift. It used to be said that Bryan was Stella's child, because in a cautiously phrased clause in her will she left him a small legacy. Mrs Le Brocquy bases her theory on the evidence of Stella's goodness and undemanding love, on the correspondence between Swift and Vanessa, and on a sentence in the Van Homrigh Petition. It refers to Vanessa's impending marriage and was drawn up in the early days of her love affair with Swift. It seems to me that the letters alone afford the strongest evidence for Mrs Le Brocquy's contention. Swift constantly urged discretion but neither lover was good at dissembling and Vanessa did not even try. They had a secret code but used it so recklessly that it is easy to decipher.

After two centuries Swift still seems to be the greatest figure in Irish literature. Ireland, which he disliked, shaped his mind and his moods, and with her sufferings constantly rekindled the savage indignation that has made him the greatest satirist in the world. He is as Irish as a storm cloud that comes from across the sea, breaks upon our mountains and inundates our fields, destroying some things, reviving others.

His real enemies were not, as one might infer, Marlborough and Queen Anne, his Uncle Godwin and the Bishop of Meath; these were just accidental victims of his spleen. He was at war with the whole world of his time, and unless he had had some faint glimpse of heaven, he could not have battled against it so effectively. Our grandchildren will understand him better than we do and because of that we should cherish every faint trace of his sojourn among us and, if that is the thing to do, cover it with ruberoid.

[1963]

34

ENID STARKIE

Why has there been no great Irish novelist? Has it something to do with the adhesiveness – Miss Starkie helps us to distinguish this from the cohesion of love – of the Irish family? Emotional freedom, if it is not claimed at adolescence, can seldom be achieved again, and without it a writer can never be more than a virtuoso or an exhibitionist. Exhibitionism, though, is perhaps an unjust word, for much so-called exhibitionism is in the nature of a self-justification: 'Why I wasted my talent.' *The Portrait of an Artist* will survive as a magnificently convincing apologia of this order. George Moore, too, in *Ave atque Vale* raised a monument to this emotional unfreedom, which, in Ireland at least, will survive his novels, and yet he, compared to most Irishmen, was free as the wind.

This is not the popular conception of the Irishman, but I think it is true of him as it is of the Jew. There are devices by which other races conclude or pension off their dear ones, their tender and bitter memories, but these two will not or cannot.

This may seem a very roundabout way of approaching Enid Starkie's autobiography,* which is above all immediate and Irish. Indeed in Ireland it is impossible to read it without the sense that somewhere not far off feelings are hurt, old bitternesses revived. It is inevitable that a picture taken at so close a range and so individual an angle should often be out of focus, that certain features should be given an unjust and cruel prominence, others blurred or effaced. Yet in spite of that it is possible to see it as a portrait not

---

* Enid Starkie, *A Lady's Child.*

of an Irish family but of the Irish family in one of its characteristic phases, and there seems as much to be said for it and no more than there is for a skilful and humane vivisection operation. At a certain price, it adds to the sum of human knowledge and may like many another uncompromising autobiography contribute to the relief of human suffering.

It is not trivial at the present time to be interested in these long-forgotten family squabbles in Killiney and Blackrock. The problems that Miss Starkie has raised cannot be settled by wars, how we are to love without possessiveness, be good citizens and yet good fathers, writers and musicians and yet loyal daughters. The answer, which is implicit but which she has not given, is that in the present social framework it cannot be done. The family is too small a unit for tenderness and talent to prosper side by side in its shade, the state is too large. In a certain sense her father is the saddest figure; a distinguished civil servant, he spent the warmth of his nature in impersonal service to the State, what was left for his children he transmitted to them through his wife. A year or two after his death his lifework was overthrown by social forces, which he had ignored because they were based on a more personal and emotional view of life than he had time for, and his family was dispersed, because that affection and understanding, which he had for them and which might have reconciled them, was withheld.

Miss Starkie has written a distinguished book. It will be a pity if Irish readers criticize only the details and particular judgments and do not see that it is at a society and not at a single family that she has flung her challenge.

[1942]

35

W.B. YEATS

Lawrence of Arabia wrote how once, as he passed W.B. Yeats in Oxford, 'he had wanted to call the whole street to attention for lack of power to make the sun blaze out appropriately'. Yet in his own country, even when he was acknowledged to be the greatest poet of his age, Yeats was in no sense a national figure, least of all in that small portion of the nation from which he sprung. Someone has said that to the average Anglo-Irish provincial the name Yeats vaguely recalls an optician in Nassau Street and nothing more, and even at the end of his life when he came forward more and more as the champion of the Protestant minority, this remained nearly true. This indifference, whether we attribute it to sluggishness or to a certain perverse nimbleness at dodging the obvious, was remarkable enough but scarcely stranger than Yeats' refusal to be bruised by it. As he grew older, he acquired the dignity and authority of a man who has found his place and is satisfied with it. There was never anyone less frustrated or embittered.

In his case it was not simply that he obtained outside Ireland that recognition that Ireland refused him, nor was it his contempt, clothing itself ultimately in reach-me-down political formulae, for mass opinions and the verdict of any but the distinguished spirits. Admittedly he was not indifferent to pensions, royalties, Nobel prizes, but Ireland was the source of his highest inspiration, the focus of all his thoughts, of most of his enterprises. It was naturally to the Irish response that he listened most attentively; that response must have disappointed him, yet he was not, as others have been, in any way disillusioned. How did he manage it?

Perhaps we must reckon here with the advantage the poet often has over the man of action even in practical affairs. He can always withdraw into an ideal world, where achievement is possible, when the real world closes its doors, so he does not take its values too seriously. Yeats' invasions into practical life were often effective just because he clearly had no fear of getting cornered there. About Ireland his ideas had always been clear and consistent. Mr Hone says that his mind was haunted by the question of how to bring the aristocratic and Protestant tradition of Swift, Berkeley, Burke into line with the modern 'Gaelic' nationalism, or, in Yeats' own words, 'how to help the two Irelands, Gaelic Ireland and Anglo-Ireland so to unite that neither shed its pride'.* Such a faith is easier to practise than to preach, for public life in Ireland seldom gives it a platform, but, when in the theatre, the Senate, the world of letters, the opportunity came, he used it nobly. Perhaps it was only in his verse that he achieved a fusion of the Gaelic and Anglo-Irish spirit, but in all his activities he never lost sight of this aim.

Sometimes it exposed him to misinterpretation. Mr Hone finds it difficult to believe that a poet could be as excited as Yeats was about such 'an unphilosophic legal compromise as divorce'. Yet scarcely anything, he declares, except the censorship of books stirred him so deeply. He was deathly pale when he rose to give his celebrated speech in the Senate. To his friends it was clear that it was not a particular view of marriage that he was championing but the liberties of a minority that were being assailed. Yet to the average Catholic he appeared to be trying to introduce a foreign laxity of morals, to the average Protestant he seemed a busybody who had much better left well alone. Divorce is seldom an important issue among Irish Protestants but if it became so, social considerations, apart from legal ones, would always incline them to settle their matrimonial affairs outside their own community. Yeats was an Irishman who scorned such evasions. It was the right of the Anglo-Irish to make their own impress on Irish laws that he saw challenged, but were not proud enough of their country to claim their rights in it. It was to them I think as much as to his opponents that he addressed his peroration, 'We against whom you have done this thing are no petty people. We are one of the great stocks of Europe. We are the people of Burke; we are the people of Grattan; we are the people of Swift, the people of

---

* J.M. Hone, *W.B. Yeats 1865–1939*.

Parnell. We have created most of the modern literature of this country. We have created the best of its political intelligence.'

W.B. Yeats in Ireland was an Irishman and a European. Exploring foreign cultures he often seems something of a provincial and a tourist. From Italy and from India he collected some queer fantasies that consorted badly with the eighteenth-century furnishings of his mind. He set them on the mantelpiece but they really belonged to the box-room. Mr Hone picks them up and puts them down again, that is all we too can do. There is no comment to make. Their interest is that a great man was once interested in them.

This biography, completed last year in Kilkenny, is a masterly one. Mr Hone is the most distinguished survivor of that inner circle of Anglo-Irishmen and women among whom Yeats' life was passed. Some day perhaps he will write a more personal account of that circle. At the moment its stock is low, its dreams and ambitions seem far away and ineffectual. The dragons they fought have mostly died of old age or been domesticated, but time, which brings increasing disillusionment to the Anglo-Irish and the Gaelic extremists, has not obscured the vision these men had of an Ireland where the two streams of culture will one day flow peacably together.

[1944]

36

VIENNA IN 1938

I have always admired Edward Crankshaw as a balanced and scholarly recorder of the terrible forties and, recalling that it was in Vienna that Eichmann made his first appearance in history, I thought that here was another book about the part Hitler and his Austrian fellow-countrymen had played in the destruction of what had once been a centre of civilization and learning. To my initial disappointment, this is a reprint of an old book published in 1938* and 'the decline of culture', which is Crankshaw's concern, had begun generations before Hitler was born, indeed before Maria Theresa herself, whose reign he describes as 'the autumn flowering of Vienna, the irridescence of decay'. Crankshaw has chosen Vienna, which he first saw as a young man, as the European city in which the art of civilized living (for the few, maybe, as in Ancient Greece) once reached its zenith and in its slow decline he saw an image of what had been happening all over Europe. After a few pages I saw that his arguments are as pertinent in 1976 as they were in 1938 and my regrets vanished. This is an essential book.

Many factors contribute to the growth and decline of a culture and to reach the heart of the labyrinth the historians must follow several different strands, so it would be surprising if writer and reader did not sometimes get tangled in the complexity of the search. In his chronicle of cultural decay he sees the year 1791 as an important landmark, for it was then that Mozart died alone and in bitter poverty in the *Rauhenstein gasse*. In earlier generations the

---

* Edward Crankshaw, *Vienna, the Image of a Culture in Decline.*

artist had been in tune with society: 'as he grew in stature, society grew with him. He climbed and it climbed with him.' As a child Mozart had been feted at Schonbrunn and other royal palaces of Europe. 'But as he grew up, his music grew up with him and passed the easy comprehension of his hearers.' An ever-widening gulf was opening between the people and the artist. Slowly it came about that the grandchildren of the men who had loved Handel and Gluck went to Coward and Lehar for their spiritual sustenance. How had this irrevocable recession begun?

All over Europe the industrial revolution and the rise of commerce were changing the old social patterns and slowly converting art into a marketable commodity. With them came the advance of democracy showing itself first at the top in the breaking up of the Habsburg dictatorship of culture and the passing of patronage to the nobility, the Liechtensteins on the Swiss frontier, the Esterhazys in Hungary. Following on that came nationalism and patriotism. The Habsburgs had administered their polyglot 'empire' as a private estate; they had, except for the ghastly interlude of the Thirty Years War, been as free from racial or political or religious discrimination as the average eighteenth-century landlord was in the treatment of his employees. The only patriotism they acknowledged was loyalty to themseves. Great landlords can in a few years carry through revolutions that democracies take generations to achieve. Maria Theresa, a devout Catholic, curbed the arrogance of the Church, and her son, Joseph II, in his idiosyncratic way, as the arbiter of enlightenment, fostered a spirit of independence and made the finest hospitals in the world. There were deplorable emperors like Ferdinand II but in general the Habsburg empire jogged along unchallenged, feudally pampering the working classes and suppressing as far as it could the rising bourgeoisie.

The industrial drabness that swept over England in the early nineteenth century was held at bay by Habsburg arrogance, by Joseph II's passionate resistance to the dingy tide and in the nineteenth century by Dr Karl Leuger, the mayor of Vienna, who, in Crankshaw's words, 'saved Vienna from the disgrace of being ruled by financiers and inflated tradesmen'. Crankshaw's argument is subtle and I am not surprised that he here dodged saying what he certainly knew. Lueger, whom he reveres, was one of the heroes of *Mein Kampf*, in the Führer's own words 'the greatest German mayor of all time', and the inspiration of his anti-Semitism. Yet he was chivalrous and decent and many Jews, like Stefan Zweig, honoured and loved him. What he was attacking was the evil power of finance. Yet this is an abstraction, and those whom he wished to educate needed concrete, almost unsummoned symbols; the image of the Jew presented itself.

To hand out ideas to those who can only think in pictures is as dangerous as to give weedkiller to a child or sophisticated weapons to men incapable of inventing a pea-shooter. Yet it is what everybody does.

Crankshaw builds his story of Vienna chapter by chapter around the famous buildings, which in his eyes illustrate the stages of its decay. Apart from its prophetic qualities, it has the charm of a very good guide-book.

[1976]

37

DENMARK'S FINEST HOUR

Fifty years ago Denmark was greatly admired in Ireland and an attempt was made to imitate in Ireland the Danish co-operative system. Our creameries survive as memorials to this abortive movement, but the admiration has largely gone. It is fashionable now to believe that the Danes have sold their souls to the electrician and the plumber and the marketing board. Life is so well regulated that it has nothing more to offer them. Therefore, since they do not believe in a hereafter, they will souse themselves with Danish beer and, well-clad and well-fed, will end their lives painlessly with special pills, in an air-conditioned sun parlour.

Occasionally the Danes reply to this, saying that they keep good statistics and tell no kindly lies about 'unsound minds' and that, in any case, there are relatively more suicides in Austria. Francis Hackett also derided a current view of the Danes but, if you wish to see it blown sky-high, you must read Mr Flender's account of a stupendous Danish achievement.* The Danes have not talked about it much, yet historians of the future will relate how in the Second World War, when Christianity was obliterated over most of Europe, it survived in Denmark as creedless and as churchless as when it first came into the world. Once more fishermen and tax collectors began to love their neighbours as themselves and to lay down their lives for them. And the plumbers and the electricians joined in, as did taxi drivers and civil-servants and policemen and schoolteachers and clergymen. A trapeze artist and a book-binder and a king and a detective were among the leaders.

---

* Harold Flender, *Rescue in Denmark.*

The story lends itself to commercialized sentiment, and in the preface the words 'documentary film' and CBS Religious Programme, 'Look Up and Live,' fill the mind with foreboding. Is it only through these cardboard archways that the truth can now reach us? Possibly. But anyway here she is, Veritas herself, with very little TV make-up on her face. Mr Flender has padded out the story a little with some flat chunks-of-life dialogue. 'The cod is very nice and I have some fresh shrimps,' may not have been said by Mrs Niel, the fishmonger, to the two Jewish customers, who were soon to involve her in rescue work, which was to bring her in the end to Ravensbruck. Yet these chunks correspond well enough to the authentic documents, the letters and the diaries. We cannot now take our medicine without a dab of supermarket jam, and this jam is fairly good. Mr Flender has rejected as spurious most of the Scarlet Pimpernel romance. The king never made the celebrated remark about wearing the Star of David, nor did he say: 'There is no Jewish question in this country: there is only my people.' Emphatically he did his best, but no one made epigrams.

There is, of course, some substance in the two Irish views of the Danes. Probably it is because they are phlegmatic that they co-operate well both about butter and about human rights, not squabbling unprofitably or sacrificing themselves vainly for hopeless causes. When the Germans invaded in April 1940, the Danes put up the feeblest resistance, capitulating with the loss of thirteen soldiers. Most small peoples have to treat modern war as if it were a thunderstorm; they do not bombard the clouds, they run for shelter, carrying with them whatever is valuable and damageable. At the beginning of the war the Danes seem to have decided that armies, navies and even frontiers were expendable elements in their independence, for in 1939 the army was halved and a year later the navy was to surrender without firing a shot. They submitted to the ignominy of being called by Hitler a '*Musterprotektorat*,' or model protectorate, and as a reward were allowed to retain their parliament, their law courts, their Jews. They must have watched with shame the heroic resistance of Norway, and perhaps consoled themselves with the thought that the Norwegians in defeat gave up their Jews and accepted a Quisling government. Till about September 1943 they remained as they were, moderately independent, moderately docile. Co-operative societies have always to purchase harmony by a certain sacrifice of autonomy.

What was it that turned them all at once into the most efficiently obstructive of all Hitler's subjects? The Danes are sober in their self-esteem and they would probably put two material reasons first. (1) Rations were curtailed. (2) The Germans were losing. But a third cause suddenly lifted Danish resistance onto the heroic plane and gave them a victory such as no other subject nation had achieved. A telegram came from Ribbentrop to Governor Best ordering the deportation of all the Danish Jews.

Best, a strong Nazi, had always advised against this. He considered Denmark 'a ridiculous little country,' but he had a premonition that an attack on the Danish concept of citizenship would be more dangerous than the occupation of Denmark itself. No sooner had Ribbentrop's order come than the Germans seemed to suffer a sharp psychological setback. There was sufficient idealism in the Nazi movement to make it vulnerable when it encountered an idealism higher than its own. The confidence of the German authorities in Denmark began to sag. The Chief of Transport tried to dissuade the Governor, the army commander said the deportations would 'impair the prestige of the Wehrmacht,' the Gestapo officer in charge of embarkation said they might mean less Danish meat and fats. Finally, Duckwitz, the head of German shipping, after fruitless efforts in Copenhagen, Sweden and Berlin to have the plan cancelled, betrayed it to a Danish parliamentarian. He, in his turn, informed the leading Jews that ships were waiting in the harbour to transport all the 8000 Danish Jews to Poland, and that the date fixed for their embarkation was 1 October.

They had only three days left, but the Chief Rabbi gave out the news in the synagogue and straight away Jews and Christians, students, taximen, shopkeepers, doctors, policemen, raced round the town searching for Jews to warn, and arranging for their concealment in Danish homes. In this way all but 472 Danish Jews were in hiding when the SS arrived to collect them.

On 3 October the Lutheran bishops sent a letter to the German occupation authorities saying that it was to fulfil God's promise to the Chosen People that Christ had been born in Bethlehem, that the Danes respected the right to religious freedom, which they themselves valued more than life, and would fight to preserve for their Jewish brothers and sisters. The letter was read in every church, and Pastor Lange was not unique in adding: 'I tell you I would rather die with the Jews than live with the Nazis.'

As far as I know, no hierarchy in all occupied Europe, with the exception of the Patriarch of Bulgaria, made so brave and unambiguous a pronouncement. One of the pastors hid the Chief Rabbi in his rectory, and though this is a story of predominantly secular heroism, the aid of the pastors could always be counted on.

It soon became plain that the Jews could not long remain in hiding without being discovered. Shortly before, the Danes had scuttled their navy and Admiral Vedel had been arrested. Now he was offered freedom if he disclosed the whereabouts of the Jews. He answered: 'There's no point in exchanging one Dane for another Dane.' Co-operation is certainly the best training in non-co-operation, and every Dane was equally unhelpful. It was necessary to ship the Jews to Sweden, and here the great Jewish-Danish nuclear physicist Niels Bohr, enters the story. The Allies had wanted him to work on the atom bomb in the USA, so he had been smuggled to meet their representative in Sweden. He refused to stir until he had persuaded the Swedes to admit the Jews. While his English escort fidgeted impatiently, he put all the pressure he could on the Swedish government and the king and the press, and it was not till he had got his way that he agreed to leave for the USA.

The escape of the Danish Jews to Sweden, by every variety of fishing boat and pleasure steamer, and the neat co-operation of a dozen different rescue groups, are among the wonders of the century. It was a sophisticated and ruthless campaign of mercy. Informers were shot or drowned. Small children were anaesthetized before the passage. The fugitives, aware of what was at stake, had often secured capsules of cyanide from the family physician. Respectable housewives stole bicycles and clergymen blew up railway lines.

In contrast, the Germans lost their nerve and acted senselessly. Why, for instance, did they use the stomach pump on Jews who had poisoned themselves and whom they intended to destroy? The Germans were, in fact, at war with their own natures, while almost by accident the Danes had discovered an ecstacy that men rarely enjoy, a marvellous consonance between belief and action. What they did was not merely right, it was also acute pleasure. Looking back on it afterwards, many expressed gratitude to the Jews, who had given them something meaningful to do. 'We were never happier. We were together. Nowhere were we refused,' said a professor's wife. Another woman said: 'It's as if we never realized before what it means to live,' and one, a doctor, after he had seen off a boatload of Jews to Sweden, said: 'What a strange feeling! It's almost like experiencing again the overwhelming love of one's youth!' And a trapeze artist said: 'I feel like throwing myself down on the beach and saying "Thank you!" '

It was as though the Danes, by ignoring the official war, which is fought between conscripts for obscure, complex and usually unattainable ends, had discovered the true war and were fighting as free men, with co-operation and skill, for the things in which they personally believed and for which most men struggle in haphazard isolation.

[1963]

38

THE ANT ON TOP OF THE HILL

Long ago I read in a French journal an attack on 'scholarly objectivity' that I have never forgotten.

'Would Zola', the writer asked, 'ever have defended Dreyfus, if he had been objective? No, he would have waited till he could examine all the files at the French War Office.' David Irving is one of several historians who in the past decade have tried to reassess Hitler in the light of secret files and forgotten documents.* He has been charged with whitewashing the Führer and in this book he ably defends himself. He certainly does not like Hitler at all, and yet and yet ... Like raindrops on the window-pane, like autumn leaves on the footpath, this spate of tiny revelations and reappraisals blurs what once was clear, a vision of evil that forty years ago set a million hearts ablaze.

These scholarly investigators are all the same. X discovers the general's widow in a home for the aged and is thereby able to prove that the bishop's diary, on which Y based his interpretation of the Foreign Minister's murder, was a forgery. Then Z seeks out the bishop's niece and she says ... It is all fascinating and an extract from Z's book with good photographs of the bishop and his niece will make a splendid trailer for it in a Sunday supplement. Yet the result is that the pursuit of truth begins to look like a race, in which Z outruns X and Y and wins the Lloyd-Padmore Prize and the Chair of History at the University of Iowa.

One would suppose that if Irving really believed that the truth could rescue us from the abyss of rich and murderous despair

* David Irving, *The War Path*.

into which the world fell forty years ago, he would be glad if he was anticipated. But no, by no means! 'Other writers', he complains, 'have overtaken me, I have been scooped more than once.' Prof. A.J.P. Taylor, reviewing his book, goes one better. 'I formulated these views', he comments cattily, 'nearly twenty years ago and I am delighted that Irving follows loyally in my footsteps.'

The 'views' concerned Hitler's attitude to Britain. Now, if the attitudes they were interpreting were those of some innocent creature like a crocodile or a boa constrictor, one could forgive the petty competitiveness of rival zoologists. But Hitler was not, like the crocodile, a child of nature. He and his comrades were obscene artefacts cloned (is that the word?) by our technological society. It is of no significance whether or not Hitler knew of the Final Solution for the Jews, a question that Irving thinks important, since such a solution was the inevitable result of his words and actions. Indeed there was something inevitable about Hitler himself.

All this was understood forty years ago. In the early days of the dictators, Ortega y Gasset, the Spanish Republican writer, in his great book, *The Revolt of the Masses*, wrote:

Owing to the disarticulation of knowledge science has progressed, thanks in great part to men astonishingly mediocre or less than mediocre, constructing mindlessly like bees on a honeycomb, cell by contiguous cell ... The specialist is a learned ignoramus with all the petulance of one who is learned in a special line. Though strongly opposed to the mass-man, he will behave as one in almost all spheres of life.

Hitler certainly understood that this was the source of his power. Walter Hewel, one of his oldest and most devoted disciples, said: 'If you want to understand the way the Führer's mind works, you must look on the human race as being just a swarm of ants.'

And indeed there is something entomological about the collapse of Czechoslovakia, which Irving relates most brilliantly. The Czechs, a brave, cultured people, were submerged not like men struggling, but like ants, chemically sprayed. How did it happen that, without a shot being fired, they handed over all their magnificently equipped armaments and their vast gold reserves, outlawed their Jews (in this, according to Irving, their academics had already taken the lead), and finally came to love their oppressors and in particular, Heydrich, Deputy Chief of Gestapo and Protector of Bohemia and Moravia. Had he not got pensions for Czech officers, big contracts from the Reich for Czech industrialists, social security for Czech workers? Had he not solved unemployment (he had been helped in this by the robbery and deportation of many thousand Jews)? When Heydrich was murdered by two members of the Free Czechoslovakia army parachuted in by the British, the Czech ants were deeply grieved. 30,000 of them filed past the catafalque bearing flowers, ant-sextons tolled the cathedral bells, ant-clergy said a Requiem Mass. (To be fair, though Irving does not mention this, the murderers were given asylum by the priests in the Borromaean Church, where they were besieged and killed.)

I wish I had space to quote how President Hacha, signing the capitulation in Munich, had a heart attack and was treated by Hitler's own personal physician, who thereafter regularly sent the prescription to Prague; how Hacha's daughter's room was filled with yellow roses, sent with a kind note by the Führer himself, and how in return Hacha sent him a valuable picture. See how it pays to be polite! When the Nazi army entered Prague, one road bridge was blocked by Czech patriots singing the national anthem. The Nazi troops halted and presented arms. After such courtesy, what could the Czechs do but withdraw?

It is all very well told and yet I believe that Irving never discovered what Hannah Arendt called 'the banality of evil' and secretly likes ants. He calls the lonely young Jew, Grynszpan, 'deranged', because on his own he had tried to kill the German ambassador in Paris, in revenge for the barbarous deportation of his family to Poland. Yet I know Irving would accept that the killers of Heydrich and the plotters of 20 July were heroes. This would be because there was something semi-official about their enterprise.

And why does he contrast 'the flabby structure' of Italian Fascism, which collapsed so easily, with the 'stoicism' of the Germans, who battled on for Hitler when all seemed lost. Did it ever occur to him that Fascism was 'flabby' because the Italians had never wholly surrendered their souls, whereas the Nazis were staunch, because they had killed, expelled or intimidated all those in whom the great traditions of liberal Germany survived?

This book in its unsatisfactory way is very good. Read it, but it is more important to press for a reissue of *The Revolt of the Masses*, for that famous book not only explains Hitler, it explains Mr Irving too.

[1978]

39

SOME IRISH SAINTS

The writings of Celtic scholars do not now get the attention they deserve and once received. Sometimes there is a reason for this. The scholar has become increasingly a specialist and, like a psychiatrist giving evidence at a murder trial, he makes his comments in a special jargon. He is not greatly attended to, but while the ordinary man may distrust his arguments and repudiate his conclusions, he seldom feels qualified to say so. A dense, quickset hedge of esoteric knowledge often stands between the educated outsider and the elementary error that he has detected and would like to expose. Hardly anyone, for example, now believes Professor O'Rahilly's theories on the origins of the Irish people, yet no one has effectively disproved them. They are based on faulty reasoning of a familiar everyday type, but protected by such a jungle of learned appendices and footnotes that the critic, whose only weapon is common sense, is daunted at the outset.

Professor Carney's book is quite different.* He addresses himself to us as equals, appealing to our reason and intuition. He uses his knowledge to persuade and not to intimidate. I do not mean that his is an easy book, but he has never forgotten that the course of history was determined by ordinary men and not by grammarians, and ordinary men should pay him the compliment of reading him.

This book is so rich in detailed speculation that it would be an impertinence to try to summarize it in a few paragraphs. Much of it

---

* James Carney, *Studies in Irish Literature and History* (Dublin: Institute for Advanced Studies).

concerns the relationship of Irish legend to Irish literature, which Professor Carney traces to an educated elite, far more susceptible to literary influences from outside than is generally acknowledged. Because of this, it is possible to find parallels between the Irish sagas and the Anglo-Saxon epic of *Beowulf* or the ancient stories of China and Greece.

Most of these affinities are tentatively suggested, for to discover a literary likeness, to distinguish the original from the imitation, is as much a poet's job as a scholar's, and Professor Carney seems to me to use his equipment with modesty and skill. Readers of this paper should be specially interested in the parallels that he draws between pagan stories and the lives of such saints as Kentigern and Moling, and in his reconsideration of the Patrick legend.

Most of us find it more exhilarating to criticize than to commend. Conscious of this human failing, I would suggest that Professor Carney is too deferential to orthodoxy in his account of St Moling. He calls him 'an undoubtedly historic Irish saint,' whereas he seems to me to be among the most obviously fabricated. A pagan Moling, half-brother of Fionn, preceded St Moling at St Mullins on the Barrow. Professor Carney says of him that he is 'of course identical with the saint of the same name, but by a genealogical fiction is made to belong to an earlier period'. There was also in precisely the same spot a tribe called the Ui Linga, whose ancestor Ling was 'by a genealogical fiction' made a brother of the ancestors of the neighbouring Ossory tribes and a descendant of all the Ossorians.

There are thousands of instances of fictitious beings, who have been judged real – Ling and his brothers undoubtedly belong to that category – but Professor Carney would put this natural process into reverse and argue that our predecessors converted a perfectly real saint into a fiction. Admittedly he could claim that Santa Claus developed in this way out of St Nicholas of Myra. But did St Moling give rise also to Ling and to the Ui Linga? Surely not, yet that there was some link between saint and tribe is obvious, and has not been denied. St Moling's most memorable activity was jumping three times over some rushes. He was on that account called Moling Luachra, since '*ling*' means 'jump' and '*luachra*' rushes. Christianity would in no way be impoverished if he was relegated to fairy-land, and all would be explained if we accept the Ui Linga tribe as the only reality and that their hypothetical ancestor Ling was elaborated by legend first into the pagan Moling and then into the Christian St Moling.

Canon Ledwich, Rector of Aghaboe and one of the fathers of Irish archaeology, is still in great disrepute because he linked a sceptical view of the Irish saints with a very arrogant imperialism and some out-of-date notions of Irish origins. But was he not right in saying that it is corrupting to the mind to believe that which is not true, and was he not in this supported by the best traditions of Anglo-Irish scholarship from which his successors out of politeness or policy often departed?

In fact nobody is nowadays very much interested in the Irish saints at all, and the ten thousand saints who lived in the two or three centuries after Patrick are deemed 'undoubtedly historical' simply because their histories are tedious to investigate in a critical spirit. Life is short, and I do not think Professor Carney can have had time for a thorough investigation, or he would scarcely state as a 'general rule' that where continental saints or heroes overcome serpents or dragons, the Irish overcome watermonsters. 'It was well known that Ireland harboured no venomous creature of the serpent, hence dragon-type.' This is an incorrect deduction. St Attracta, for example, had to battle with a quite normal dragon in Lugna, Co. Sligo. It had tusks and ram's ears and roamed the countryside. St Senan had to deal with a poison-breathing monster on Inish Scattery. St Ciaran had to expel an ordinary dragon from Achadh Draignige in Galway. St Ternoc's nurse, on St Fursey's advice, threw a dragon into Loch Bel Dragain in the Galtees. And though it is true that Irish monsters often lived near a lake or a sea, it must be stated in general that where a dragon was necessary to explain a place-name or embellish the life of an island saint, the hagiographer was seldom embarrassed by the fact that St Patrick expelled them all.

Such flaws are of little consequence in Professor Carney's argument. The best books are provocative, and it is to Professor Carney's credit that many will disagree with him about many things.

[1950]

40

HORACE PLUNKETT AND THE IRISH CO-OPERATIVE MOVEMENT

I

Nowadays we talk very little about the co-operative movement and not at all about Sir Horace Plunkett.* We accept the creameries of the I.A.O.S as a natural product of the Irish soil, and nobody recalls the great pioneer of voluntary association in rural communities. How often, I wonder, is Plunkett mentioned at the Annual Rural Week or at the conferences of Young Farmer's Clubs or Countrywomen's Associations? Very rarely, I expect. Yet, if the good seed scattered by the speakers does not always fall on stony ground, it must often be because Plunkett and his fellow-workers, over long laborious years, shifted the stones and tilled the soil. Except for Plunkett House, built in his lifetime, there is no official monument to Plunkett in Ireland, but that would not worry him. *Circumspice*! Every co-operative creamery is a reminder of his imaginative insight and devotion. All the same, I am sorry that the ruins of Kilteragh were not preserved as a monument, not to Plunkett, but to our barbarism and ingratitude. Whenever there is some unwholesome outburst of national complacency, compulsory tours, like those for Weimer citizens to Buchenwald, could be organized. 'That is the way', it could be explained, 'we treated one of the most constructive minds of our century.' Kilteragh was for many years a focus of social and intellectual life in Ireland, but when in the September issue I tried to write that once-honoured word, even the printing press yawned and gave us Kiltimagh instead.

---

* Margaret Digby, *Horace Plunkett. An Anglo-American Irishman.*

Plunkett was a very rich man and enjoyed great social 'advantages,' but I incline to think that these were fully counterbalanced by his perpetual ill-health and a shyness, which looked like rudeness. He was better with his pen than with his tongue, and this was a disaster for him, for much of his work lay among the illiterate (or rather those who read newspapers but not books). They would have been susceptible to warm, wise words, but were not moved by his well-expressed, well-considered writing. His book, *Ireland in the New Century*, is exceedingly well-written but has always been grotesquely undervalued.

Plunkett was deeply aware of his limitations, and overcame them by his power to communicate his ideas and something of his enthusiasm to others more articulate than himself. His greatest interpreter was, of course, Æ, and in *The Irish Statesman* Plunkett founded an organ that bridged the gap between agricultural and intellectual Ireland. Looking back over the procession of weeklies and monthlies that have succeeded it in the past twenty years, can we deny that nothing better happened in the whole history of Irish journalism? But the most arduous part of Plunkett's work was probably never recorded at all except in diaries and letters. Miss Digby quotes some of these and we can see how mercilessly he drove himself:

'Omagh. Long speech to a small meeting. It was a dreary experience. They were nice to me but very apathetic and I am not the man to rouse. My thoughts germinate in other brains and, when the brains are attached to the proper physique, the enthusiasm works all right.'

'Two long speeches to two small meetings. Did good, I think, but oh, so boring and tiring!'

'A two hours' crawl in the Major's brougham to Longford.'

Miss Digby summarizes very well a long life with many divergent interests, and perhaps few Irishmen could have done such justice to Plunkett's work in America, where he was the confidant of Roosevelt and Colonel House and during the First World War was able to influence the relations of the English and American governments. Yet when I reached the epilogue by Gerald Heard, a subtle observer of character who was Sir Horace's secretary, it seemed to me that it was he who should have written this book. No great man could have had a more brilliant Boswell. Yet Heard found the 'ethos' of Ireland, the 'recessionalism' of its nationalism, wholly repugnant. He knew all about Jacob Boehme and the function of the pituitary gland in the coloration of frogs, and balanced the aridity of such knowledge with dreams of ideal communities. Sir Horace, juggling with banalities and vulgarities, checkmating gombeenmen with Credit Banks, and potato blight with Carnegie Libraries, won his admiration and loyalty, but never his enthusiasm. And therefore I think there is something missing in the observant and moving study of Sir Horace with which the book is ended. What is it? Surely Plunkett felt a sense of dedication to his country as irresistable as that which his kinsman, the Blessed Oliver, once felt to his Church. It was an unfashionable feeling in his circle and is even more so now, but it was the categorical imperative that drove him to those dreary meetings in remote villages, and which for opposite reasons made him face the censure of Cardinal Logue and the Kildare Street Club, the hostility of Redmond and the disfavour of his own sister, as well as a multitude of snubs from self-important nincompoops. He compared himself once to a dog on a tennis court, chased and cursed by both sides at once.

It needs great courage for a clever man to consent to be a bore. In his old age Sir Horace had simplified his creed of co-operation into a series of pithy maxims that could still kindle the imagination of the young. Long afterwards I wished that, when I had known him, I had been more susceptible to earnestness and less to atmosphere, for it was impossible not to be influenced by the evidence that those around him were yawning their heads off. Catchy aphorisms about butter and brotherhood and business methods had been dinning in their ears for a quarter of a century, and Sir Horace believed that a maxim outlived its uses not when it became tedious but when it became unneccessary.

I am sorry that Miss Digby shies abruptly away from George Moore's witty, silly disparagement of Plunkett and will not quote it. H.P. was a great and substantial figure, and detraction only boomerangs back on the detractor. It is her only serious failure of scholarship and I hope that this excellent book will revive an interest in Plunkett and the movement that he began, which, as time goes on, new minds may quicken into new activity.

[1951]

THE APPLEMAN AND THE POET

Patrick Bolger has done his work well.* The Co-operative Movement in Ireland started in idealism and poetry and ended – but some would say fulfilled itself – in proficiency and prose, good prose. Fifty years ago George Russell (Æ), by means of that unique threepenceworth *The Irish Statesman,* was the interpreter to thousands of young people in a young state of Sir Horace Plunkett's plans for the regeneration of the Irish countryside. He believed that through the co-operative movement we could 'carve an Attica out of Ireland'. And, in fact, in hundreds of Irish villages, through his and Plunkett's inspiration and vigorous personal effort, creameries did spring up and long lines of donkey carts streamed towards them. On the road to Attica, co-operative bee-keeping associations were formed, societies for vegetable marketing, fishing, meat-processing, poultry and eggs. Affiliated to them were at least thirty pre-Carnegie village libraries, and fifty-three Home Industries.

Then Plunkett's home was burnt by the republicans and many creameries were burnt in reprisal for other reprisals by the Black and Tans. The great co-operative library in Plunkett House was moved from Dublin to London and at the end of his book Mr Bolger sadly reveals that Ireland never after all became very like Attica.

Yet he is an optimist as well as a realist. Co-operation did in fact continue and become, one might say, bigger and better but very different. Æ's ideal had been to create at every level 'true social organisms'. The efficient marketing of butter and eggs was only a step on the road to a wider co-operative commonwealth. Unfortunately, efficient people often make efficiency their goal, whereas for the wider commonwealth it is only one consideration out of many.

Co-operation had been an electric word. Read the story of Paddy the Cope and his battle with the gombeenmen in Donegal. It raised vital issues, which caused him to be denounced from the altar and sent to Derry jail by his shopkeeping neighbours in Dungloe. His friends got the Lord Lieutenant to liberate him.

Many village creameries have had equally stormy stories. Remembering the local ructions, when my father was chairman

*Patrick Bolger, *The Irish Co-operative Movement: Its History and Development.*

of the first creamery, at Bennettsbridge, I took Mr Bolger's advice and enquired what is happening today. I found someone who remembered those lively, quarrelsome times, and it was with a tinge of sadness that he admitted that everything was going very smoothly indeed. Our creamery does not now even need a name. If you buy a bag of cement or turf there (and there is little else you can buy), the bill comes from Avonmore Farmers Ltd, Kilkenny area, Branch No 10, a vast factory fifteen miles away to which the milk sucked from a thousand churns in three counties travels for processing. There are no arguments about the price of milk, no scandals about the misappropriation of funds since we don't handle either the milk or the funds locally. A year or two ago I read of an Avonmore milk lorry being wrecked on the way to Belfast, but it was not our affair and I do not remember why. The milk is good and so is the butter and most of the employees dismissed from the villages have been taken on by Avonmore. There is still a local committee that meets now and then to listen to a report from Avonmore Farmers Ltd. There is nothing much to discuss, so it ends in a happy drinks party, with pleasant hosts. There is a little grumbling about not getting cream or skim milk now in the village, but that is all.

What would Plunkett, or the other pioneers, of whom Bolger writes most interestingly, say of all this: Robert Owen, John Vandaleur, William Thompson? I do not know. And what saddens me is no one cares either.

Indeed, as Bolger writes, few would be able to distinguish Horace Plunkett from the other famous Plunketts; the Count, who was Sinn Fein MP for Roscommon, or Joseph Mary, the poet after whom Waterford Station has been rechristened. Like them, Plunkett was a man with a mission. He was fuelled by his own convictions and did not need applause. It may well happen that creameries survive railway stations and someone will ask how they got there. Someone else may remember.

[1977]

41

GOOD MAN AND TRUE

Dag Hammarskjöld once said jokingly that to be Secretary General of the UN was like being a secular Pope. He too occupied a lonely eminence; it was his character rather than his training that so notably qualified him for it. He was a Swedish civil servant, but so self-contained in spirit that he could resist all ordinary pressures towards conformity and compromise. This diary,* which he left behind as the 'only correct profile of himself', is a collection of impersonal aphorisms as unlike as possible to the usual gossiping, self-justificatory memoirs of the great. There is not a word about the intricate and nerve-wracking international problems to which his active life was devoted. He seems to have believed, like a Greek philosopher, that the decisions of a good man must be good and that, therefore, if you are to study and master society, you must apply yourself first to the study and the mastery of yourself.

Ever since President Wilson, who was once just such a 'secular Pope' as Hammarskjöld, the exponent of abstract principles has been deeply distrusted in politics. His idealism is supposed to disqualify him from the jungle war of international affairs. But Hammarskjöld, unlike Wilson, belonged to a disillusioned generation or rather to the more desperate one that succeeded it and which believes as he did that sometimes 'self-delusion is necessary to life'. He was a sad and sceptical economist, who saw that the power of the reasonable man to influence society had become very small. Yet you cannot contract out of society: 'In our age the

---

* Dag Hammarskjöld, *Markings*. Translated by Leif Sjoberg and W.H. Auden. With a foreword by W.H. Auden.

road to holiness necessarily passes through the world of action.' You can at least do what is right, even if its effect is negligible. And for doing right, there are still rules that can be followed.

He had no doubt about these rules, though as he expounds them they may seem somewhat banal, sometimes highly idiosyncratic. Most good men regulate their lives primarily by venerable platitudes, and Hammarskjöld tries to rejuvenate them by some rather tired images, 'the Labyrinth of Life and Ariadne's Thread,' 'the Devil's Pack of Cards,' and so on; he worked eighteen hours a day and they may be less awful in Swedish. Where his principles diverge from the norm, he is simpler.

Though he was not a churchman, he said that his life had been given direction by the formulae of religion, even when his intellect had rejected their validity. He recognized the 'Divine intention' behind what is, in fact, only 'a sacrificial rite in a still barbarian cult', a 'feeble creation of man's hands'. He had been granted 'a Faith, which required no confirmation, a contact with reality, light and intense, like the touch of a loved hand'. To find this Faith, you have to listen Quakerwise to the 'voice within you' and to follow 'a fleeting light'.

Auden reproaches him for his spiritual self-sufficiency, his indifference to that communal worship by which Faith is strengthened, 'when two or three are gathered together'. Auden suggests that he shrank from committing himself to any particular Church so as to be neutral between east and west, yet it is clear that his isolation, his introversion, which he often called 'loneliness', was an essential part of him.

From what did it derive? Was it 'pathological?' 'Psychology' has enabled nincompoops 'to dismiss the perplexing mystery with a label that assigns it a place in the list of common aberrations,' so he gives few clues, yet resents the dissimulation that has been forced on him: 'Upon your continual cowardice, your repeated lies, sentence will be passed on the day, when some exhibition of your weakness in itself perhaps quite trivial deprives you of any further opportunities to make a choice – and justly.'

His isolation is traced by Auden to some failure to achieve happiness in love, to which he only half reconciled himself. He asks whether the bleakness of his world was 'a reflection of my poverty or my honesty, a symptom of weakness or of strength, an indication that I have strayed from my path or that I am following it? – will despair provide an answer?'

And, at one point, he answers himself, 'Love has not matured till you no longer expect a response.' But elsewhere he says: 'Without the strength of a personal commitment, your experience of others is at most aesthetic.'

He was already at the peak of his influence when he was complaining to his diary that it was impossible for his life to acquire a meaning. Then, in 1961, he records a crucial moment when he made a great decision. Was it political, religious, personal? He does not say: 'From that hour I was certain that existence is meaningful and that, therefore, my life in self-surrender has a goal.'

Hammarskjöld did not idealize himself or others. He believed that we all have in us something that wills disaster even to those we love and the cause we serve. He believed in self-effacing service, yet this is not easy when one's withdrawal enables some scheming non-entity to inflate himself. A mature man does not hide his strength out of fear. He reproached himself, too, with 'brooding over his pettiness with masochistic self-disgust'.

Yet in regard to others his critical sense occasionally relaxed and he wrote of 'the aura of victory that surrounds a man of good will, the sweetness of soul that emanates from him – a flavour of cranberries and cloudberries, a touch of frost and cloudy skies'.

Is this like Epictetus? Is it like Ella Wheeler Wilcox? There are different opinions about the quality of Hammarskjöld's writing, but in his life he became very close to being what he most admired, a man of good will.

[1964]

42

THE ONE AND THE MANY

Hans Küng, whose sincerity and courage no one who heard him speak in Ireland can doubt, makes in this fine book a massive attempt to recover for the Christian Churches the ground that has been lost.* He addresses himself to a world in which there is neither passionate belief nor passionate unbelief. In two world wars the Churches, Catholic and Protestant, disgraced themselves, and thereafter, in the contemporary phrase, 'lost credibility'. It was surely on apathy rather than opposition that Vatican II foundered. Like stones into a stagnant pond, Küng tosses at his Church a series of necessary reforms. Bishops must be elected by representatives of clergy and laity, likewise the Pope himself, and many questions of morality, of sex and of marriage must be decided by the individual conscience, 'in the light of medical, psychological and social criteria'. Because of all this, like many of the opponents of Infallibility at Vatican I, he has been charged with being a crypto-Protestant.

It is true, of course, that these are all issues that Protestants have fought over for generations and about which one or other of our 260 sects reached conclusions that the rest of us are now adopting. Yet it is clear that Küng believes in a universal Church and the Primacy of Rome, whereas the heresies that have kept Protestantism alive have mostly been centrifugal. The fragmentation that ecumenists deplore, has seemed to many more like the bursting of a seed-pod than the rending of a robe.

Yet the One and the Many, though they converge on it from

---

* Hans Küng, *On Being a Christian.*

opposite poles, have the same goal, the gospel of Jesus Christ and that new commandment: 'As I have loved you, so are you to love one another.'

The book is so detailed and scholarly that it would be rash to raise criticisms of any particular passage because in all probability it would be answered elsewhere in its 600 pages. It is only in a very subjective way that one can talk of what one has missed. I do not find that he has applied his 'social and psychological criteria' to the question of loving one's neighbour in our faceless, rootless world. Who is one's neighbour? To Jesus they were those who were nearest, imperfect men and women, one doubted, one denied, one was Judas. For the average man, some dim reflection of the divine love might light on such individuals but Küng does not refer to the great gulf that yawns between the love we cherish for the known individual, the goodwill we feel for the half-known neighbour, the concern (it would be affectation to call it more) that we sometimes manage to warm up for 'the masses' or for distant peoples. He seems to me to accept too readily these great divides and to depersonalize without regret – 'In the modern mass society, it is not only a question of the relation of one individual to another but of group to groups' – and he talks of the evils of race discrimination. Yet if Christians had goodwill, let alone love, for their neighbour, black, white or yellow, discrimination would dissolve at its source. Here in Ireland the seeds of neighbourly hate were sown in the village, though of course it is in the forcing house of the cities that they flourish.

Goodwill for our neighbour is such a precarious trickle that nothing should be done to divert it into wider channels.

So surely Küng is on the wrong lines when he asks for Christian involvement in the poverty and misery of the oppressed in Latin America. He is making an appeal to our hearts, which should be addressed to our intellects. The Latin Americans are the victims of 'modern mass-society' and it is through modern mass communication that we know about them. Mass methods must be used for their relief and for the survival of 'the dying sub-cultures in Chile' and all the other distant sufferers from our civilization. But must we accept 'modern mass-society' simply because it is all round us? I think we have to reject it, as the first Christians rejected the gods of Rome.

What an inadequate account of a splendid book!

[1977]

43

TEILHARD DE CHARDIN

Teilhard de Chardin,* who came of a small but independent-minded landowning family in Auvergne, had from very early on interested himself, via geology and palaeontology, in the origins of Man. The Jesuit Order, which he joined as a young man, had with other Orders been expelled from France in the wake of the Dreyfus trial (they had been strongly anti-Semitic and even the son of a converted Jew was not eligible for the Society). He followed them to Jersey and later to Hastings, and there made the acquaintance of Charles Dawson, the discoverer and later, as it emerged, the manufacturer of the famous Piltdown skull. Teilhard had been an enthusiastic collaborator and it was with intense sadness that some forty years later he discovered that even 'the interlocking canine', which he himself had found, must have been fraudulently planted. He could never accept that Dawson himself had been responsible.

Yet there were other Missing Links, most famous of them all the Peking Man, in whose discovery Teilhard, sent by his Order to China, so as to be out of mischief, once more observed from nearby. Evolution became to him not, as it is to most scientists, a hypothesis that works but a vital element in religion. 'Evolution', he wrote, 'is a light illuminating all facts, a curve that all lines must follow.' If one can compress a long and learned book *The Phenomenon of Man* [1955] into half a sentence, Teilhard believed that over aeons of time man had evolved from inorganic matter, through the 'complexifications' of matter folded in on itself and

* Mary and Ellen Lukas, *Teilhard de Chardin* (1977).

through consciousness becoming conscious of itself. *The Phenomenon* was introduced to English readers by Julian Huxley, the scientific Humanist, who believes that Teilhard has indeed opened the door between Science and Religion and 'forced scientists to see the spiritual implications of their knowledge'.

Whatever the ultimate fate of his theories may be, Teilhard was a noble and fearless figure, who loved the Church into which he was born and the Jesuit Order, which he had entered at the nadir of its fortunes in France. As a young man he had been forced to sign a profession of faith in a literal Adam and Eve. His sympathetic colleagues persuaded him that his signature was 'a purely mechanical gesture and not a sign of intellectual assent'. Yet he felt he had capitulated to 'dolts and ignoramuses' and that to redeem his honour he must either leave the Order he loved or bring about such an intellectual revolution within it that hypocrisy and self-deception became impossible.

When he was in America Teilhard was astonished to find that the cleavage that he had observed between science and religion was scarcely deeper than that between science and humanism, of which he was not aware. Yet perhaps it is the more important of the two abysses. A few years ago there was a Humanist Conference at Malahide. It was centred on Teilhard, the mediator between science and religion, from whose reconciliation the organizers thought that Humanism would profit. It was a strange belief for Humanism, which like the Ten Commandments draws its strength from negation. In its great days it was anti-Church; it had clubrooms and libraries and eminent lectures instead of churches and Ministers of God, for the Theory of Evolution and the Higher Criticism of the Bible needed strong support against ecclesiastical orthodoxy. Then in England the Churches largely capitulated to both heresies, Humanism lost its *raison d'etre* and most of its adherents. After Hiroshima the survivors tried to recover the enthusiasm of their godless days by opposing science instead of championing it. They joined with the Churches in Aldermaston marches, and campaigned against pollution and the abuse of Technology. If Humanism has any future that, surely, is where it lies.

Teilhard's life was in many ways a sad one, with periods of deep depression and loneliness, condemned by his vows of obedience to withhold his writings from publishers till death should free them from the censor, to travel widely in search of people, many of them Jesuit colleagues, with whom he could speak his thoughts freely. He was frequently unlucky in his timing. When he went to Rome to try to persuade the new General of the Jesuits, Jannsens, to permit the publication of *The Phenomenon of Man*, the powerful Sicilian cardinal Ruffini had just published an anti-evolutionist book, and Pius XII had given a new lease of life to Adam and Eve. Whether you call them mythology or truth the old images persist. The same year that Teilhard signed his declaration of belief in Adam and Eve, the famous Monkey Trial took place in the USA, but the ban on teaching evolution in Tennessee was not lifted till 1967. The fundamentalists of Ulster and the Bob Jones University still maintain it.

Mary and Ellen Lukas write in the lively manner of *Time* magazine (Mary was once on its staff). They have clearly researched deeply and have made Teilhard the man as interesting as his theories. It is strange though that they have not mentioned that the Peking Man (really a woman, christened Nellie by her discoverers) was allegedly stolen by the Japanese over thirty years ago and that her authenticity has been challenged. Have any serious attempts been made to answer the detailed criticisms of Father Patrick O'Connell, who was in China at the time of her discovery?

Teilhard believed that if God was shown to be 'the universal centre of unification' and Jesus Christ 'the principle of universal vitality', and the Redemption 'the general ascent of consciousness', he was opening a gateway through which lost sheep would return to the fold. Yet surely the reason why many sheep still prefer to stay outside is no longer the conflict of Science and Religion, an old, old story, but the failure of both to meet the ruthless cruelty of our time, the dire absence of love. To Teilhard, the kindest of men, these were the things that time would cure. The evidence of the appalling experiments of the doctors at Dachau, the fact that, as Mary and Ellen relate, most of the French bishops collaborated with the Nazis, were in his eyes mere temporary set-backs. After great and far-reaching changes had been made in the structure of the Churches, Science and Religion would march hand in hand towards that distinct Omega-point, which is the goal of Evolution.

How did they know that Pere Garrigou, Teilhard's formidable adversary, 'made a gesture meant to deprecate the burden of celebrity he was forced to bear'? It does not matter. He was that sort of man.

[1977]

44

REBECCA WEST IN YUGOSLAVIA

I am glad that this famous [1941] book has been reissued.* Emotional, digressive, highly subjective, it will always puzzle and infuriate the professional historian, yet in no other way could Rebecca West have recreated so perfectly a vanished era, as well as a country and a people, which have been changed beyond recognition. When she made her journey round Yugoslavia in the late thirties, the glow of hope and excitement that had gilded the years after the First World War had not faded. Though the League of Nations was dead, the PEN Club dowdy and the *Wandervogel* sinister, those who have lived through that springtime can never forget it. Miss West writes of the ecstacies of the newly liberated peoples:

They were all like young men stretching themselves at the open window in the early morning after long sleep. To eat in public places in these countries, to walk in their public gardens, was to fill the nostrils with the smell of happiness. Nothing so fair has happened in all history as this liberation of peoples, who during centuries of oppression had never forgotten their own souls.

All the succession states, the Irish Free State included, had been carved out of one or more powerful empires, and each one was confident that the genius of the land and its ancient culture could assimilate all those of their fellow citizens whose traditions were different.

The fact that the alien soul could be captivated was not a delusion. Just as Ireland owed much of its cultural nationalism to

---

* Rebecca West, *Black Lamb and Grey Falcon*.

men of English and Anglo-Irish descent, so it was that the sub-merged culture of all the Slav subjects of the German, Austrian and Russian empires had first been roused by foreigners, like Johann Herder, a Prussian, and the Catholic Bishop Strossmayer of Djakovo, an Austrian. Miss West devotes several pages to this far-seeing and generous patron of Croats and Serbs. These men were all humanists and the arrogant racialism to which their teachings sometimes seemed to lead would have appalled them.

Soon after Miss West returned home all these once young and happy peoples had been engulfed in the Nazi empire. To what extent were they themselves to blame? This is a question that Miss West frequently asks. Like Thucydides, she tells much of her story in dialogue, real people making unreal speeches to each other, long, shapely and logical. Croat talks to Serb, Orthodox to Catholic, Christian to Moslem, and her husband [H.G Wells], whom I remember as articulate and intelligent but not given to page-long monologues, draws suitable conclusions.

As it seems to me that they are usually right, I do not quarrel with this artform. We are kept in touch with reality by Gerda, their German travelling-companion who is agonizingly true to life. Arro-gant and stupid, she is like an early blueprint of a Belsen wardress.

In the twenties, the small self-governing state, forging anew its cultural identity, had seemed the only answer to imperialism, Communism and international capitalism, yet hardly any small people were ready to grant to others the liberty they claimed for themselves. Instead they toadied to the big ones and despised each other. Arthur Griffith's book, *The Resurrection of Hungary, A Parallel for Ireland*, was ominous, for Hungary, defending her culture against the Austrians, trampled on all the small peoples, Serbs, Croats, Slovaks (Griffith calls them 'the Slav hordes'), that came within her power. To quote Miss West: 'Kossuth declared he would suppress the Croatian language by the sword and intro-duced an electoral bill that omitted the name of Croatia and described her departments as Hungarian counties.'

Miss West, who once told me she is Irish by birth, writes else-where (thirty years ago, remember): 'The nationalism of Ireland and Hungary have always been intense but Hungary has always been industrially ambitious and resolute both in maintaining a feudal land system and in oppressing the alien within her frontiers, while Ireland, though she desires to annihilate Ulster, wishes to be a peasant state with industries well within manageable proportions.'

As for the Croat-Serb tensions, it is Henry Andrews, who brings a long dialogue to a conclusion.

'Is it not the tragedy of the situation here', suggested my husband to Valetta, 'that you Croats are for the first time discovering that your religion and your race run counter to one another and that you are able to evade that discovery by putting the blame on the constitution of Yugoslavia? The Croats, like all Slavs, are a democratic and speculative people. You lived for long under the Habsburgs, whom you could blame for everything ... Now the Habsburgs are swept away you should see the Roman Catholic Church as it is; not at all democratic, not at all in favour of speculative thought ... You should proceed to the difficult task of deciding whether you can reconcile yourself to this bias of the Church for the sake of the spiritual benefits it confers on you. But you are postponing this task by letting the Church throw the blame for all its suppressions of free speech and free press on Belgrade.'

I am sorry that Miss West, who used Valetta, a mutual friend, as a spokesman for the Croats, overlooks his colleague Dr Milan Curcin, the editor of *Nova Evropa*, a man of much greater stature. A Serb, living in Croatia and a convinced Yugoslav, he saw his country's racial and religious problems against a European background. A PEN Club enthusiast in the challenging days of H.G. Wells, he came to Ireland from the Edinburgh Conference to harvest impressions that he could use in Croatia ('the Ulster of Yugoslavia'). He wanted to come back, when the Conference was in Dublin, but Yugoslavia was in disgrace here at that time and I could not get an invitation for him

In her epilogue Rebecca West tells magnificently of Yugoslavia's epic resistance to Hitler. Though its army was overwhelmed after three days, guerilla war burst out spontaneously in the mountains and played a noble part in Hitler's defeat.

Yet it was those first three days that electrified Europe. 'The news that Hitler had been defied by Yugoslavia travelled like sunshine over the countries that he had devoured and humiliated, promising Spring.'

It is on this note that the book ends. With all its faults it is surely a memorable work, and after more than thirty years has lost nothing of its freshness and vigour.

[1977]

45

RONALD REAGAN AND THE AMERICAN WALL OF SEPARATION: A VIEW FROM IRELAND IN 1985

The American elections are over. Have any before been watched so intently? Half the world has been sitting beside its television set and a new type of man has come into being to match the new technology. Reagan can project his complete personality, body, clothes, voice and appropriate gestures, into a billion homes with his arguments, promises and rhetoric in the same package. Mondale claims he has been defeated largely by television, which in the hands of an expert reduces all politics into personalized snippets.

When over two centuries ago the thirteen American colonies were claiming their rights, Edmund Burke almost alone stood up for them. His two great speeches on American Taxation and on Conciliation must have taken a couple of hours each to deliver. He was a boring speaker with a bad manner and towards the end he was addressing almost empty benches. Yet in print these speeches have survived, many times reproduced, because on almost every page there is some penetrating observation about politics or human nature whose relevance is not only for 1774–5 but for today.

Will posterity be able to rescue anything of the kind from the mountain of triviality that enveloped the Reagan victory? It was unique, because for the first time television had brought the Fundamentalists out from their strongholds in the Bible Belt. They spread themselves over the network and all America was theirs. Even here in Ireland I have heard the principal Televangelist on a cassette. The Rev. Jerry Falwell is the founder of 'The Moral Majority' and he boasted that he could bring eight-and-a-half million voters to the polls for Reagan and that he had 'activated' millions more: 'I think we will easily put 10 to 15 millions at the polls nation wide.'

I keep in touch with the United States through my American son-in-law, and before the 1984 elections I received from Jerry Falwell, as did many thousands of Americans, a moving appeal to take part 'with a million other Christians' in a Day of National Fasting and Prayer from sundown on Sunday 4 November to sundown on 5 November. We are to pray that on election day God will lead Americans to vote for righteous men and women at all levels of government. He writes, 'I am not talking about Democrats or Republicans.' All the same it is fairly clear who the top-righteous man is. He has often been photographed with Jerry Falwell at prayer breakfasts and other religious occasions.

Counter-attacking, Mondale's supporters circulated a Petition to President Reagan, which recipients were to sign. As it is concise I will quote it in full:

The Founding Fathers of America made a wise choice about the Separation of Church and State and the prohibition against the establishment of Religion by the government. Hundreds of years of bloody religious warfare and persecution in Europe led them to write the Constitution as they did.

For over two hundred years America's religious institutions and the religious liberty of its people have flourished without government endorsement or advocacy for their viewpoints. This, the American Way, has proved best for all of us.

I am alarmed by your recent efforts to inject ultra-fundamentalist Christian doctrine into the laws and policies governing all of America's citizens. I urge you to reconsider your position on these complex issues. The Presidency is an office of all people, not a forum for one particular dogma.

What in fact are Jerry Falwell's religious views? They are probably much like those of Ian Paisley, who is on the board of the Bob Jones University in Greenville, South Carolina, in the Bible Belt. Falwell, as Chancellor of a Baptist college at Lynchburg, Virginia, now called Liberty University, lately told an interviewer that all his faculty members have to sign a statement of faith in the iner-rancy of the scriptures and the biblical account of the Creation. He believes he has a divine mission to Christianize America and, with Reagan's support, he is heading an attack on the decisions of the Supreme Court during the Sixties when the Justices interpreted the Separation of Church and State with the utmost strictness. Fal-well's main targets are the 1962 decision banning religious devo-tions in public schools and the 1973 decision to legalize abortion. These are sensitive issues and the Fundamentalists have not hesi-tated to call their opponents atheists and murderers.

Reagan's way of handling Jefferson's Wall of Separation of Church and State is to ignore it: 'The truth is', he said, 'politics and morality are inseparable and morality's foundation is reli-gion; religion and politics are necessarily related. We need reli-gion as a guide.'

To what religion is he referring? There are some 280 different sects in the USA and at least seventy million who belong to no Church at all. Reagan himself was raised as a Disciple of Christ but became a Presbyterian and we saw him attend a Catholic church in Ballyporeen. He does not go to church in the USA because, say his aides, the necessary security precautions might disturb other worshippers. He has endeared himself to the Fundamentalists by his belief that the biblical account of the Creation should have equal authority in the schools with the Theory of Evolution and by his obsession about the imminence of Armageddon, that great battle between Good and Evil, which will be fought before the Day of Judgment. He has no doubt where the Powers of Evil are to be found.

The anti-abortion campaign threatens to be bitterly divisive. To the anti-abortionists it is as crucial an issue today as slavery in the last century. Their opponents compare it to Prohibition, which became law in 1919 only to be repealed as unworkable fourteen years later.

The Justices of the Supreme Court hold their office for life, so that popular pressure cannot influence their decisions. Fortu-nately for Reagan five of the nine are seventy-five, so he may be able to replace one or two of them with men favourable to the mandatory school prayer and to the banning of abortion.

It is clear that in the USA, as in Ireland, the Fundamentalists are more politically assertive than the mainstream Protestants who mostly cherish the Separation of Church and State and, while condemning abortion, have no wish to make it illegal. A characteristic statement came from Bishop Paul Moore of the Episcopal Diocese of New York, who believes that 'the soul of America has gone wrong'. 'The nation', he said, 'was being conned into false judgment by the slick veneer of religious verbiage.'

Of school prayers, he said: 'If a school becomes a place where children are taught to pray, it is a short step to their thinking of the State as an instrument of God and that leads to the most demonic of all Church-State confusions, a tendency to mingle patriotic and religious fervor.'

He saw a dearth of compassion and serious thought: 'Abortion is an issue not to be dictated by governments. If a woman is considering one, her decision is one of the most agonizing and painful she will ever address. She needs to have freedom to work through her decision.'

There is an unspoken question here. Is Ronald Reagan one of the silliest and most dangerous of all American presidents? Or is he merely an astute politician who has captured the South from Democrats by his 'slick veneer of religious verbiage'?

I was in America in 1962 when the Supreme Court made the decision that Ronald Reagan and Jerry Falwell now wish to revoke. The Justices, voting eight to one, declared the recital of a state prayer in the public schools to be unconstitutional. It was a very short prayer and seemed innocuous and undenominational, but when four parents, Unitarian, Jewish, Agnostic and Ethical Culture, objected, the Supreme Court upheld their objection. Justice Black, who delivered the opinion, quoted President Madison in justification:

There are more instances of abridgment of freedom of the people by gradual and silent encroachments of those in power than by violent and sudden usurpations. It is proper to take alarm at the first experiment on our liberties. Who does not see that the same authority, which can establish Christianity in exclusion of all other religions, may establish with the same ease any particular sect of Christianity in exclusion of all other sects.

Madison recalled the circumstances that had induced the Founding Fathers to erect their Wall of Separation. Though they were for the most part classically educated country gentlemen, they had been real revolutionaries. They upset many century-old traditions and overthrew at least nine established Churches. The

Church of England was established in New York, Virginia, Maryland, and the two Carolinas and Georgia, Congregationalism in Massachusetts, New Hampshire and Connecticut. In some states there was discrimination against Catholics.

The men who drew up the Constitution and its amendments were aware that those who have suffered religious persecution often become the most experienced persecutors. Twenty years after the Pilgrim Fathers had fled from English bigotry to Massachusetts, they were themselves expelling Quakers, Catholics and others under pain of cruel punishment and even death. Nor can the Framers of the Constitution have been surprised by the fury they aroused in the Churches they disestablished. Would Jefferson, an Anglican himself, have succeeded in disestablishing the tax-supported Anglican Church in Virginia if their clergy had not for the most part sided with Britain and left their parishes when war broke out in 1775?

Jefferson justified the intransigence of the Founding Fathers by a clause in the preamble to the Statute of Virginia for Religious Freedom. Abridged a little, it runs:

Almighty God hath created the mind free ... (But) the impious presumption of legislators and rulers, civil as well as ecclesiastical, who being themselves but fallible and uninspired men, have assumed dominion over the faith of others, setting up their own opinions and modes of thinking as the only true and infallible and as such endeavouring to impose them on others, hath established and maintained false religions over the greatest part of the world and through all time ... To compel a man to furnish contributions of money for the propagation of opinions, which he disbelieves, is sinful and tyrannical.

Jefferson himself, like Benjamin Franklin, was a Deist, but said he would have been a Unitarian had there been a Unitarian Church in Charlottesville. Of all the Founding Fathers, he was the one most concerned with religion and the freedom of religion. He wrote of Jesus that 'he presented to us a system of morals the most perfect and sublime that has ever been taught to man ... To the corruption of Christianity I am indeed opposed but not to the genuine precepts of Jesus himself.'

He was the part-author of the First Amendment of the US Constitution, which runs: 'Congress shall make no laws respecting the establishment of religion or prohibiting the free exercise thereof.'

The precise meaning of this has often been disputed. Jefferson himself interpreted it in the following way in his *Notes on Virginia*: 'The legitimate powers of government extend to such acts only as are injurious to others. But it does me no injury for my neighbour to say there are twenty gods or no god.' This is very far from Reagan's claim that 'Religion and politics are necessarily related.'

Time has fully justified the Founding Fathers. No country in the world has been so free from religious conflict. Nowhere has religion been so freely practised. Yet Jefferson was as unpopular in his day as those who defend the Wall of Separation now. In 1962 Justice Black and his colleagues were told they were atheists in league with Moscow. Yet on the whole the Church and the leading newspapers approved. Cardinal Spellman protested but President Kennedy said the children will just have to pray that much more at home. The Catholic Church has often had some difficulty in meeting the Wall. There was a famous occasion in 1949 when Cardinal Spellman told Mrs Roosevelt she was unworthy to be an American mother because she had approved of the Barden Bill by which Federal money was to be devoted to public and secular schools only. The bill, he said, represented 'a craven crusade of religious prejudice against the Catholic child and his inalienable rights'.

The most telling criticism of the 1962 decision concerned expediency. Could the Supreme Court afford to take so many unpopular measures? The survival of the Court is more important than any single one of its measures. The Wall of Separation has often been breached. Does not the state provide chaplains for the army and compulsory chapel for West Point cadets? Would it not have been prudent to fob off the four parents somehow?

The answer is that the United States was founded on nonconformity and its leaders are pledged to protect the rights of the individual who will not conform. Time and again the One has overturned the smooth and settled orthodoxies of the Many. Sometimes he is a believer, as when some Jehovah's witnesses refused to salute the American flag, because it was a 'graven image'. Sometimes he is an unbeliever, as when Mrs Vashti McCollum successfully challenged the 'released time' system of Bible classes in Illinois public schools, on behalf of her son, Jim, who had been brought up an agnostic. If the most insignificant of West Point cadets were to claim that compulsory chapel was unconstitutional, the Supreme Court might feel obliged to support him. It would no doubt be the end of his military career but also it would be the end of compulsory chapel.

In no country in the world are there so many religious organizations, all of them voluntary and functioning without interference from the state. But the Wall of Separation that protects their liberty also defines its extent. All America is there to evangelize, but the law as interpreted by the Supreme Court enjoins that they must not ask a single cent from public funds or a single minute from a public servant's time for the diffusion or the defence of a private belief.

[1985]

ENDNOTE BY RICHARD CRAMPTON

Butler's theses reverberate today. He judiciously dissected the dangers of mixing religion, politics and government. Not only have his views illuminated worldwide perturbations and atrocities of the twentieth and early twenty-first centuries before and after his death, but also those threats to the American Wall of Separation he so carefully examined and portrayed a generation ago now flourish, much magnified by social media.

The late Joe Bageant pointed out that Fundamentalist Christian students and Fundamentalists constitute 25 per cent of those entitled to vote in state and national elections. Twenty of fifty million Fundamentalists voted in 2000 and 2004. A Gallup Survey disclosed that a quarter to a third of the US population identifies itself as 'born-again' evangelicals. They stand apart from mainstream America and hope to scrap the US Constitution and institute 'Biblical Law', the rules of The Old Testament. Like their Scots-Irish ancestors, they wish to create a theocratic state. The Religious Right always claim America was founded as a Christian nation (*The Covert Kingdom: They Plead upon the Blood of Jesus for a Theocratic State in Deer Hunting with Jesus: Dispatches from America's Class War, 2007, Three Rivers Press, New York*). Bageant cited Fred Clarkson, who agrees with Butler's perceptions, in his classic *Eternal Hostility: The Struggle Between Theocracy and Democracy*. Clarkson observes that the Religious Right 'seek to restore a theocratic order that never was, not since the ratification of The Constitution. The Framers of The Constitution overthrew 150 years of colonial theocracies and theocratic wannabes. And when it was accomplished, Benjamin Franklin said, 'You have a republic if you can keep it.' So let's keep it.

Butler's concerns about theocrats eroding the Wall of Separation are amply justified. Christian Fundamentalists participate vigorously in contemporary social media. Jennifer Preston described Dr Aaron Tabor's Facebook Page for Jesus with Highly Active Fans (*New York Times* 4 September 2011) where he posts the words of Jesus four or five times daily. The *Jesus Daily* has 8.2 million fans with 3.4 million interactions weekly. Social media expedited 'friending' an online faith community. The Bible Facebook page run by the United Bible Societies, Reading, England, has eight million fans. Will Facebook and other social media change how people worship? Thirty-one per cent of American Facebook users and 24 per cent of users outside the USA list religion in their profiles. Preston found over 43 million Facebook users have at least one page categorized as religious. Will worship via social media so popularize and politicize religion that we can anticipate new threats to the Wall of Separation as perceived by Butler in Reagan's 1984 campaign rhetoric? Indeed we can. These threats are precisely those identified by Butler nearly thirty years ago.

For example. Butler foresaw Frank Bruni's report ('The God Glut', *New York Times* 11 December 2012). Blake Page, an atheist cadet, resigned six months before graduation from the publicly funded US Military Academy at West Point. He could no longer bear widespread discriminatory bullying by faculty officers and fellow cadets. He identified the problem as evangelical Christian 'unconstitutional proselytism'. Yet Page did not contest his resignation legally, so it was never examined in the US Supreme Court. By contrast, when the US Military Freedom Foundation asserted that Air Force Academy cadets should not have to swear 'so help me God' in their entry Honor Oaths, this phrase officially became optional (*New York Times*, 26 October 1913).

As of March 2013, Butler's clairvoyant disquiet about threats to the Wall of Separation rests on solid bedrock. The biased rhetoric and theocratic agenda of six US Republican politicians, Bachmann, Gingrich, Paul, Perry, Romney and Santorum, were imbued with Fundamentalist, Catholic and Mormon beliefs. Despite Romney's loss in the 2012 election to President Obama, very wealthy threats to the Wall of Separation abound. The Christian Fundamentalist Jerry Falwell Ministries, Liberty Counsel and Liberty University and The Christian Broadcasting Network and Regent University of TV preacher Pat Robertson yearly take in respectively $523 and $435 million. Eight like-minded organizations of the Religious Right add $216 million more (*Americans United for Separation of Church and State*, www.au.org). This massive thousand-million-dollar warchest pours into the evangelical Christian Crusade to insert God's wishes about Creationism into public schools, deny raped women abortions and block civil marriages of same-sex partners. These religious and gender-based threats menace rights embodied in the First Amendment of the US Constitution. In June 2013 controversy at the Wall of Separation erupted again.

Senator Wendy Davis filibustered for eleven hours in the Texas legislature, but failed to block the ani-abortion omnibus measure denying women's right to choose.

Butler wrote this prescient essay in 1985 after Reagan's election to a second term as President of the USA. It expands upon his earlier essays, 'American Impressions: In Salt Lake City (1962)' and 'The Bob Jones University (1977)' in *Grandmother and Wolfe Tone* (1990). Earlier versions of this essay appeared in *The Journal of the Butler Society* (2010), and in *Princeton University Library Chronicle* (2010). Butler and Richard Crampton edited it in 1985.

Butler hung a copy of The Declaration of American Independence in his house at Maidenhall in 1963. Staying with his daughter's family in Charlottesville, Virginia, in 1972 and 1974, he read *The Federalist Papers of Madison, Hamilton and Jay*. He perused The Constitution of the USA, The Bill of Rights and Jefferson's *Notes on Virginia*. He visited Monticello, Jefferson's house, and worked at the library of the University of Virginia, founded by Jefferson.

For the classicist Butler, The Commonwealth of Virginia's motto, *Sic Semper Tyrannis*, fits the spirit of his essay. As Maurice Craig succinctly put it in his Foreword to Butler's first book:

For all his elegance, Hubert Butler is no *bellelettrist*. For him an essay is a projectile, aimed at a particular target and freighted with what it needs to do its work: no more and no less. All his projectiles tend to converge on the same area of moral choice: the responsibilities of the individual to his community, and, by implication, those of the community towards him, in the special sphere where belief and conduct, dogma and decency, are so often in conflict. (*Escape from the Anthill*, 1985)

[2014]